W9-BLG-493

JOHNNY CASH

JOHNNY CASH

The Redemption of an American Icon

Greg Laurie

WITH MARSHALL TERRILL

SALEM
BOOKS
an imprint of Regnery Publishing

"A lot of books have been written about my brother Johnny since his 2003 death, but I think he might have liked this one the best. Greg Laurie and Marshall Terrill have done a marvelous job capturing Johnny's spiritual walk, which was not always easy or done in a straight line. But he reached the finish line and he finished well."

Joanne Cash Yates
Artist and co-founder of Cowboy Church

"The redemption story of Johnny Cash needs to be told to a new generation. This American music legend, the Man in Black, sang his way into our hearts and now the full story is written by my good friend Greg Laurie. This biography is inspiring as well as informative. It includes the spiritual transformation of a man who overcame his demons and finished well. I'm so glad the rest of the story is now written."

Dr. Jack Graham
Bestselling author and senior pastor, Prestonwood Baptist Church, Dallas, Texas

"Cash was definitely an original and a one-of-kind artist. Clearly his style was all his own. What lingers for me is the fact that he was able to stand up for the things he believed in, and he stood up strong. *Johnny Cash: The Redemption of an American Icon* beautifully captures his spirit, which will live on forever."

Will Turpin
Bassist, Collective Soul

"Johnny Cash experienced a life of diamonds and dirt, heart and hurt, mixed with mishap and majesty. *Johnny Cash: The Redemption of an American Icon* is a tragically beautiful journey into the vastness of God's heart and a world that few can imagine."

Ken Mansfield
Waylon Jennings & Jessi Colter producer
former US Manager, Apple Records

"As Johnny's brother-in-law for over thirty years of his life, I have had the pleasure of spending quite a bit of time with him. So many people have written books, songs, and other things about his life, but no one until now has captured the true essence of Johnny Cash. This book is an amazing itinerary of his spiritual quest to be more like his Lord. Ups and downs, ins and outs, but when put all together Johnny would have heard these greatest words, 'Well done, thou good and faithful servant.' "

Dr. Harry Yates
Co-founder and pastor of Cowboy Church

Scriptures marked ESV are taken from the The Holy Bible, English Standard Version®. Copyright© 2001 by Crossway, a publishing ministry of Good News Publishers. Used by permission.

Scriptures marked KJV are taken from the King James Version, public domain.

Scriptures marked MSG are taken from *The Message*, copyright © 1993, 2002, 2018 by Eugene H. Peterson. Used by permission of NavPress. All rights reserved. Represented by Tyndale House Publishers, Inc.

Scriptures marked NIV are taken from The Holy Bible New International Version®. Copyright© 1973, 1978, 1984, 2011 by Biblica, Inc.™. Used by permission of Zondervan

Scriptures marked NKJV are taken from the New King James Version®. Copyright© 1982 by Thomas Nelson, Inc. Used by permission. All rights reserved.

Scriptures marked NLT are taken from the *Holy Bible*, New Living Translation, copyright © 1996, 2004, 2015 by Tyndale House Foundation. Used by permission of Tyndale House Publishers, Inc., Carol Stream, Illinois 60188. All rights reserved.

Regnery® is a registered trademark of Salem Communications Holding Corporation

Salem Books™ is a trademark of Salem Communications Holding Corporation

Cataloging-in-Publication data on file with the Library of Congress

ISBN: 978-1-62157-974-8

Ebook ISBN: 978-1-62157-980-9

Published in the United States by
Salem Books, an imprint of
Regnery Publishing
A Division of Salem Media Group
300 New Jersey Ave NW
Washington, DC 20001
www.salembooks.com

Manufactured in the United States of America

2019 Printing

Books are available in quantity for promotional or premium use. For information on discounts and terms, please visit our website: www.salembooks.com

CONTENTS

Introduction		9
Prologue		17
CHAPTER 1	The Grapes of Cash	19
CHAPTER 2	Cottoning to Christ	31
CHAPTER 3	Meet Me in Heaven	41
CHAPTER 4	Finding His Voice	49
CHAPTER 5	High School Confidential	57
CHAPTER 6	The Man in Blue	65
CHAPTER 7	A Cherry Pink and Apple Blossom White Dream	73
CHAPTER 8	Cash Rich and Spiritually Poor	81
CHAPTER 9	I Walk the Line	87
CHAPTER 10	Go West Young Man	93
CHAPTER 11	Say Goodbye to Hollywood	99
CHAPTER 12	The Black Hole	105
CHAPTER 13	One Man, Two Personalities	113
CHAPTER 14	El Paso Times	121
CHAPTER 15	End of the Line	127
CHAPTER 16	Free Man Freefall	133
CHAPTER 17	The Cave	139
CHAPTER 18	Cleanup Time	145
CHAPTER 19	Folsom	151
CHAPTER 20	Good Times, Bad Times	161

CHAPTER 21   Country Superstar   167

CHAPTER 22   Brother Billy and Tricky Dick   175

CHAPTER 23   A Cog in the Wheel   183

CHAPTER 24   Let's Talk About Jesus   189

CHAPTER 25   The Gospel Road   199

CHAPTER 26   A C-Plus Christian   207

CHAPTER 27   Fair to Middling   215

CHAPTER 28   A Contrast in Kings   223

CHAPTER 29   Swimming in Different Directions   231

CHAPTER 30   Where's Waldo?   237

CHAPTER 31   Rock Bottom and Top of the Pops   245

CHAPTER 32   Kicked to the Curb   253

CHAPTER 33   Into the Fire   263

CHAPTER 34   Then Came Branson   273

CHAPTER 35   The Wanderer Comes Home   279

CHAPTER 36   Resurrection   287

CHAPTER 37   Hip Icon   295

CHAPTER 38   (Spiritual) House of Cash   303

CHAPTER 39   The Man Comes Around   311

CHAPTER 40   Unshakeable Faith   319

Epilogue   329
Acknowledgements   333
Selected Bibliography   335
Sources   337

ENDNOTES   359

INTRODUCTION

I'm standing at the gravesite of Johnny Cash. There's nobody else around here at Hendersonville Memory Gardens. It's just me and "The Man in Black"—a one-on-one in death I wish I could have had with him in life.

Overhead, massing clouds threaten rain. All week long, it's been hot and muggy in Nashville, which is to be expected in July. My main purpose in coming here was to deliver a pep talk at a convention of Southern Baptist preachers, but it was also a golden opportunity for a personal pilgrimage I've long had in mind. It started at the Johnny Cash Museum just off Nashville's Broadway District, also known as the "Honky Tonk Highway." The name certainly lived up to its billing with its souvenir shops, cowboy hat and boot stores, three-story bars, trendy lounges and live country music blaring from door to door. For that matter, there's no mistaking you're in Music City, USA as soon as you deplane at the Nashville airport. There are singers performing as you make your way to the baggage claim area. The Las Vegas airport has slot machines; the Nashville one entertainers.

My very first stop was The Johnny Cash Museum. It houses the largest and most comprehensive collection of Cash artifacts and memorabilia in the world. It includes interactive exhibits, clips of his performances and TV appearances, old guitars, gold records, costumes, handwritten notes and letters, all spotlighting different periods in Cash's life—his childhood in Arkansas, his hitch in the Air Force, his marriage to June Carter, the famous prison concert tours. I spent hours there, soaking it all up, finishing up at the gift shop, and shelling out a small fortune on T-shirts for the whole family. We're all big fans of Johnny Cash.

My own fandom comes from a very personal place. "The Man in Black" was a touchstone in my life dating back to my childhood. I remember watching him perform on television with my grandparents and hearing that deep booming voice—once called "The Voice of America." An even more indelible memory is of my grandfather, who read the newspaper religiously, coming across a mention of one of Cash's frequent brushes with the law (he was arrested five times in one seven-year span).

When that happened, the man we called "Daddy-Charles" would give the paper a quick shake, shoot my grandmother a disapproving look, and say to her, "Well, your cousin's in trouble again."

Whoa—were we related to Johnny Cash?

A man named Nettie Cash Fowler was a relative on my grandmother's side. I know nothing about him, but have an "Old West"-style photo of him in my family album. He has a distant look on his face, and his arms are crossed. There's a gun in one hand and a large knife in the other.

He looked like trouble.

Fowler was my grandmother Stella's last name when she married Charles McDaniel. So, even if she was only a distant relative of the famed entertainer, Daddy-Charles never let her forget it.

The possibility isn't that far-fetched. Johnny Cash was born in Kingsland, Arkansas, and my grandparents hailed from Friendship, Arkansas, about an hour's drive away. When they moved to Southern California in the 1930s they brought their Southern Baptist values and work ethic with them. They were like parents to me when I was sent to live with them while their daughter Charlene—my mother—was living her wild life.

It was almost like I was being raised in another century.

Among the old-fashioned values they instilled in me was showing respect for and obedience to your elders . . . or else! More than once, Daddy-Charles applied the "board of education" to the "seat of understanding."

I absorbed those values as thoroughly as I lapped up the tasty Southern dishes my grandmother prepared: fried chicken, mashed potatoes, black-eyed peas, okra, cornbread—and her crowning achievement, buttermilk biscuits made from scratch.

The large gilt-edged slab of black marble now in front of me is inscribed in gold lettering:

John R. Cash
Feb. 26, 1932
Sept. 12, 2003

PSALM 19:14
Let the words of my mouth,
and the meditation of my heart,
be acceptable in thy sight,
O Lord,
My strength,
And my redeemer.

As a Christian for almost fifty years and a pastor for decades, I know that verse well. I also find it interesting that it was chosen for Johnny's memorial.

"Let the words of *my mouth* . . ."

That's ironic, given that nobody had a voice or cadence like Johnny Cash. He could tell a story, like he did in his iconic 1969 song "A Boy Named Sue," and he could quote Scripture chapter and verse, like he did in his recording of the entire New Testament.

Therein lies the paradox of Johnny Cash.

He was both a sinner and a saint.

To many sinners, he was a saint, even a prophet-like figure, admired by idols of days gone by ranging from Elvis Presley, Paul McCartney, and Carl Perkins to modern-day rockers like Bono, Jack White, and Trent Reznor.

To many saints, he was a conflicted man, struggling with drugs and the law and a lot more most people don't know about.

In reality, John R. Cash was a lot like you and a lot like me.

Who else could be friends with Willie Nelson and Billy Graham at the same time?

Who else could play a large Las Vegas showroom and a Billy Graham Crusade in the same week?

Who else could play a gospel tune to a roomful of murderers, rapists, and thieves and have them eating out of the palm of his hand?

It's often said that it's best not to meet the people you admire most because you'll end up wishing you hadn't, but I doubt that would've been the case with Johnny Cash.

The closest I ever got to him was in Portland, Oregon. I was there assisting Billy Graham on one of his Crusades. I was just beginning my evangelistic ministry then, and Billy's was slowly coming to a close. Johnny and his wife June Carter Cash sang that night, and at intervals, I staked out the stage area during sound check and their dressing room, but I never even got within shouting distance of him. I should've tried harder.

Like millions of people, I was touched personally by Cash's life and music. When I became a Christian in 1970, the "Jesus Revolution," as *Time* magazine dubbed it, was in full swing. The high-water mark for many of us was a massive event called Explo '72 in Dallas, Texas, that brought new forms of worship into the church and paved the way for contemporary Christian music. Adding star-studded legitimacy was the presence of Billy Graham and a host of performers such as Kris Kristofferson, Love Song, Andrae Crouch and the Disciples—and Johnny Cash.

Having the famous and infamous Johnny Cash identify as "one of us" was a big deal. No disrespect intended, but Ernest Tubb just wouldn't have cut it.

Cash was many things to many people: a country music artist who sang and acted in a rock 'n' roll context; a social activist and a jailbird; an evangelist and an addict; a humanitarian who often stood up for the underrepresented and often butted heads with authority figures; a master storyteller and a world-class embellisher; an outlaw with the soul of a mystic; an impossible, tortured man who pinballed back and forth between extremes.

In addition to being "The Man in Black," Johnny Cash was also "The Godfather of Cool."

To me, being cool is to be real and authentic. It's not the person who morphs with the latest trends; it's the person who stays true to who he is. It's authenticity—being real, and original.

He also was an American icon, though he never copped to that.

"I see the pimples on my nose and I see a fat jaw where the pain has left me severely swollen, thinning hair, whatever," Cash said. "Icon? No. I don't see him. He's not in my mirror . . . no, thanks anyway."

But Cash was that icon—and he also was an unashamed follower of Jesus Christ.

During his heyday, Cash was constantly in the news. Not all the headlines were stellar. He was often embroiled in scandal or controversy stemming from high-profile arrests, car accidents, and other drug- and alcohol-induced escapades, including one resulting in a forest fire that devastated 508 acres. His music and social activism gave light and hope to others, but Cash's dark side often overruled his true nature.

"I confess right up front that I'm the biggest sinner of them all," Cash admitted. "But my faith in God has always been a solid rock that I've stood on, no matter where I was or what I was doing. I was a bad boy at times, but God was always there for me, and I knew that. I guess maybe I took advantage of that."

Maybe? He never killed anyone, but the other nine of God's Commandments seemed to be fair game. Cash's enormous successes were often rivaled by a litany of personal tribulation.

He had an angel on his shoulder, but the devil was always on his back.

Cash was a walking, talking contradiction who identified with the Apostle Paul—often ashamed and lacking the courage to stand up for Christ—in the first half of his life. All of these traits and foibles were rolled up in a larger-than-life, one-of-a-kind personality that put its own unique, indelible stamp on popular music and pop culture.

He was a devout Christian who divided his time between sinning and seeking forgiveness, frequently going from jail to Jesus. He was arrested several times on account of his addiction to pills and sophomoric shenanigans, and he knew almost every hymn and gospel tune ever sung, often performing them on stage between such hit songs as "I Walk the Line," "Ring of Fire," and "Cocaine Blues." He acknowledged God as the Number One power in the world, but viewed Satan as a close second.

"I learned not to laugh at the devil," Cash was once famously quoted as saying.

He was introduced to Jesus Christ as a dirt-poor child in the midst of the Great Depression. On his twelfth birthday Cash attended a revival meeting and went forward as the congregation sang the hymn "Just as I Am." But his brand-new faith was shaken to its core when he lost his older brother Jack, described by Johnny as his "hero, my best friend, my big buddy and my mentor," in a gruesome accident.

Cash had the understanding, the knowledge, the instincts, and the yearning, but he was torn between his spiritual life and his love of everything the secular, material world had to offer—fame, money, and their open invitations to sin. His behavior caused collateral damage to his family and friends, resulting in heartbreak, betrayal, and sadness. When living by the Word, he was inspiring. When diverted by temptation, his life became ugly and out of tune.

Like so many entertainers, Cash had two personas—the down-to-earth, doting family man at home and the defiant outlaw on the road. Dinners at home were warm and inviting, with lots of prayer, family time, and down-home music, everything from traditional hymns to rock standards. On the road, Cash was often distant, hard-driving, pill-popping—a full-tilt party-time outlaw who secretly carried a Bible in his briefcase. It was either black or white with Johnny . . . depending on what day or town it was. The struggle was constant, a never-ending competition.

Put another way, you could say Cash's image in the Highwaymen was the cowboy version of the British John in the Beatles. He was the mysterious and moody one who was noticeably different . . . the one you couldn't quite get a handle on.

According to a recent Pew Research Center study, Christianity is in steady decline in the United States. There are now more than 56 percent religious "Nones" in this country—people who either don't practice religion or don't ascribe to a particular faith. Six out of ten Millennials do not identify with any branch of Christianity at all. Turn on the TV news or open a newspaper (if your city still has one) if you don't believe me. Godlessness is on a roll.

Young people today, especially those who have never been introduced to the Bible or its figures, need modern-day examples in the flesh—as they say, "God with skin on."

The life of Johnny Cash offers one such stellar example. He felt his trials and tribulations were akin to those endured by the Apostle Paul. Like Paul, Cash stumbled, fell, dusted himself off, and got back up again. Understanding his triumphs, defeats, redemption, and story arc offers a way for people to relate to the Bible, which is why I have embarked on this project.

My approach to this book will be the same as in *Steve McQueen: The Salvation of an American Icon,* my 2017 bestseller. This won't be a straight biography. Anybody can look up the bare facts of Johnny Cash's life and career by going on Wikipedia or consulting a number of standout Cash books like Robert Hilburn's *Johnny Cash: A Life*; Michael Streissguth's *Johnny Cash: The Biography*; or Steve Turner's *A Man Called Cash.*

This offering is a lean and mean spiritual biography, tracing the roots of the faith instilled in Cash long before he became a household word. That faith was tested over and over—often in tortuous, turbulent ways—and I'm going to talk to friends, acquaintances, business associates, musicians, and close relatives who knew Johnny to learn how he faced and dealt with those tests to become the man he was. I'm not going to cover his scars with make-up or his failures with syrupy idolatry. And I'm not going to get into every granular detail of his epic life.

The truth of the whole man is compelling, and the story of Johnny Cash is a roadmap for every conflicted soul for whom redemption too often seems a destination far off the beaten path.

Thank you for accompanying me on this very personal and meaningful journey.

Greg Laurie
March 2019

PROLOGUE

When Johnny Cash entered the dark underground cave, he didn't intend to come back out.

Not alive.

The country music superstar was fed up, strung out, at the end of his emotional rope, and filled with self-loathing. He was an inconsiderate husband, an AWOL father, and a selfish person who had used and trampled over lots of people.

All because of the amphetamines Cash was addicted to.

They also made him hear voices—demons.

Once, sitting in his camper in the middle of the night, stewed to the gills on Dexadrine, he put his hand over his face and peeped through his fingers at his reflection in the rearview mirror.

"Let's kill us," the demons urged.

"I *can't* be killed," Cash told his reflection. "I'm indestructible."

"I dare you to try."

So Cash started up the camper and headed down the side of a steep mountain. The vehicle rolled over twice, and Cash broke his jaw in two places. But he'd showed those demons—he was indestructible.

Now he didn't want to be indestructible anymore.

His twelve-year marriage to a loving, dutiful wife had crumbled, and he had left four daughters in his self-destructive wake. He had financial problems, and his credibility with concert promoters was shot. Thanks to a diet consisting mostly of amphetamines, he had wasted away to a gaunt 150 pounds—almost skeletal for his six-foot-two frame. And when the tremors caused by the pills had him climbing the walls, he switched to barbiturates to calm himself down. He gulped down lots of beer in between.

The love of June Carter was the only bright spot in his life, but his addiction was driving her away, too. Cash had repeatedly asked her to marry him, but June always said only when he got clean— a prospect farther away than ever. Now he was even getting stoned in front of his parents.

His drug use had isolated him from everyone, and many had written him off. Cash felt abandoned, lonely, and completely hopeless. He had wasted his life, drifting so far from God and every good and stabilizing influence that there was no point in going on.

So, in early October 1967, he descended into the byzantine arrangement of caves that ran beneath the mountains from Tennessee to Alabama.

For decades, the caves had attracted the curious and provided shelter for fugitives. Cash had explored them with friends looking for Civil War and Native American artifacts, and he knew that several people had died there after getting lost in the dank passages.

He crawled underground for hours until his flashlight died out and he was exhausted. Then he lay still and waited for the pervasive blackness to claim him.

1

———

THE GRAPES OF CASH

"A midwife delivered me,
Mary Easterling.
The doctor came several hours later
and gave my mom two aspirin."

—JOHNNY CASH

Growing up in rural Arkansas, there was no avoiding God's existence in the daily life of Johnny Cash. He was at the center of the
Cash household because the family's faith was simple and trusting.
He was with them in the fields when they picked cotton; He was with
them at church on Sundays, and He was in their midst each night at
suppertime when they asked Him to bless their hard-earned bounty.
God was their protector and provider, there for them in the good
times and the bad.

I also believe God was watching over and guiding Johnny's Scot-
tish antecedents, starting with William Cash, a twenty-something

master mariner who captained his own wooden brigantine called the *Good Intent*, which transported cargo and pilgrims to America in the 1600s. A voyage from the United Kingdom to Salem generally took two months and was fraught with all manner of danger—unpredictable storms, rough seas, and the dreaded disease scurvy that was a common and ruthless affliction on long sea journeys.

Intrepid William Cash helped establish the routes used in the British Isles-American colonies commerce that followed. Among the passengers on one of his voyages to America was his nephew William, who planted the Cash family flag in Westmoreland County, Virginia. A few generations removed, the first John Cash was born in 1757 and fought in the war for American Independence. In 1829, he moved from Bedford County, Virginia, to Henry County, Georgia. A grandson named Moses Cash served in the Confederate Army.

William Henry Cash, Johnny's grandfather, was born in Elbert County, Georgia, in 1852 and migrated to Toledo, Arkansas, a town that virtually disappeared overnight when the new railroad went through nearby Rison.

"Billy" Cash, as Johnny's grandfather was known, was a God-fearing man and a rough customer if crossed. He was a farmer and a circuit rider—a traveling Baptist preacher who served four widely scattered congregations, riding to and fro on horseback. In addition to the Bible he used to preach the Gospel, Billy always packed a hog leg pistol—some said it was two feet long—and he wasn't afraid to use it if someone got in the way of the Lord's work.

Billy Cash was what today might be called a hellfire-and-brimstone preacher. Some people complain there are too many preachers today cut from that cloth, but quite frankly, there are not enough of them. I see lots of preachers on TV, but can't remember the last time I heard a message on judgment and hellfire from them.

That's not all preachers should talk about, but when they leave it out completely, they are not delivering an authentic Gospel message.

The world could use a few more good old-fashioned, hellfire-and-brimstone, Gospel preachers like Billy Cash today.

This seemed to be Billy's grandson's mindset, as well.

Johnny Cash sang about a final judgment and facing the consequences for your sins often in his songs. One—a traditional folk song called "God's Gonna Cut You Down"—comes to mind:

You can run on for a long time,
Run on for a long time,
Run on for a long time.
Sooner or later, God'll cut you down
Sooner or later, God'll cut you down

Looks like Johnny had more than a little of his grandfather's blood in him.

Reverend Billy Cash never received nor asked for a single dime for his services, but members of his far-flung flocks often expressed their appreciation for his efforts by gifting him livestock from their farms. It helped feed his dozen children, who were birthed over a twenty-two-year period.

The youngest of Billy Cash's brood, Johnny's father Ray, was born in 1897 in Kingsland, Arkansas. In his first autobiography, Johnny said of his dad, "I don't believe a man ever lived who worked harder and was more dedicated to providing a living for his family."

Cash family historian and biographer Mark Stielper views Ray differently.

"His early years were misspent wandering between neighboring counties, never keeping a job long or leaving a mark," Stielper said. "Every so often, Ray Cash would hop a train, but according to a relative 'didn't have the initiative to go very far' and always ended up back in Kingsland."

Stielper's summation: Ray Cash was "a non-starter and stayed that way."

The available evidence supports the latter verdict. Ray had no high school diploma (he quit school at fourteen to help his widowed mother), no job training, no safety net. He lived on wit and grit, and when he did work, it was as a day laborer scraping out a hardscrabble existence through a variety of odd jobs and back-straining work in the midst of the Great Depression.

Ray was a hard case with a short fuse, and it didn't help that he lived in the shadow of his older brother Dave after their father passed away in 1912 of Parkinson's disease at age sixty. The brothers Cash had butted heads since childhood and grew even more distant and disparate as the years passed. While Ray barely kept his head above water doing menial work, Dave was ruthless in his pursuit of wealth, building up an empire as a land and cattle baron. He became a county sheriff and later a judge.

At age eighteen, Ray joined the Arkansas National Guard. When World War I broke out, the Guard was federalized as part of the U.S. Army. Ray was about to ship out to France when the Armistice was signed in November 1918. Ray told Johnny that his military company was dispatched to pursue Pancho Villa after the Mexican revolutionary invaded the USA in 1916 and killed seventeen American citizens, but Mark Stielper found no evidence supporting the claim. The fact is Ray was as hapless at soldiering as he was at everything else. Assigned to guard a military supply train, he left his post to visit a girlfriend, returning to find the train he was supposed to watch was gone. Somehow, Ray avoided a court-martial, and on July 1, 1919, he received an honorable discharge from the Army.

By then, Kingsland was a rural outpost with more trees than people, so devoid of charm and interest that Johnny Cash would remember it as merely "a place on the side of the road." It was originally a railroad town and in its heyday boasted six hundred residents, three hotels, a furniture store, a lumber mill, four mercantile stores, three drugstores, and a grocery. That was before the timber mills—Cleveland County's major industry—closed down. The cotton trade also tanked, spiraling the local economy into a tailspin. A local bank closed and never reopened, businesses were shuttered, homes foreclosed, and residents moved on in search of better lives.

"It wasn't a place that time forgot," said Mark Stielper. "Rather, it was simply a place that time never knew."

When Ray Cash returned home, Kingsland's population was down to just seventy-five people. One of them was Carrie Cloveree Rivers. Born in 1904, she was the eighth child of John and Rosanna Lee Rivers, a farm couple who also led the choir at the Crossroads Methodist Church. Four of their offspring had already died by the time Carrie came along, and three more siblings died before her eighth birthday, none living past the age of two.

Ray boarded with the Rivers family during the brief time he worked cutting lumber for a bridge built across the Saline River. He paid the Rivers a dollar a day for room and board. He also paid a lot of attention to fifteen-year-old Carrie.

The twenty-two-year-old Cash wasn't viewed as a model citizen in Kingsland, and when he began courting Carrie, some town folk went so far as to express their objections with threats and their fists. Ray took to openly packing a sidearm.

He and Carrie were an oddly matched couple, physically and otherwise. She was tall and slender, towering over the broad, stocky Ray, who stood five-foot-eight. The difference in personalities was just as stark. She was graceful, eternally optimistic, and consistent; he was dour, unrefined and unpredictable. Carrie wasn't much for drinking, dancing, or smoking and was wholly devoted to God. Ray was considered a backslider; he liked hooch and rolled his own cigarettes.

Most of what has been written and said about Ray Cash over the years has been negative. Even in *Walk the Line*, the highly praised 2005 Johnny Cash biopic whose script Johnny himself personally approved, Ray was portrayed as a sullen, domineering, and bad influence in his son's life.

It's important to keep in mind that every hero's story requires a special villain or nemesis. For Elvis, it was "Colonel" Tom Parker. Allen Klein filled that role for the Beatles in their last days together. Muhammad Ali had "Smokin' " Joe Frazier. In the great sprawling saga of Johnny Cash, the black hat has been plopped on the head of his father, but I'm not sure that's altogether fair. Ray was far from a model father, but Johnny loved him and spent his lifetime craving his approval. Ray grew up in hard times, and hard times make hard people. We are all, to a certain extent, products of our environment. Maybe Ray Cash didn't have much of a sensitive, nurturing side, but he didn't abandon his family and, for the most part, did the best he could.

But there were times—even into Cash's adulthood—where his ugly nature would rear its ugly head.

When Johnny was at the peak of his career, he welcomed famed evangelist Billy Graham and his wife Ruth to his home for dinner. Ray and Carrie Cash were also invited. After the Grahams departed, according to Mark Stielper, Johnny turned to his father and said, "Well, that was worth something, wasn't it?"

Replied Ray Cash, "You ain't nothing, boy!"

He and Carrie Rivers were married on August 18, 1920. A year after that came their son, Roy. Three years later, daughter Margaret Louise was born. Jack Cash joined them in 1929.

Moving from job to job as he did, Ray could not offer much financial stability to his growing family. When times got especially tough, he swallowed his pride and worked clearing land, tending cattle, and cutting wood for his older brother Dave. One time, his brother ordered him to slaughter fifty of his poorest cattle, handing him a shotgun and a couple of shell boxes. He was paid only a couple of dollars and suffered nightmares as a result of his handiwork.

Ray and his family lived in what was no better than a wooden squatter's shack on the property. A family of sharecroppers lived in similarly squalid digs next door. One night, their shack caught fire, and everyone inside perished except for a young girl. The day after she was sent away, one of Ray's jobs was to help build a new shanty on the site of the burned-down one to lodge a new family of dirt-poor sharecroppers.

Sharecropping, also known as feudalism, developed in the post-Civil War American South, not all that different from the slavery the War Between the States was fought to end. In sharecropping, a landowner allowed a tenant to live on and farm a portion of his land in exchange for a share of the crop the tenant raised. The landowner also leased farming equipment to his sharecroppers and offered seed, fertilizer, food, and other necessities on credit. Unpredictable harvests and usurious interest rates systematically kept tenant farm families deep in debt and existing at a subsistence level. There was no recourse for the sharecroppers because laws written by and in favor of landlords rendered them powerless and established them as a permanent underclass.

Being the big bossman's brother didn't get Ray any better treatment than the other tenants barely eking out a living in the fiefdom of Dave Cash. Not once in the time Ray worked for Dave were he, Carrie, and their kids invited to Dave's large, comfortable house for a family gathering, a holiday celebration, or just Sunday dinner. To Dave, his younger brother was just another cog in the machinery designed to increase the almighty profit margin.

"What this meant," said Mark Stielper, "was even before the boy (Johnny) Cash was born, there was instilled in his family and the fabric of his town, an attitude of defeat, of worthlessness, and not being able to ever measure up."

My grandfather, Charles McDaniel, was cut from the same cloth as Ray Cash.

Not one to dream, he just went out and worked hard from morning to night. And he expected others to do the same.

But Johnny Cash was different. He was a sensitive young boy, and he was a dreamer. He may have not been much in his father's eyes, but he had a Heavenly Father who did love him.

King David comes to mind here.

He was not always the king.

When a prophet named Samuel was told to go to the house of a man named Jesse in Bethlehem to find the next king of Israel to take the place of the disobedient King Saul, he met the "magnificent seven."

Jesse trotted out seven strapping sons, each more handsome than the other. But as the prophet Samuel walked down the line, none of them seemed to fit the bill.

Exasperated, Samuel asked Jesse, "Do you have any more sons?"

Yes, Jesse admitted reluctantly, there was one ... young David.

David spent much time in the field, tending his flock.

He also was a talented musician who composed his own songs of praise to God.

Jesse did not know what to do with him.

But David had both his feet on the ground. If any predator tried to harm his flock, he was fearless and very accurate with his sling and stone.

When summoned, David bounded in, full of youthful energy, and the Lord whispered into the prophet's ear, "That's the next king of Israel!"

Who could have seen the massive potential in young Johnny Cash?

His father didn't, but God did.

Of course, God seems to go out of His way to choose the undesirables, the failures, the undeserving, for His special tasks.

Another biblical character comes to mind.

Gideon was a farmer like Johnny and Ray, and he was hiding from his enemies when an angel of the Lord appeared to him and said, "Mighty hero, the Lord is with you!" (Judges 6:12 NLT)

Gideon was not feeling like much of a hero then. More like a zero.

But God does not merely see us for what we are. He sees us for what we can become.

When the angel told Gideon that God had chosen him to rescue Israel, Gideon protested: "How can I rescue Israel? My clan is the weakest in the whole tribe of Manasseh, and I am the least in my entire family!" (Judges 6:15 NLT)

But God did rescue Israel through Gideon.

And the Lord also touched the world through the life and music of Johnny Cash.

The house Johnny Cash was born in is no longer there. It wasn't the shack his parents had on Dave Cash's land, but rather Carrie's parents' house. It wasn't much of a step up. There was no running water, no electricity, no windows, and the floor was dirt, not wood. But John and Rosanna Rivers wanted to ensure their daughter had a safe labor and delivery, and a midwife was on hand to assist in the process.

The baby arrived on February 26, 1932, weighing in at a hearty eleven pounds.

A few days later, a rare winter storm swept through southern Arkansas, dumping snow on the ground and plunging temperatures down to dangerously low levels. In an effort to protect her infant son from the deadly cold, Carrie lined the inside walls of the house with blankets and huddled with him till the arctic conditions eased up.

Carrie wanted to name the baby John Rivers Cash, but Ray had something way more grandiose in mind. He had named their second son Jack after Jack Dempsey, the heavyweight boxing champion of the world. For his newborn son, Ray's idea was to name him after another famous American also born on February 26—Buffalo Bill Cody, the legendary scout, Indian fighter, and Wild West show impresario. To Carrie, that made as much sense as a boy named Sue, and it was a whole month before they finally settled on the name John R. Cash, though the locals and his family called him J.R. He would go by that until he joined the Air Force in 1950. The recruiter insisted on a full name, not initials, so J.R. became John R. Cash—again. A few years later, when his music career took off, he became Johnny Cash.

The Great Depression undermined crop prices and virtually shut down the cotton industry, and the ones who soldiered on barely scraped by. A government report called sharecroppers "dependents without control over their own destinies, with little chance for self-respect with so little hope."

In an effort to change that, different colonies and experimental communities were started around the country in 1934 to retrain sharecroppers. The largest of them was on sixteen thousand acres of drained swampland in Mississippi County, Arkansas. The idea was to build a model farming community whose residents would pull themselves up by their bootstraps; learn modern, efficient farming techniques; and share in the communal bounty. Each family accepted into the program would receive a new house, twenty acres of land to clear and cultivate, a barn, a mule, a milk cow, and a hen coop. They didn't have to put any money down or pay it back until the first crop came in. The government also planned to build a town hall, cinema, cotton mill, cannery, school, hospital, churches, cotton mill, and shops. To ensure the best market price, all the cotton grown would be sold in bulk, with the proceeds divided equally among its residents.

As soon as Ray Cash heard about the New Deal program, he practically sprinted to the courthouse in nearby Rison to apply. So did just about everybody else in Kingsland.

"When word got out about this new opportunity, the whole town lined up to get out," said Mark Stielper. "Imagine people wanting to get out of a place so badly they're willing to relocate to a swamp!"

By November 1934, two families had been chosen from Kingsland to move to the new model farm cooperative in Dyess, Arkansas: The Doster and Tatum families were the ones from Kingsland on the initial list. But in March of '35, Ray Cash was notified that his family would also be moving to Dyess.

How that happened was a subject of great speculation. Some said the fix was in and that the man behind it was Judge Dave Cash.

Ray was never happy working for his successful older brother and made no bones about it. Dave personally couldn't have cared less, but the constant friction between the Cashes was an open secret in Cleveland County and therefore a potential political liability. When Dave heard that Ray wanted to go to Dyess, it's not beyond the realm of possibility that he saw it as a golden opportunity to get his grumbling sibling out of his hair once and for all and pulled strings to make it happen. Who knows—perhaps Dave even did it as an act of mercy and pure brotherly love.

However it happened, the growing Cash family said goodbye to Kingsland.

Young J.R. had just turned three when Ray and Carrie loaded him, thirteen-year-old Roy, eleven-year-old Louise, five-year-old Jack, and one-year-old Reba into the back of a truck to their new home in Dyess. The two hundred-mile journey took two days, and when storms turned the dirt roads into gooey impassable mud, Ray pulled over till it was safe to continue driving. In the bed of the truck, the kids listened to the rain drumming on the tarpaulin over their heads and to their mother singing up front next to Ray. Sometimes they joined in, and ever after, Cash recalled the first song he ever sang was on that trip—the hymn "I Am Bound for the Promised Land." It was a fitting, glorious soundtrack for the odyssey taking the Cashes to new hope and opportunity.

Dyess was built on swampland, and the omnipresent mud there (called "gumbo" by residents) was so impenetrable that the pilgrims had to abandon their truck well before arriving at house No. 266 on Road Three, two and a half miles from the town center. Ray carried J.R. and his younger sister on his back to the just-completed house constructed by a thirty-man team that built one dwelling every two days. The paint job—green trim, white everywhere else—was barely dry when the Cashes entered their new home; five empty paint buckets were still on the living room floor.

The Cash homestead had two bedrooms, a living room, dining room, and kitchen. Outside were an outhouse, barn, chicken coop, and a smokehouse.

"There was no running water, of course, and no electricity," Johnny Cash wrote in his 1997 autobiography. "None of us even dreamed of miracles like that."

It was miracle enough that they were there, together, in a house grander than any they had ever known, on the cusp of a future that was beyond their imaginations just a few weeks before. "The Promised Land" indeed. Amidst the paint cans, the Cashes went to their knees and thanked God for their deliverance.

2

COTTONING TO CHRIST

"The hardest thing I ever did in my life?
That's easy: cotton . . .
I picked it, I chopped it, I hauled it.
It was drudgery."

—JOHNNY CASH

I don't imagine much has changed in Dyess, Arkansas, since J.R. Cash and his family lived there more than eight decades ago. On a recent visit, I discovered several things. The population hasn't wavered much over time, except that it has dwindled since its heyday—it hovers around the four hundred mark. The land is still owned by many of the same families that settled the New Deal colony, having been passed down through the generations. The "gumbo" is as dark and thick as ever. Cotton is still grown in Dyess and the outlying area, though the harvests aren't as large as they used to be.

The church where the Cash family worshipped is still there. The movie theater where J.R. watched his favorite Westerns and serials as a kid is now a museum and souvenir shop. The bridge over the Tyronza River, off of which J.R. once tossed his younger brother Tommy to teach him how to swim, remains sturdy and dependable. The house in which Cash received the first and only singing lesson he ever had in his life from instructor LaVanda Mae Fielder is dilapidated and abandoned.

Dyess seems to exist more in the past than the present. Launched in 1934 by the federal government as the largest experiment in agrarian living in the continental United States, it is mostly known today as the place where Johnny Cash grew up, and most visitors to Dyess nowadays come for a look at what has just been listed on the National Register of Historic Places as "Farm 266—Johnny Cash Boyhood Home." Most of the other fourteen original houses on that road are long gone. Road Three leading to the Cash house is still unpaved.

It was in that house where Johnny Cash tapped into his passion for music.

"I think for the first time I knew what I was going to do was when I was four years old," he recalled. "I was listening to an old Victrola playing a railroad song. The song was called 'Hobo Bill's Last Ride.' I thought that was the most wonderful, amazing thing I'd ever seen . . . that you could take this piece of wax and music would come out of that box."

As idyllic as their new surroundings seemed to the Cashes at first, it wasn't long before they learned that their Mississippi Delta paradise was not invulnerable to the whims and furies of nature. One of Cash's most vivid memories was of the Great Mississippi River Flood of 1937 that submerged the entire town and seventeen adjacent counties that January. He was four years old at the time. Most residents of Dyess were forced to evacuate as floodwaters invaded their homes. While Ray and Roy Cash stayed behind to try to protect their house from the rising tide, Carrie and the other children went back to Kingsland until the coast was clear.

"According to my dad, the waters reached halfway up the walls," said Joanne Cash Yates. "He spent days filling up sandbags, but it was of no use. The water was too swift and rising."

When the Cashes returned to No. 266 in February, they found the house not only covered with mud inside and out but also full of animals that had taken refuge there. The sofa in the living room had fresh-laid hen eggs on it.

Years later, Cash would draw on his memories of the flood to write his classic song "Five Feet High and Rising." A more immediate silver lining came in the spring of '37, he recalled, when "Daddy and my older brother Roy cleared a lot more cotton land and the cotton grew tall in 1938."

It was all hands on deck in the cotton fields. When J.R. reached middle childhood, he carried water to his parents, brother Roy, and sister Louise as they tended their crop. At eight, he worked alongside them filling a six-foot-long canvas sack with cotton. Sometimes, he also used the sack to entertain his little sister.

"He used to call me 'Baby' because I'm the baby sister," Joanne Cash Yates said. "He'd say, 'Baby, you can come and ride on my cotton sack.' He watched over me for hours while he picked cotton. That was really the start of our relationship."

Cash's childhood friend A J Henson recalled J.R. as a prodigious cotton picker.

"J.R. was an extremely hard worker and on a good day could pick up to three hundred pounds," Henson said. "The most I ever picked was about 175 pounds. He pulled his own weight, that's for sure."

The work was monotonous, dirty, and tiring—ten hours a day during harvest season. The boll of the cotton was sharp, and even with gloves, pickers ended up with sore, bleeding hands. Then there were the Delta summers, which were usually brutally hot and steamy. Air-conditioning at the Cash house consisted of opening all the doors and windows and lying on the linoleum floor to cool off.

Even if there was air conditioning for some folk, it's a pretty sure bet the Cashes would not have been able to afford it. They were the very definition of dirt poor, according to Kelly Hancock, whose mother Reba was Johnny Cash's sister.

"It wasn't an easy existence because they didn't have anything," Hancock said. "Grandma Cash made a dress out of a flour sack for my mom, and she had to wear it to school. The kids made fun of her, and she was embarrassed. She told me this story more than once. It was horrible for her."

In the fields, the family often sang hymns to ease the drudgery and lighten their hearts. Recalled Joanne Cash Yates, "J.R. would lead sometimes, and we'd all join in. We got pretty good in those cotton fields and before we knew it, the day would be over. We'd sing every old church hymn you could imagine—'The Uncloudy Day,' 'Amazing Grace.' My mother would go back early from the fields to fix supper. When the food was ready, she'd come to the back door and sing 'Suppertime.'"

Many years ago in days of childhood,
I used to play till evening shadows come home,
Then winding down that old familiar pathway,
I'd hear my mother call at setting sun,
"Come home, come home, it's suppertime,
The shadows mean come fast,
Come home, come home, it's suppertime,
We're going home at last."

Most of their food they produced themselves. From their garden, they had lima beans, corn, potatoes, tomatoes, okra, cucumbers, watermelons, and cantaloupes. Carrie wrung a chicken's neck like her son later played a guitar; her fried chicken was an eagerly anticipated staple of Sunday dinners. A pen full of hogs provided smoked ham, bacon, pork chops, pork loin roast, pork rinds, and that classic Southern delicacy, pickled pig's feet. (For the rest of his life, the mere scent of hickory smoke would instantly transport Cash back to the wooden smokehouse in the backyard of No. 266.) From the potbelly stove in the kitchen came delicious baked biscuits, cornbread, sliced tomatoes, fried okra, candied sweet potatoes, and green beans with fatback.

That takes me back to my own childhood. My mother Charlene was the classic prodigal daughter; she ran away from home and eloped while still a young girl. Her parents, Charles and Stella, were strict Southern Baptists, and as I've mentioned, my grandfather was a strong disciplinarian. When my mom was a young girl and once dared to wear pants—not allowed in the McDaniel household—Daddy-Charles made her take them off, and he threw them into the fireplace.

In between her seven husbands, Charlene had a fling with a sailor from Long Beach, and I was conceived. She had no interest in being a mother, and I was sent to live with her parents. I remember the delicious meals Mama Stella made for us—fried chicken, okra, black-eyed peas, collard greens, mashed potatoes, cornbread, and fresh buttermilk biscuits.

Food for the soul for the Cash family came from the Bible. It was read daily and was supplemented with frequent prayer and hymn singing. Sundays and Wednesdays were strictly reserved for worship at Dyess Central Baptist Church. The three-story wooden building had a capacity of four hundred, and most Sundays it was packed—an impressive feat considering the size of the town and the fact that the Central Baptist competed with the Church of Christ and several other houses of worship in the area.

The Church of Christ was a non-denominational derivative of the American Restoration Movement (also known as the Stone-Campbell Movement), which had its roots on the United States frontier during the Second Great Awakening of the early nineteenth century. Its aim was to be practical and spiritual and to restore the church of the New Testament through doctrines, ordinances, and faith.

"The simple doctrine of the Church of Christ is to follow the teachings of the New Testament, not pick it apart or skip the things you don't like or add things to do," said A J Henson, whose mother attended the church in Dyess. "We speak where the Bible speaks and are silent where the Bible is silent."

Church of Christ services were relatively staid, no-frills affairs. Congregants sang, but decorously and without accompaniment from an organ or other musical instruments. A J Henson's dad was a Baptist, and he would occasionally go with him to services at Central Baptist, where the boisterous hymn singing and general let-it-all-hang-out atmosphere made his jaw drop. The traditional Baptist altar call especially fascinated him—except for the unnerving time his friend J.R. Cash playfully nudged him to join the procession.

The rides to church are what stick in J.R.'s little sister's memory.

"My daddy would put us in the wagon with a team of horses, and we'd ride to church down that dirt and gravel road," said Joanne Cash Yates. "It was about two and a half miles. When we got there, he'd tie the horses to a tree across the road. That was thrilling to me as a child."

The service itself was usually the opposite of thrilling thanks to the fire-and-brimstone sermons of Rev. Hal Gallop, designed to scare and shame his audience into immediate and total redemption. There was little uplifting, lyrical, or life-affirming in his message. It was "Be saved right now, by God, or go to hell!"

As I've said, there is a place for talking about the reality of hell and final judgment. Jesus himself spoke more about hell than all the other preachers in the Bible put together. But the Bible also says, "It is the goodness of God that leads us to repentance" (Romans 2:4 NKJV). People need to know that God loves them and desires a personal relationship with them. I don't know that my mother, who ran from the church, understood that until much later in her life.

Cottoning to Christ

It was even worse for the impressionable youngsters at the Road 14 Pentecostal Church that Carrie Cash sometimes attended with members of the family in tow. There the fiery, relentless harangues totally unleavened by optimism and hope pitched some listeners into fits of moaning and writhing on the floor.

"That really scared me," Joanne Cash Yates said. "I remember one incident where I was asleep and awoke to see a fire in a wooded area. It scared J.R., too, and he went to Mama and asked, 'Is that hell coming?' He was really scared, and she said, 'No, son. That's just some farmer that started a fire.' But because of those preachers preaching so strong and we were so young, it was really scary."

Kelly Hancock said this style of preaching turned off her mother Reba Cash to religion almost her entire adult life.

"Whenever you have something shoved down your throat, it always has the opposite effect of what your parents wanted," Hancock said. "It was real fire-and-brimstone preaching, and it was a part of their everyday lives."

Cash himself later remembered walking on a lonely country road one night, seeing the red glow of a fire in the distance, and thinking with a shiver, *That is that hell I've been hearing about!*

In his 1975 autobiography, Cash recalled one preacher's over-the-top performance at a Pentecostal service his mother took him to:

"He was a young man in an old, brown tweed suit with a necktie that I thought must have been choking him to death, for he could get out only three or four words between breaths. I would count them. When he got to where he could shout only two words between breaths, I just knew he was going to die—or explode."

The preacher's respiratory distress didn't prevent him, however, from diving into the congregation now and then to yank someone out of his seat and shout in his face, "Come to God! Repent!" Cash recalled holding onto his seat so hard his knuckles turned white after one woman began flopping around on the floor and making guttural sounds, and the pleased preacher stood over her triumphantly,

37

wheezing, "She's got the Holy Ghost!" She looked like she had the dreaded St. Vitus's Dance. What was joyful and inspiring about that? These kinds of preachers were not giving a balanced view of the Gospel and what it really means to know God and have a relationship with Him.

At least the church choir used musical instruments to sweeten its hymns—guitar, mandolin, banjo, and piano. The effect was enchanting and stimulating to young J.R. His dad had recently bought a Sears Roebuck battery-powered radio for the living room at home, and the whole family loved listening to music and programs such as *Gangbusters*, *Inner Sanctum*, *The Squeaking Door*, and *Supper-Time Frolics*.

One show in particular caught their fancy, recalled sister Joanne Cash Yates.

"The *Grand Ole Opry* on Saturday night was a real treat for us. J.R. and I would sit facing each other in straight-back chairs, and Jack and Tommy and my sisters would listen as well," she said.

J.R.'s burgeoning creativity wasn't limited to music. He also wrote poetry and short stories and according to sister Joanne, was a gifted doodler.

"He drew Mighty Mouse with the stroke of his pen and paper and did a drawing called 'Flight of a Beautiful Bird,' and they were great pieces," she recalled. "Later on, he wrote songs and was an extremely talented photographer. He'd take pictures of bugs and then enlarge them. He was always doing something creative."

A J Henson remembered the time he had to write a poem for school with a Western theme and turned to his imaginative friend J.R. for help. Seven decades later, Henson recalled the closing lines of the poem that earned him a grade of A:

The top hand mounted his trusty steed
And rode across the plain.
He said, "I'll ride until setting sun
Unless I lose my rein."

The horse gave a jump and then a jerk
And Bob drew up the slack.
He rode his trail until setting sun
Then rode a freight train back.

Spiritually, by the time he was eleven, J.R. had started to sort things out for himself.

"I knew there was two distinct ways to go in life," he wrote in his first autobiography. "The people who had their hearts right—I recognized them as being different from the ones who were playing checkers over at the service station during the church service."

He sought God's presence through prayer and music. Songs like "I'll Fly Away" transported him to another place. "To me, songs were the telephone to heaven, and I tied up the line quite a bit," Cash reflected.

J.R. attended a revival meeting in Dyess shortly after his twelfth birthday on February 26, 1944. When it came time for the altar call, the choir started singing the hymn "Just as I Am."

Just as I am, without one plea,
But that Thy blood was shed for me,
And that Thou bidd'st me come to Thee,
O Lamb of God, I come, I come!

This was a well-known hymn in the South, further popularized by Billy Graham in his Crusades, sung as thousands of people streamed forward to make their public profession of faith to follow Jesus Christ.

"Just as I Am" brings back a very personal memory.

My mother called me one night when she had been drinking. I was a young pastor, and I prayed constantly for her to come to Christ. Slurring her words, she asked if I would sing "Just as I Am" if she would go forward to commit her life to Christ at one my services. I would have sung anything if she did that. When I brought it up to her the next day, when she was sober, she had no recollection of our conversation and wouldn't talk about it.

In the front row at that revival in Dyess was Cash's older brother Jack, whom he idolized, his eyes closed as he sang along with the choir. Up till then, J.R. hadn't been particularly moved or affected by anything he'd heard that night; in fact, when the song started, he was thinking of cutting out and going home. But all of a sudden, he felt his soul touched by the music, the words, and the inevitable choice facing every child of God going back to Adam and Eve: to accept Jesus Christ as Lord and Savior or to reject Him. It was an easy decision. Cash walked to the altar and knelt with the other converts.

"I left feeling awfully good that night," he later recalled, "feeling joy and relief at having made my decision."

He was formally baptized shortly thereafter by Rev. Hal Gallop at the Blue Hole, a favorite fishing and swimming spot on the Tyronza River.

Faith is a wonderful and powerful thing, and young Cash reveled in the peace and contentment it brought him. But he would soon find out that it doesn't automatically inoculate us from pain, misery, temptation, doubt, pride, and all the other frailties that are our birthright as mere human beings.

3

MEET ME IN HEAVEN

"Jack was an inspiration not only to the whole community, but to me—like a beacon for me to look back to as years went by. When a moral issue or decision comes up, I put myself back to 1943 and say, 'What would Jack do?'"

—JOHNNY CASH

Johnny Cash's brother Jack was two years older. Jack was his protector, best friend, fishing buddy, and mentor. The brothers were inseparable; no one who knew them back then can remember a cross word between them.

"Jack was the essence of a Christian and very godly," said Joanne Cash Yates. "He was very kind. I do not ever remember him raising his voice. He prayed all the time and was forever encouraging J.R. 'You need to be sure you follow the Lord in your life and in whatever you're doing,' he'd say. When J.R. would say, 'I know I'm gonna sing,' Jack would respond, 'I know I'm gonna be a preacher.'"

By the time Jack was fourteen, the small print Bible he carried with him everywhere was close to being worn out. Cash remembered that while he listened to the radio every night before bedtime, Jack intently studied Scripture at the dining room table by the light of a kerosene lamp.

Jack was dependable and worked hard in the fields. He also delivered the *Memphis Press-Scimitar* in Dyess, impressing everyone with his easy-going personality and work ethic.

He was so devout that J.R. never forgot the one time he heard his brother cuss. They were hunting cottonmouth snakes in the drainage ditches bordering the farm, one of their favorite pastimes in summer. They'd whack the snakes with their fishing poles while the reptiles sunned themselves on low-hanging branches of willow trees.

On this excursion, they came upon one of the biggest cottonmouths Johnny had ever seen. Jack crept up, and as he took a mighty cut at the snake with his pole, he yelled, "Die, damn you!"

J.R. was as stunned as if Jack had hit him instead. "I didn't know you cussed," he said.

Jack immediately apologized and promised it wouldn't ever happen again.

"I think it bothered Jack that he had come down a notch or two in my estimation," wrote Cash in his first autobiography. "He told me later he had asked God's forgiveness, and again, he was all right in my eyes. Because he knew his influence over me had been temporarily endangered, he made it a point to heal the wound."

Jack more than made up for it the time he and J.R. went to the co-op store in Dyess run by a man named Steele. Steele belonged to a rather extreme church and thought everyone who didn't was doomed to eternal judgment, and he never passed up an opportunity to tell them so to their face.

"Jack," he said to the older Cash brother, "you know if you don't belong to my church you're going to hell, don't you?"

A cussword or two would have been an understandable response this time, but instead Jack started to sing the hymn "Are You Washed in the Blood?":

Have you been to Jesus for the cleansing power,
Are you washed in the blood of the Lamb?
Are you fully trusting in His grace this hour,
Are you washed in the blood of the Lamb?

Steele's face turned beet red, and he ordered the Cashes out of the store. Jack left smiling.

God clearly had his hand on young Jack Cash.

The Bible is filled with the stories of very young men and women of God who were wise beyond their years. Shadrach, Meshach, and Abednego were most likely young teens when they took their courageous stand not to bow before the golden image that Nebuchadnezzar had erected. Esther, the beautiful girl who saved the Jewish people, was very young when she was selected. Some scholars believe the prophet Jeremiah was around seventeen when God called him. The Lord even told him to not use his youth as an excuse not to respond. "But the Lord said to me, 'Do not say, "I am too young." You must go to everyone I send you to and say whatever I command you" (Jeremiah 1:7 NIV).

Mary, who was hand-picked by God to have the privilege of being the mother of the Messiah of Israel and the Savior of the world, may have only been fifteen years old when called by God.

Of course, her pregnancy was a miracle, but a lot of people never bought it. She bore that shame for the rest of her life.

Paul wrote to the young Timothy and said, "Don't let anyone think less of you because you are young. Be an example to all believers in what you say, in the way you live, in your love, your faith, and your purity" (1 Timothy 4:12 NLT).

Jack Cash was that in spades.

He was an example to his younger brother and others, even if he got angry at snakes that would not die quickly enough every now and then.

As much as Jack witnessed to others, he never did so to Johnny.

"I don't think he ever tried to talk religion to me or make it a point to try to tell me about salvation," Cash recalled. "He and I were so close that I'm sure he knew I was seeing it in him, for I admired and looked up to him."

Even when J.R.'s behavior fell short of his brother's high standards, Jack never called him out on it. When J.R. was twelve, he started stealing tobacco from his father's pouch and bumming cigarettes from older kids. Jack knew and disapproved but said nothing. He credited J.R. with enough sense to eventually make the right decisions.

On a Saturday morning in May 1944, Johnny wanted to go fishing and asked his big brother to come along. But the always-industrious Jack worked Saturdays cutting fence posts at the Dyess High School's agricultural building; the $3 he earned helped the family out, and he dutifully placed the money in a pint fruit jar and stored it in an old cracker tin. The boys headed out together, and, till they went their separate ways a mile down the road, J.R. begged Jack to blow off work and come fishing instead. But that wouldn't have been the responsible thing to do—and besides, the teacher who oversaw the post-cutting project at school was on vacation and had put Jack in charge that day. It was a big responsibility for a fourteen-year-old boy, but if Jack Cash couldn't handle it, nobody could.

J.R. was walking home at noontime when a Model-A Ford pulled up alongside him. Rev. Hal Gallop was behind the wheel. Ray Cash was next to him in the front seat.

"Throw away your fishing pole and get in," Ray said forcefully.

At the Cash house, Ray and J.R. exited the car, and Ray steered him into the smokehouse out back, where he grimly removed from a brown sack the khaki pants and shirt Jack had been wearing when he and Johnny left the house a few hours earlier. The clothes were ripped to shreds and blood-soaked.

In a voice twisted by anguish, Ray told his son what happened: as Jack and another student were sawing posts on the pendulum saw at school, Jack had somehow been yanked onto the oversized razor-sharp blade and sliced wide open. Jack hadn't fallen or screamed but calmly walked out of the building and lay down beneath a tree, holding his stomach to prevent his innards from falling out. An ambulance was called, and Jack was rushed to the Dyess Hospital. The ambulance driver later said that Jack sat in the front seat and was holding in his own stomach. He said Jack told him, "Tell me something happy because I'm going to die."

That was also apparent to Ray Cash.

"We're going to lose him, J.R.," said Ray to his son. It was the only time J.R. ever saw his father cry.

Jack clung to life for a week. Decades later, son John Carter Cash asked his father if he believed in angels, and Cash disclosed that he had been visited by one after Jack's accident. He had fallen asleep on the porch at home, he said, and awakened in the dark to find that he wasn't alone there. In a nearby chair sat a man in a gray suit, idly leafing through a Bible J.R. recognized as the one he kept in his room. It slowly dawned on Cash that his visitor was an angel, and he pleaded with him to save Jack, to even take his own life if it would spare his brother's.

"No," responded the angel. "It's not your time."

The fact is, angels are actively involved in the life of a Christian.

The Bible has over three hundred references to their constant work and activity in our lives. Angels protect us, guide us and sometimes even speak to us. The Bible tells us to show kindness to strangers because in doing so, we may be showing kindness to an angel without knowing it. Angels generally work undercover. They are like "God's Seal Team": you don't always know what they are doing, but they are busy on our behalf.

So maybe Cash did have a talk with an angel after all.

The entire community offered up fervent prayers for Jack, but as gangrene set in, the doctor told the Cashes it was hopeless. The family maintained an around-the-clock vigil at Jack's bedside. On May 20, J.R. was sleeping in an empty hospital room adjacent to his brother's when his father woke him and said it was time to come say goodbye to Jack.

Jack was under heavy sedation for the pain, and his entire family was at his bedside. "He was saying strange things that I didn't understand as a child," recalled Joanne Cash Yates. "Jack called me 'Jana,' which was kind of a nickname for me. He said, 'Jana, tell me goodbye.' I was scared and told him, 'No, I don't want you to go nowhere.'"

J.R. took Jack's hand and brought his cheek close to his brother's. "Goodbye, Jack," was all he could get out.

Jack looked at his father and asked, "Will you meet me in Heaven?"

Ray Cash did the most unexpected thing—he fell to his knees and prayed, asking Jesus Christ to be his Lord and Savior. Sure, there were some changes in Ray's life following, but he still was a "work in progress," to put it delicately.

Then Jack looked at Carrie. "Why is everybody crying over me? Mama, don't cry over me. Do you see the river?"

On one side of the river, he said, was fire; on the other side was Heaven. "I thought I was going toward the fire, but I'm headed in the other direction now, Mama. Can you hear the angels singing?"

Jack squeezed her hand, and tears of happiness rolled down his cheeks. "Mama, listen to the angels. I'm going there, Mama."

A moment later, he said, "What a beautiful city! And the angels singing! Oh, Mama, I wish you could hear the angels singing!"

Then he was gone.

But death for a believer is not the end.

The moment you take your last breath on earth, you take your first breath in Heaven.

The community visitation for Jack Cash was held the next day in the living room at No. 266, preceding his funeral. In the constant procession of mourners was a farmer the Cashes had never met before who told Ray and Carrie that Jack had always encouraged him and once even prayed with him for rain to ensure a bountiful crop.

The sight of Jack's corpse was unnerving for some of the Cash children, including sister Reba, who hid underneath her bed, according to her daughter, Kelly Hancock.

"It really scared her, and she said John comforted her," Hancock said. "He put his arm around her and said, 'Reba, it's okay. He's not there . . . he's in Heaven. That's just what's left.' He tried to reassure her, but she recounted to me several times throughout her life that it really frightened her."

After the funeral service at Dyess Baptist church, Jack Cash was buried in a cemetery in Bassett, about a dozen miles away. The day before, while J.R. was helping to dig his brother's grave, he stepped on a nail that went through his shoe and pierced his foot. The next morning, the foot was so swollen J.R. couldn't get his shoe on. He went barefooted to Jack's funeral and the cemetery.

At Jack's graveside, Rev. Hal Gallop read John 14.

In this passage, Jesus talks about his "Father's house" having many rooms. "Let not your heart be troubled; you believe in God, believe also in Me. In My Father's house are many mansions; if *it were* not *so,* I would have told you. I go to prepare a place for you" (John 14:1-2 KJV).

A better translation would be, "In my Father's house there are many rooms."

The idea of "My Father's house" suggests spaciousness, like a massive estate. The word "rooms" suggest coziness. A private space.

Jesus gave these words to His disciples, who were extremely stressed out.

The reason was that Christ had dropped the bombshell that He was indeed leaving them, and they could not wrap that minds around that horrible reality. So Jesus said, "Don't let your heart shudder!"

When one has a glimpse of the glory that awaits us, it puts our earthly problems in their proper place.

That passage read by Rev. Gallop brought much-needed comfort to the grieving Cash family that day, but they would struggle with young Jack's passing for the rest of their lives.

After the coffin was lowered into the ground, a group of Jack's fellow Boy Scouts filled in his grave. Later, a marble headstone was erected that bore the Boy Scout crest, and under "Jack D. Cash 1929-1944" was inscribed, "Will You Meet Me in Heaven?"

There was still cotton to be picked, and the next day, it was back out to the field. In his 1997 autobiography, Cash recalled one of the most affecting scenes of his life. His mother was picking cotton when suddenly she sank to her knees in exhaustion and grief. Ray rushed over, took her by the arm, and started to help her back to her feet, but Carrie brushed him off.

"I'll get up when *God* pushes me up," she said.

A moment later, she slowly arose on her own and stoically resumed picking cotton.

4

——

FINDING HIS VOICE

"The memory of Jack's death, his vision of
Heaven has been more of an inspiration to
me, I suppose, than anything else that has
ever come to me through any man."

—JOHNNY CASH

For the rest of his life, Johnny Cash was visited by his brother in dreams. It wasn't the fourteen-year-old Jack but one who aged through the years as he would have in life. The last time Jack appeared in a dream, a few months before Johnny's death, he had gray hair and a snowy white beard.

When loved ones die, and even more so when they are taken from us unexpectedly, as was the case with Jack Cash, it takes years to process.

Seeing those who have passed over to the other side is not an "appearance" as much as a super-charged memory. It's a combination of sudden loss mixed with hope. I know this from experience with my own son Christopher, who died in an automobile accident in 2008.

To be connected with someone every day and then to have them suddenly taken from you is, for a parent, the worst-case scenario. My son has appeared to me many times in dreams over the years. Like Jack in Johnny's dreams, Christopher does not offer me advice. He is simply "there." I usually find myself overjoyed to see him; but then he always has to leave for somewhere, and I am heartbroken all over again.

Jack, a committed Christian and would-be preacher, was clearly in Heaven. But J.R. at times felt he was experiencing "hell on earth." His relationship with his father was, for the most part, a complete disconnect. No warmth or fatherly nurturing was forthcoming from Ray Cash—just coldness and apparent perpetual disappointment with young J.R. In dramatic contrast, Jack was more than a brother and friend to J.R. He was also a guide in life and someone who cared deeply for J.R. long before he became "Johnny Cash" the icon.

Johnny missed Jack with all of his heart, and he never really got over it.

As he had been in life, in J.R.'s dreams, Jack was never openly critical of his brother or judgmental, even when J.R.'s behavior—abusing amphetamines, infidelity—warranted it. But Cash always sensed when his brother was disappointed in him and wanted him to straighten himself out. At times, he sensed Jack was ashamed of him, and he vowed to do better at those times.

It wasn't really Jack that J.R. was reaching out to—it was Jesus, Who he would grow to know better down the road of life. But Jack Cash was the closest representation of Christ that J.R. had known at this point of his still-young life.

In the immediate aftermath of Jack's death, there wasn't much time for dreaming. Roy Cash, J.R.'s oldest brother, lived in Texas and had no interest in moving back to Dyess to help with the farm. So twelve-year-old J.R. had to shoulder a man-sized load of responsibility. He did his grieving in the cotton fields.

His mother did her best to carry on, but J.R. frequently found Carrie in tears, beseeching, "Why, Lord? Why? Why? Why?"

For Carrie Cash, to lose a child was something beyond comprehension—a fate worse than death. Most parents would gladly trade their life to save the life of their child, and she missed Jack deeply. The why question, of course, is unanswerable. So one must address the "who" question—as in, "To whom shall I turn?" The answer for Carrie was Jesus. And though He comforted her, the pain lingered, and the loss was like an unbearable weight on her chest.

Ray Cash's acceptance of God at his son's deathbed culminated in a stunning appearance in the pulpit of the Baptist church one Sunday in the spring of 1945, filling in for the vacationing Rev. Hal Gallop. Ray preached from Second Chronicles chapter seven, verse fourteen, and he talked stirringly about the grief that comes from not obeying God, putting it in the context of the Second World War that was then raging. After the service, he was heartily congratulated by congregation members impressed by his delivery and knowledge of the Bible. His father William, the wild-eyed circuit-riding preacher, would have been proud.

This passage is addressed to believers and tells them how to be restored spiritually. "If my people which are called by my name will humble themselves and pray and seek my face and turn from their wicked ways, then I will hear from Heaven and forgive them of their sin, and heal their land." It's a passage that has been preached by more than a few men in the pulpit (present company included) to urge people to pray for a spiritual revival in our land.

For Ray Cash, it was a roadmap he sometimes followed—but then disregarded.

This would be a pattern throughout his life, and in a very real sense, it made the verse "The sins of the parents will be visited on the children" come to life. Ray Cash was most definitely a dichotomy.

Ray pinballed between the Bible and the bottle and, when under the influence of the latter was capable of great callousness. More than once he scolded J.R. for not convincing Jack to go fishing instead of to work that fateful day, and he even went so far as to lament in Johnny's earshot that "God took the wrong son."

I can't even begin to imagine how young Cash felt hearing those words.

Whether malicious or just thoughtless, his father's words seared young J.R.'s psyche as if inflicted with a red-hot iron. The rest of his life was spent trying every balm possible—fame, riches, drugs—to extinguish or at least dull that pain and his never-diminished case of survivor's guilt.

For now, his own mourning turned J.R.'s focus even more inward. In class photographs from that time, he wears a brooding expression while those around him look like they don't have a care in the world. The poems, stories, and songs Cash scribbled began to reflect his deepening introspection and newfound morbidity. Up to then, he'd never given much thought to mortality—his own or that of mankind in general. Now such dark considerations seemed to infuse most of J.R.'s creative output.

The Sears & Roebuck guitar Carrie had bought for J.R. mysteriously disappeared after Jack's death. Later, he surmised it had been sold to help get the family through a financial rough spot. When he wasn't needed in the cotton fields, Johnny began spending time at the home of Jessie "Pete" Barnhill, who lived three miles from the Cash farm. Pete had an old Gibson flattop acoustic guitar he played like a virtuoso despite a right arm severely withered by polio.

Barnhill taught his young protégé songs by Hank Snow, Ernest Tubb, and Jimmie Rodgers, astonishing J.R. with his dexterity and finesse. Cash later said he tried to copy Barnhill's unique picking style—playing rhythm and leading with his thumb.

That wasn't even the most valuable thing he learned at those freewheeling after-school symposiums. One time as Barnhill demonstrated a guitar lick, Cash shook his head in wonder and exclaimed how amazing it was that he could play like that with his disability.

Barnhill looked at him meaningfully and said, "Sometimes when you lose a gift, you get another one." Cash never forgot that.

As his passion for music grew, J.R. avidly listened to music on the radio during lunch breaks and every night for fifteen minutes before hitting the sack, getting a feel for different sounds and styles.

He got zero encouragement from his father.

"You're wasting your time listening to them old records on the radio," Ray told his son. "That ain't real, you know. Those people ain't really there. That's just a guy sitting there playing records. Why d'you listen to that fake stuff?"

It was just Ray Cash being the way his hardscrabble life had made him. To him, if something didn't pick cotton or couldn't be traded for a few bucks, what earthly good was it? With growing frustration and worry, he regarded Johnny's growing obsession with music as a frippery that would ill serve him in the dog-eat-dog, survival-of-the-fittest real world.

"You'll never do any good as long as you've got that music on the mind," Ray admonished. Ray was off by a country mile. That music on Johnny's mind would do him and a lot of people good—most especially Ray—for decades to come.

Words are powerful stuff. The Bible tells us that "death and life are in the power of the tongue."

Luckily, his father's dour attitude was countered by the fervent encouragement J.R. received from his mother. Carrie recognized that he had inherited the passion for music passed down to her from her father. John L. Rivers led the choir in his church and was said to be such a good singer that he might have made a living at it if he'd been so inclined. People came from all around the county to hear him; he was that good.

Carrie sang well, too, and could play the guitar and fiddle. To her, music was an expression of joy and faith, a way of coping with life and its travails. Everything Ray found in a bottle of applejack, Carrie got out of a song or a Bible verse. To her, J.R.'s burgeoning musical talent was a blessing from God to the entire family, bringing relief and solace from misery and despair.

J.R. sang pop and country songs he heard on the radio as he chopped cotton. At home with his family, it was what Cash called "hillbilly and novelty songs," such as "I'm My Own Grandpa" and "Don't Telephone, Tell a Woman." J.R. and his mother loved rousing gospel tunes and also melancholy ones like "Life's Evening Sun is Sinking Low," which they sang at the end of every evening.

At the time, J.R. had a high tenor voice. Carrie had great hopes for him as a soloist in the church choir and, eventually, as a gospel singer, but the few times they tried it, J.R.'s singing and Carrie's piano accompaniment lacked synchrony, and he bowed out.

Across the street from Dyess High School lived La Vonda Mae Fielder, a music teacher who offered private singing lessons at $3 a pop. Carrie took in laundry to earn money for her son's first—and, it turned out, also his last—lesson.

Joanne Cash Yates accompanied Carrie and J.R. to Fielder's home that day and vividly remembers what went down in her living room.

"Ms. Fielder said, 'Well, J.R., let me hear what you can do,'" she said. "So he sang a song—I don't remember what it was—and she said, 'You can stop now.' He hung his head and said, 'You mean I'm no good?' She said, 'On the contrary—you have a gift from God that I wouldn't dare touch! You're a song stylist. Always do it your way.' And that encouraged him greatly because he knew he had that calling."

Those words, in contrast to the withering ones from his father, impacted Johnny dramatically. No doubt it was alcohol that sharpened his dad's tongue.

"My dad used to drink all the time, and it didn't make things so happy at home a few times," Cash later confessed. "Maybe that's the reason I'm so set against it."

By the time J.R. was sixteen, he'd gone from tenor to the rich, earthy baritone voice the world would know and love, the one with that dramatic Old Testament delivery. The change didn't happen overnight, but it seemed that way when J.R. finished cutting fire-wood one day and broke into song as he drew water from the well in the backyard.

Recalled sister Joanne Cash Yates: "Mama did all of her biscuit making in a big wooden bowl in the kitchen, and I was standing with her looking out the window when all of a sudden, we heard this booming voice—real deep and strong."

As soon as J.R. entered the house, Carrie pleaded with him for more. He sang "A Wonderful Time Up There," and tears ran down his mother's face.

When he finished, she exclaimed, "You sound exactly like my daddy!"

Then she looked him square in the eye and added portentously: "God has His hand on you, son. Don't ever forget the gift."

For the first time since Jack's death, J.R. Cash felt suffused with God's grace and imbued with hope that his life had a purpose after all.

5

HIGH SCHOOL CONFIDENTIAL

"Songs were my life. I feasted on them."

—JOHNNY CASH

Now armed with a soulful voice and a purpose, J.R. Cash began putting his gift to use in earnest, singing in church and at school assemblies, recitals, and talent contests.

Fellow students recall seeing him step out at school assemblies in the cafeteria to sing "That Lucky Ole Sun," "The Whiffenpoof Song," "Trees," and "Drink to Me Only with Thine Eyes." Cash had no accompaniment and no microphone, but with that big, booming voice, they would've been superfluous.

"J.R. liked to be out front. He was always an extrovert," said A J Henson. "I was afraid to be seen, and J.R. was afraid he wouldn't be seen. He liked being on stage, and it didn't matter if it was in a play or [he] was called on to sing or make an oral report in class. They had to threaten to kill me to get me to stand up before the class. Not him."

That was not unusual for a person wired to do what Johnny Cash would ultimately do, transforming the dirt-poor child from Arkansas into an American and international icon. So often those who stand out from the crowd with unusual talent, especially entertainers, actors, comedians, and artists, develop this skill set out of necessity. What may come off to some as a simple "need for approval" may in fact be something they developed to diffuse tension and change the temperature of a room. Music and art are also avenues of escape for a person in pain. Cash had more than his share with his brooding father and the loss of his brother. He not only discovered music but how specific songs could lift the spirits of someone who was hurting, starting with his mother and eventually encompassing millions of people around the world who had lost hope.

Being raised by my Arkansas-born alcoholic mother Charlene and while waiting for her in smoky bars, I turned to the world of art, specifically cartooning, for relief. I also developed a sense of humor to diffuse tense situations while my mom engaged in nightly alcohol-infused conflicts with her myriad husbands and in-between boyfriends.

In essence, Cash and I had both developed survival mechanisms. His was music—mine was drawing. It kept our spirits up, and it kept us from falling into a dark hole.

J.R.'s favorite radio show was *High Noon Roundup*, aired every day from 12:30 to 1 p.m. on WMPS in Memphis. The show, hosted by Mid-South personality "Smilin' Eddie" Hill, offered a mix of music, interviews, and cornpone comedy. Cash's favorite act on the show was the Lonesome Valley Trio, comprised of Hill and the Louvin Brothers.

When "Smilin' Eddie" announced on the air one day in the spring of 1947 that *High Noon Roundup* was coming to the Dyess High School auditorium for a special show, J.R. was beside himself with excitement. The night of the show, he arrived at the high school a whole two hours early, before anyone else, and gaped in open-mouthed astonishment when a long black limousine pulled up to the auditorium door. He'd never seen anything like it before. From the car emerged "Smilin' Eddie," Ira and Charlie Louvin, and the technical staff of *High Noon Roundup*. As the latter started carting musical instruments, a sound system, and other equipment into the auditorium, Charlie Louvin himself walked up to the mesmerized youngster and asked where the restroom was located.

Cash had never seen a radio star up close before—nor, for that matter, from afar, either. His instinct was to blurt out how much he loved the show and the Lonesome Valley Trio, but he was so dumbstruck all he managed to croak was, "I'll show you." He ushered Louvin inside and then snagged a front row center seat for the show.

Two spellbinding hours later, Cash watched as the instruments and equipment were loaded back into the limo. "Smilin' Eddie" and the Louvins signed a few autographs before they got in. As the massive car headed down dusty Road One toward the Memphis Highway, Charlie Louvin waved at the gangly teenager standing agape outside the auditorium door. Which one would have been more surprised to know their positions would be virtually reversed in just a few years?

As natural as it had become for J.R. Cash to stand up at a moment's notice and entertain his classmates and fellow Baptists with a song, his mouth hardly worked at all when it came to just having a normal conversation with a member of the opposite sex who wasn't his mother or a sister.

One of his first girlfriends was Louise Nichols, whose family moved to Dyess after the flood of '37. She and Cash were classmates through grade, middle, and high school. They also attended the same church.

"We were all from farming families, we were all poor, we all picked cotton, and we grew up together," recalled Louise, now in her late eighties. "My dad had a truck, and if he didn't attend services on Sunday, Mr. Cash had a truck, and he'd go around to all of the neighbors and pick us up for church."

She recalled J.R. as popular (he was voted class vice president his senior year), a bit of a prankster, and very upstanding.

"Back then, there were no alcohol or drugs around, and no cursing," Nichols said. "One night, about fifteen of us were walking to the movies, and a car passed by us with a bunch of boys in it. They slowed down and hollered something untoward, and J.R. said, 'Wait a minute, fellas. I don't think you know the Lord Jesus Christ— because if you did, you wouldn't have said that!'"

When sixteen-year-old J.R. invited a younger classmate, Evelyn Shaddix, to a movie, he ended up with more female companionship than he wanted thanks to ten-year-old sister Joanne.

"J.R. loved Westerns," she recalled, "and somehow I talked Mama into letting me go with him on his date. He didn't want me to, of course, but I did. When we got to the theater, J.R. bought me a bag of popcorn and a small Coke and said, 'Now, you sit in front of us and be quiet, okay?'

"They showed a serial and cartoon before the main feature. When the movie finally started, I turned to J.R. and said, 'I'm sleepy. Please take me home.' So we had to leave the theater and go back home. He wasn't happy that I cut his date short that night and didn't let me forget that for a while."

Cash's greatest high school heartthrob was Virginia North. He wrote her love letters but couldn't bring himself to deliver them. North was dating a boy from Osceola—a nearby town considered (mostly by Osceolans) more upscale and refined than Dyess—who had his own car. J.R. couldn't compete with that; the Cashes' rattletrap half-ton truck might've been all right for ferrying people to church, but it was hardly the kind of chariot a fellow wanted to go courting in.

But then Ray bought a used dark green 1935 Ford. It had no heat, erratic brakes, and the glass in the side and back windows was completely gone. But next to that Ma and Pa Kettle truck, to J.R., it was almost as spectacular as that *High Noon Roundup* limo, and on a rainy Saturday afternoon, he was feeling his oats as drove to the Dyess Café, hangout of the local teenagers. Cash sped around the town circle and as he approached the café, slammed on the brakes. They didn't catch right away, and he ended up skidding onto the café's front porch sideways. Virginia North happened to be out there at the time, and she had to leap back to avoid getting wiped out.

The nonplussed Cash promptly invited her out on a date that night.

"I might go with you sometime if you had *windows* in your car," sneered North as she turned on her heel and huffed into the café.

"So long, Virginia North," muttered Cash to himself as he drove away. "I'll have a car with windows in it someday—and you'll be stuck picking cotton somewhere up around Osceola."

Even then, young J.R. Cash had a sense of destiny.

He knew instinctively that a better life was ahead and whoever would share it with him would care more about him than his ride.

As his senior year of high school approached, J.R. began to think about more than a car with windows. College wasn't even on his radar, and cotton farming held no appeal for him as a livelihood. The government program in Dyess had given people like Ray Cash the chance to survive but not flourish. Even if J.R. had been interested in living off the land, the fact was that the great New Deal experiment there had just about run its course.

From the beginning, the plan was to enable colonists to eventually purchase their farmsteads at reasonable rates, based on the initial costs of the property, buildings, improvements added by the government, and a prorated share of other infrastructure costs. It was not until 1937, however, that prices were established and contracts offered, and by then, many residents were disgruntled. Some thought the contract amounts were way too high, with land inflated beyond what the government actually paid. Others chafed under the relentless federal oversight and strictures. Some were homesick or found the work too hard and moved on. Like the people who watered it with their sweat, the land itself was largely played out, yielding ever-diminishing returns. Ray Cash took whatever odd jobs he could find just to straddle the poverty line, including managing the Dyess Café with Carrie for a couple of seasons.

Two choices stood out for J.R. and most other coming-of-age males growing up on Depression-era subsistence farms in the South: the automotive factories in Michigan and the Armed Forces. A J Henson didn't even wait until he graduated from Dyess High School to decide. He dropped out in his junior year and joined the U.S. Army, where he enjoyed a long and prosperous career.

"Many people from Dyess joined the military because it was a step up from the farm," Henson said. "Anybody who grew up during that time became a man much quicker than they do today. They were more responsible. They knew what their share of the work was, and they did it without any problems."

J.R. Cash finished high school in May 1950. In his final year, he did well in everything but English and History and was elected vice president of the senior class—all twenty-two members of it. He performed in school plays and sang at his graduation ceremony. In the school yearbook, he was thanked for sharing his talent with the Dyess High School student body.

Cash's top priority upon graduating was to make a break from his father any way he could. Hearing jobs were available in west Arkansas picking strawberries, he headed for Bald Knob, a town about 100 miles away. But picking strawberries was no more lucrative (or easier) than picking cotton, and after just three days, Cash returned to Dyess. The town barber, Frank McKinney, was giving up the hair-cutting trade and going to Detroit to seek work in the auto industry. Hearing that J.R. was at loose ends, McKinney invited him to come along. As soon as the door of the bus closed behind them at the nearby Wilson bus station and all the way to the Motor City, Cash was wracked by doubt about his decision to go.

He was hired as a punch press operator at the Fisher Body plant in Pontiac, and he walked a mile and a half there and back each day from a boarding house where he was staying. He hated the tedious, repetitive work even more than he'd hated the cotton fields.

It didn't help that, as a Southerner, Cash was constantly looked down on and openly derided by his Yankee co-workers and bosses. When his arm was sliced by a fender on the assembly line, J.R. was sent to the on-staff doctor. Noting that he came from Arkansas, the doctor didn't bother trying to hide or contain his scorn as he patched Cash up. "Southern hicks" like him were always trying to game the system, he complained, faking illness and injury to get out of a full day's work.

"How long you gonna work here?" needled the doctor. "You gonna get yourself a good paycheck or two and then split like they all do?"

After less than a month, Cash thumbed his way back to Dyess.

At the time, Ray was working part-time at a Proctor & Gamble oleomargarine plant in nearby Evadale, and J.R. reluctantly accepted his dad's offer to get him in there in June 1950. Initially, he poured concrete, but his skinny frame just couldn't handle the work required for such a task. He was then assigned to clean out tanks, working in filth beyond his imagination and in heat that was almost unbearable.

When he quit after two weeks, Ray didn't hold back expressing his frustration and disappointment with his son, and J.R. himself began to wonder if the old man might not be right about him after all.

More out of desperation than anything else, Cash turned to the only avenue left open to him.

6

THE MAN IN BLUE

"I cherish all the freedoms we have, including
the freedom and the right to burn the flag. But I
also have the right to bear arms, and if you
burn mine I'll shoot ya."

—JOHNNY CASH

Before Johnny Cash transformed into the "Man in Black," he was
actually the Man in Blue. J.R. Cash became Airman John R. Cash
when he enlisted in the U.S. Air Force on July 7, 1950.

The world was far from tranquil. Five years after the end of World
War II, the United States and former ally Russia were embroiled in
the Cold War; a month before Cash's enlistment, North Korea had
invaded South Korea, and America was about to get involved in a
three-year hot war disguised as a "police action."

Airman Cash was fortunate to avoid Korea, but his tour of duty
took him to many other distant ports of call. Along the way, he saw

Queen Elizabeth's coronation in London in 1953; visited Oberammergau, Germany, home of the famous Passion Play; fished and skied in the Bavarian Alps; ogled the can-can dancers at the Folies-Bergere in Paris; and listened to flamenco guitarists play in caves in Barcelona, Spain.

In addition to his military training and cultural enrichment, Cash picked up some bad habits as he gained an education in such life skills as cussing, chasing women, drinking, and fighting. He continued in that trajectory after his Air Force hitch was over. He also excelled in his ability to intercept radio communications and transcribe Morse code signals that he learned over a six-month period at Keesler Air Force Base in Biloxi, Mississippi, because his military aptitude test indicated he was good at typing and distinguishing sounds.

Cash got his technical training at Brooks AFB in San Antonio. The most noteworthy event in his eight weeks there occurred on July 18, 1951, when he and Airman Jim Hobbs were out and about in downtown San Antonio and dropped into North St. Mary's Roller Rink. Cash's eye was quickly drawn to a pretty, exotic-looking, dark-haired girl skating with a friend. She noticed the tall, handsome serviceman staring and looked right back. When Cash pointed her out to Hobbs, the latter bet him he wouldn't be able to persuade the pretty girl with the dazzling smile to let him walk her home that night. It was just fifteen minutes till closing time, so John skated right up to seventeen-year-old Vivian Liberto and introduced himself.

They traded thumbnail biographies. She was going to be a senior at a Catholic high school. Her father owned a local insurance agency. An uncle was a Catholic priest. Cash wasn't much of a skater, and his repartee wasn't much to write home about, but he made up for those deficiencies and won the bet with his friend by singing a popular Rosemary Clooney song as they glided around the rink.

She didn't let him kiss her at her front door a while later, but Airman Cash headed back to the base with the vivacious Miss Liberto's phone number in his pocket.

Over the next eighteen days, they went skating again, to movies and cafés, and held hands strolling along San Antonio's beautiful downtown River Walk. Their first kiss happened at a drive-in. Vivian recalled later that she had never felt so alive and happy before.

But the Air Force had first call on Cash, and he got his orders for Landsberg Air Base in Germany in September. (His other option was Adak Island, in the frozen Aleutian archipelago off the coast of Alaska. It was the fastest and easiest decision he ever made.)

John and Vivian vowed to write each other every day, and over the course of the next three years, they actually exchanged thousands of letters brimming with fervent declarations of love and longing for one another. They even broached the topic of marriage and children, debating if they would be raised Protestant or Catholic.

Cash spent his military leave in Dyess before sailing for Europe on the USNS *General W.G. Haan* in late September, 1951. On the journey across the Atlantic Ocean, his bunkmate was Vic Damone, a top singing star ("I Have but One Heart") with his own radio show. Damone had even appeared in two movies before he entered the Army in 1951, but aboard ship, he mopped the deck and shot craps like everybody else. Every night, he sang for his shipmates. "Why, he's almost human," gushed Cash in a letter to Vivian about the star in his midst.

Upon arriving in Germany, Cash and others bound for Landsberg Air Base, thirty miles west of Munich, were temporarily quartered in a nine-story apartment building in Bremerhaven. From his room high above the street, Cash heard a great commotion outside, looked out his window, and saw hundreds of black and white American servicemen fighting each other. The Armed Forces had been integrated three years earlier by President Harry S. Truman, but it was easier said than done. The racial hatred, violence, and carnage he witnessed that day topped anything Cash had ever witnessed in Arkansas, and it made a lifelong impression on him.

At Landsberg, it didn't take long for Johnny to start behaving—and misbehaving—like most other red-blooded American servicemen.

He took a quick fancy to German beer and cognac and off-base benders with pals. They frequented bars, strip clubs, burlesque shows, and Munich's red-light district. In letters to Vivian, he left out some of those things but did confess to occasionally dating German girls— a disclosure he tried to leaven by writing, "Boys grow up fast over here, honey, and 95 percent of them grow up on the left side. I've been trying to be part of that 5 percent that don't, for you, so I would deserve your love."

Cash's other extracurricular activities included peddling cartons of cigarettes, cheaply available at the base PX, on the German black market, which led to an altercation with a couple of security guards in which he knocked out the front teeth of one and broke the other's nose. He got his own honker bent out of shape in a honky-tonk scrap with a paratrooper. (The distinctive scar on the right side of Cash's jaw wasn't the result of a fight; it came from having a cyst cut out by a German doctor who anesthetized himself for the procedure by getting drunk.)

His attendance at Protestant services on base steadily declined in his first year at Landsberg and then ceased altogether. Clearly, the Air Force had changed more than J.R. Cash's name.

The problem with temptation is that it is so tempting, and John R. Cash was not made of stone. Perhaps adopting the philosophy of Oscar Wilde, who said, "The only way to get rid of temptation is to yield to it," Cash began a downward spiral that would repeat itself over and over for many years. At times, he would forget all about God, but God never forgot about him and indeed had big plans for this young man.

One thing Airman Cash didn't abandon was music. He bought a Hofner Congress guitar for $5 and practiced on it relentlessly. Another young musician would discover the Hofner brand a bit later, choosing the violin electric bass that would become iconic to him and his band, the Beatles. His name was Paul McCartney.

Cash and three other servicemen formed a band they called the Landsberg Barbarians, playing country and "hillbilly" songs like "The Wild Side of Life," "The Great Speckled Bird," "Shine On, Harvest

Moon," and "In the Evening Moonlight." A Wilcox-Gay reel-to-reel recorder Cash purchased at the base PX recorded some of their rollicking tunes—and resembled nothing akin to the music that would later make Cash famous. The Landsberg Barbarians' only public performance was at a fundraiser on the base for the United Way.

Cash also began writing songs based on his own experiences and observations. A service buddy recalled that Cash spent many a night sitting on his footlocker in his boxer shorts, scribbling down lyrics. After Cash saw a film in the base recreation hall about life at one of America's first maximum-security prisons that October, he wrote a song he called "Folsom Prison Blues." Another composition started in Germany was "Hey, Porter" about a prodigal son's return to his native South. It would be the B-side of Cash's first record.

As a member of the Twelfth Radio Squadron Mobile, Cash worked as a Morse code operator intercepting Soviet Army transmissions. The job was intense and top-secret, and in a letter to Vivian dated May 16, 1952, Cash mentioned he could get a prison sentence of twenty years to life, or even face a firing squad, if he told her or anyone else exactly how he earned his monthly paycheck of $85.

Thanks to a typing class in high school, Cash was able to transcribe quickly, and he was a skillful "dit-dot" man. Later, he claimed to have detected the signal when a Soviet jet bomber made its maiden flight from Moscow to Smolenski, and he boasted he intercepted and transmitted the first news of Soviet Premier Joseph Stalin's death from a stroke on March 5, 1953. Decades later, his son John Carter Cash said the old man still had it when it came to retaining his skills. He proved it by writing out the twenty-third Psalm in Morse code on a piece of scrap paper.

His shifts required constant, heightened concentration, and during them, Cash downed lots of coffee and smoked like a fiend. Co-workers said he was jittery on the job with a leg that continuously thumped up and down. When he returned to Arkansas in

1954, among the changes in J.R. noted by family members was his excess of nervous energy.

Cash's competence eventually earned him a promotion to staff sergeant in charge of a department of forty men—not too shabby for a twenty-one-year-old high school graduate. His pay went up to a heady $110 a month, and when there was a special top-priority assignment in Foggia, Italy, in June 1953, Cash was tapped to handle it.

Upon returning to Germany, he decided he had been without Vivian long enough and rented an apartment from a German couple three miles from the base for $20 a month. Cash intended to have Vivian come over and for them to be married immediately.

But first Johnny did what he considered the proper thing and wrote to Tom Liberto, Vivian's father, to formally ask permission to marry his daughter. It was also the legal thing, since Vivian was not yet of age. Cash even promised they'd be married by a Catholic priest.

Tom Liberto wrote back that after he and his wife prayed for divine counsel on the matter, they decided Vivian could not go off to Europe and marry a man she knew only through a whirlwind three-week courtship and the letters he sent her. Liberto advised Cash to put off all thoughts of marriage until he returned stateside and he and Vivian got to know one another better. Realizing that argument would be futile, John wisely counseled Vivian to obey her parents and turned his new apartment over to a just-married serviceman buddy. Vivian was devastated by her father's letter and didn't talk to him for an entire week.

Vivian's father gave her wise counsel despite her protests.

As his Air Force hitch neared its end, Cash's superior officers lobbied him to re-enlist. But he hadn't had a furlough in three years, and in that whole time, he had been allowed only three calls to the States. No, thanks, he said. He was honorably discharged on July 3, 1954.

"He said his military service was very hard, but he discovered who John R. Cash was away from the cotton fields of Dyess, Arkansas," said Cash niece Kelly Hancock. "He was grateful for those four years.

He later said they were the basis of his life and turned him into the man he would later become."

Cash had served his country honorably and well and saw and did things he'd never even daydreamed about while picking cotton in Dyess. Now he was itching to get started on the next chapter of his life, in which he envisioned both Vivian and music playing featured roles.

It beat making cars and oleomargarine, but years later, Cash often joked that he "spent twenty years in the Air Force between 1950 and 1954."

7

—

A CHERRY PINK AND APPLE BLOSSOM WHITE DREAM

"That was the big thing when I was growing up, singing on the radio. The extent of my dream was to sing on the radio station in Memphis. Even when I got out of the Air Force in 1954, I came right back to Memphis and started knocking on doors at the radio station."

—JOHNNY CASH

On August 7, 1954, a month and four days after he left the Air Force, twenty-two-year-old Johnny Cash married Vivian Liberto at St. Ann's Catholic Church in San Antonio. Presiding at the ceremony was the bride's uncle, Father Vincent Liberto. Twenty pounds bulkier than when he left for Germany, Cash stood tall and resplendent in the Air Force dress uniform he wore because he didn't have and couldn't afford a suit.

With money the bride and groom had saved and scraped up, plus $500 they received as wedding gifts, Cash bought a green 1954 Plymouth four-door sedan from his brother Roy, who, after a stint in the service, had relocated to Memphis and worked for the Chrysler Corporation. Johnny and Vivian also moved to Memphis, renting a furnished apartment on the west side of town for $65 a month. They couldn't afford a telephone.

After briefly considering putting his military training to work as a member of the Memphis Police Department, Johnny interviewed for a disc jockey spot at a radio station in Corinth, Mississippi, eighty miles east of Memphis. He was informed that he couldn't just come in cold and go on the air. The station manager recommended a school of broadcasting, and Cash took advantage of the G.I. Bill to sign up for a part-time course. To him, it was the first step to getting his own records on the air. (Cash didn't fare so well at the school and was advised to look elsewhere.)

Meanwhile, to pay the bills, he took a full-time job selling appliances for the Home Equipment Company. This entailed going door-to-door for eight to nine hours a day trying to interest homeowners in purchasing washers, dryers, refrigerators, and such, and it didn't take long for Cash to grow weary of constant rejection, sometimes polite but often as not expressed by slamming the door in his face as he launched into his sales pitch.

It is worth noting that Billy Graham, who later became a close friend of Johnny's, started out as a Fuller Brush man himself. So, in addition to both becoming national icons, both had humble beginnings.

There is rarely, if ever, such a thing as "overnight success."

One must persist in order to succeed. And that includes some "planned neglect."

I once heard about a concert violinist who was asked how she became so skilled. She said it was "planned neglect"—once she set a goal for herself, she planned to neglect everything that was not related to achieving it.

Coming back to King David, who one day would ascend to the throne as the second monarch of Israel, he spent a lot of time living as a nobody in a nothing town in the middle of nowhere. David's hometown of Bethlehem is revered today because it is the birthplace of Christ. In reality, it was known for its smallness—not its largeness.

But big doors swing on small hinges.

Cash's day would come, but it would take time.

Sales were few and far between, but the Cashes got by on loans and advances from Johnny's boss George Bates and Vivian's father Tom, who proved to be a soft touch.

The day after Cash arrived in Memphis, Elvis Presley recorded "That's All Right (Mama)" in a studio a stone's throw from the Home Equipment Store. Three days later, the song was playing on the radio.

Johnny's musical career got going after his brother Roy introduced him to two mechanics Roy worked with at Chrysler—Marshall Grant and Luther Perkins—later known as the "Tennessee Two." They hit it off immediately, thanks mostly to their shared passion for hillbilly music. None were seasoned—or, for that matter, very talented—musicians, but they steadily improved by rehearsing in Grant's garage every chance they could get.

The trio's first public performance was in the basement of a Memphis church. The audience consisted of a handful of elderly women, none of whom responded to what they heard in the twenty-minute set the way females did to that Presley fellow. But it was a start.

This was to be more than a significant thing in the life and career of John R. Cash—the church.

In a song he would record later called "Sunday Morning Coming Down" that was written by his friend Kris Kristofferson, Johnny would sing about the conflict he had with the two lives he wanted to live.

Walking by a church on a Sunday morning, the singer catches the familiar scent of fried chicken, reminding him of his days as a younger man at a meal after a church service.

. . . caught the Sunday smell of someone's fryin' chicken
And Lord, it took me back to somethin'
That I'd lost somewhere, somehow along the way[1]

For years, Johnny Cash would have one foot in the church, and one foot in the world.

He would have too much of the world to be happy in Christ and too much of Christ to be happy in the world. It was a miserable "no-man's land" of compromise.

Over the next year, the band developed and honed a distinctive boom-chicka-boom sound backing Johnny's distinctive voice. And when not playing music, Cash was busy writing it. No piece of paper was safe around him. Anything he got his hands on—notepads, newspapers, napkins, or a tablecloth if nothing else was available—ended up scribbled over with lyrics to some song he was working on. After he finished writing the words, he'd get out his guitar and work out a melody to fit them. It was arduous and unconventional, but the good ear for sounds that had served the Air Force so well didn't fail him now.

Eventually, Cash set his sights on Sam Phillips, a former radio announcer and engineer and now owner of Sun Records—the Memphis label that would produce Elvis, Jerry Lee Lewis, and Carl Perkins.

Once "That's All Right (Mama)" started getting heavy airplay throughout the South, Elvis wannabes streamed through the front and back doors at 706 Union Avenue, and just about came through the windows and down the chimney, too! The receptionist's phone jangled from the time she reported to work till she closed the door and went home, everyone pleading to audition for Sam Phillips. One of the most persistent callers was Cash, who was usually told Phillips was out of town or in conference. One time, he got lucky, and Phillips himself answered the phone, but as soon as Cash introduced himself as a gospel singer, the Sun Records mogul winced. He told Cash that gospel music was nice but not marketable, goodbye.

There was an irony here as Cash would ultimately distinguish himself as one of the "Kings of Country Music" while Elvis was the "King of Rock and Roll."

But in his heart, Johnny always was in many ways a gospel singer. (By the way, the word "gospel" means "good news.")

And Johnny looked for opportunities to share that message whenever he could.

Contrary to this image many would have of Cash as an "outlaw," some even believing his lyrics were autobiographical ("I shot a man in Reno / Just to watch him die"), Johnny Cash was a master storyteller— and the greatest of all stories is the one about Jesus Christ, who changed Johnny's life.

Whatever Johnny Cash sang, it rang true. He had an unmatched authenticity in his voice, a timbre, a cadence that set him apart from other artists before and after him. That is one of the reasons he endures as a true American icon.

At the peak of his career, when he had his highly rated television show, he used that platform to sing songs about his faith. One standout was "The Preacher Said, 'Jesus Said'" complete with Billy Graham himself proclaiming soundbites from his sermons.

Johnny knew exactly what he was doing.

As a door-to-door salesman, Cash was used to rejection, but this time, he was hawking something more important than a refrigerator or toaster. The direct, head-on approach had got his foot in the door with Vivian at that San Antonio roller rink; now it was time to give Sam Phillips the hard sell.

On a Monday morning in the fall of 1954, Phillips arrived at the office early and found a large man on the doorstep with a guitar. He'd been waiting there quite a while. When he said his name was John R. Cash, Phillips groaned and said, "You're the one who's been calling."

Cash figured the worst that could happen was Phillips would tell him to get lost. But instead he resignedly told him, "Come on in, and let's give you a listen."

Over the course of the next two hours, Cash played songs by Hank Snow and Jimmie Rodgers, his own compositions "Belshazzar," "Hey, Porter," and "Folsom Prison Blues," and even the old chestnut "I'll Take You Home Again, Kathleen." Phillips was intrigued, sensing Cash's unvarnished authenticity and charisma. At six-feet-two, he had a commanding presence.

When Phillips asked what kind of band he had, Johnny said they were "just three guys" without much experience performing in public. Phillips didn't care about that—he was more into feeling and vibes than polish. Come back with the other two guys, he told Cash, and let's see what happens.

Johnny returned with Marshall Grant and Luther Perkins, and they played several numbers. Phillips came out of the booth scratching his head and said, "There's something really squirrely about you guys." It didn't sound like a compliment, but then Phillips added, "I've never heard anything like it before—it's different." It turned out that Sam Phillips' mantra was, "If you're not doing something different, you're not doing anything." He dug the Cash trio's ragged sound and insistent rhythm, and especially the rawness and understated force in Johnny's voice. Most of the singers that auditioned for Phillips tried to sound like Elvis. Cash wasn't trying to be anyone other than himself.

But launching a brand-new act required fresh material. Phillips thought "Hey, Porter" had potential as a single, so Cash, Grant, and Perkins rehearsed the song Johnny penned in Germany until they had it down pat and were ready to go into the studio and cut their first record.

The question was what would go on the flip side?

The trio tinkered with the hymn "I Was There When It Happened," but Phillips was adamant about not recording a gospel song.

Cash would record the song later, and it was certainly overt gospel singing without apology.

Yes, I know when Jesus saved me (saved my soul),
The very moment He forgave me (made me whole).
He took away my heavy burdens
Lord, He gave me peace within (peace within).[2]

Then, while listening to the radio at home, Cash heard DJ Eddie Hill glibly intone, "We've got good songs, love songs, sweet songs, happy songs, and sad songs that'll make you cry, cry, cry." That final three-word refrain stirred something in him, and he picked up a pencil. Even he was surprised when just fifteen minutes later he had a complete song. He called it "You're Gonna Cry, Cry, Cry."

Cash ran it past Grant and Perkins at their next rehearsal. After a few tweaks, it was ready for Sam Phillips' consideration. The boss man approved, and at a two-and-a-half-hour Thursday night recording session in May, Cash and the Tennessee Two got it right after thirty-five takes. The finished product clocked in at two minutes and twenty-nine seconds.

Phillips liked it so much he made a series of executive decisions. "Hey, Porter" was promptly relegated to the B-side of the record, and the title of the new A-side was shortened to "Cry! Cry! Cry!"

The final decision was to overrule Cash, whose idea was to put "The Tennessee Three" under the title of the song on the record, and make it "Johnny Cash and the Tennessee Two." Cash expressed misgivings; he thought that, at twenty-three, he was too old to be "Johnny." But he acquiesced when Phillips invoked the famous Golden Rule—"He who has the gold makes the rules."

It became official when Cash signed a contract with Sun Records on April 1, 1955. It was a standard deal for the time—a one-year pact for a royalty rate of about three cents per record, with Sun having the rights to extend the agreement via two one-year options. When Cash went to the Home Equipment Store with the news, his now ex-colleagues there kidded him that any contract signed on that day was bound to be an April Fool's Day joke.

One of Cash's oft-told stories over the years was that he walked out of Sun that morning with just fifteen cents in his pocket and grandly presented it to a panhandler on the street, confident that his money worries were now over.

The day before "Cry! Cry! Cry's!" scheduled release date of May 25, the anxious Cash picked up an advance copy of the record and rushed over to WMPS. He could hardly contain his excitement as deejay Bob Neal (soon to be Cash's manager) obligingly played both sides on the air. Then, as Neal removed the record from the turntable, he dropped and broke it. Cash was horrified. Was it an omen? Would his first record crash and burn?

The next day, about a half dozen Memphis radio stations played "Cry! Cry! Cry!" The day after that, every other Memphis station got in the act. Pretty soon, almost every station across the South was airing the record, and eventually it reached No. 14 on the *Billboard* singles charts and sold approximately 100,000 copies.

The song's success resulted in a feature spot for Cash on the *Louisiana Hayride* tour with Elvis Presley. His pay was $20 a night—$30 when they played bigger towns.

In a letter to an old Air Force pal, Cash wrote, "Friend, I tell you, it just don't seem real. It seems like a big cherry pink and apple blossom white dream."

The reality would turn out to be far less picturesque.

8

CASH RICH
AND SPIRITUALLY POOR

"Once [Vivian] saw how women went nuts over
Elvis and realized I was heading into that world,
she cooled considerably on the whole idea of
my recording and touring career."

—JOHNNY CASH

A month before Johnny's first record made its debut, Rosanne Cash made hers. She was born on May 24, 1955, at St. Joseph's Hospital in Memphis. Johnny and Vivian were so elated to become parents they vowed to have seven more children. They got halfway to that goal—over the next six years came three more daughters: Kathy (1956), Cindy (1958), and Tara (1961).

Good thing Johnny didn't have a big wad of cash to bestow on that panhandler outside Sun Records. The launch of "Cry! Cry! Cry!" did not result in the immediate infusion of money into his bank account he figured on. His first royalty check was a whopping $3.30. When Vivian's younger sister Sylvia came from San Antonio to help out with Rosanne, she had to use some of her own high school graduation money to buy groceries and diapers for the struggling family. Johnny's relatives also came from Dyess to pitch in. Vivian tried stashing a few bucks in hiding places around the house, but Cash always rooted it out and spent the money on cigarettes.

A turning point, in more ways than one, came on August 5, 1955. Cash was one of twenty-two artists performing in Bob Neal's "Country Music Jamboree" at Overton Park Shell, an outdoor amphitheater in Memphis. Elvis Presley was on the bill, too, along with Webb Pierce, Wanda Jackson, and Sonny James.

Cash and James had both performed earlier that year at the armory in Covington, Tennessee. After Cash and the Tennessee Two did "Cry! Cry! Cry!" and "Hey, Porter"—their entire repertoire at the time—the audience called them back out four times to repeat it.

James was known as "The Southern Gentleman" because he always conducted himself as one, and after the show, Cash sought him out for advice about something increasingly on his mind as his musical career took off: How to handle the demands of the entertainment industry, the bright lights, the fan adulation, and temptation—and still live a Christian life.

"John, the way I do it is by being the way I am," James told him. "I am not just an entertainer who became a Christian. I am a Christian who chose to be an entertainer. I am first a Christian.

"Remember that what you are and the life you live sings louder than any song.

"And don't forget to pray."

At times, Johnny would follow that sage advice, and other times he wouldn't. John R. Cash clearly knew right from wrong. He was a husband and now a father with responsibilities to put bread on the table. The career path that he chose—which in some ways chose him—was fraught with peril, and Johnny knew it. Though Elvis was already a huge star and Johnny Cash an emerging one, as time passed, it was Johnny, not Elvis, who would both start and finish well.

The Christian life is in many ways like a race. Some start well only to never finish.

Some start late in life and finish well. Johnny would stumble and fall many times as a Christian, but he would dust himself off and get up again . . . and again. In the end, Johnny's faith would reach its zenith.

He would also produce the finest music of his career, including "The Man Comes Around" and his version of Trent Reznor's "Hurt," which ended up winning the Country Music Association award for Single of the Year in 2003. "Hurt" was also nominated for six other awards and the 2003 MTV Video Music Award, winning for Best Cinematography. Johnny Cash was the oldest artist ever nominated for an MTV music award.

Many (including John Lennon) would say that Elvis hit his musical peak right before he went into the Army. All his monster hits ranging from "Hound Dog" to "Jailhouse Rock" were a soundtrack to rebellious youth in the 1950s. But when Elvis emerged from the military with songs like "It's Now or Never," "Are You Lonesome Tonight?" and, later, "Viva, Las Vegas," it was clear the King was going in a new direction, and it wasn't the groundbreaking rock and roll he was best known for.

The Overton Shell Park event drew more than four thousand people, and hundreds more were turned away. The next day's *Memphis Press-Scimitar* ran photos of Cash and Presley superimposed over one of the big crowd with the headline, "Country Rhythm Fills a Country Park."

Elvis himself had invited Cash to perform that night. For Presley, it was a triumphant homecoming. He had played his first public show there the year before as a supporting act for featured star Slim Whit-man. Now the hip-swiveling upstart was the big noise at the event, literally. The screams for Elvis reverberated throughout Overton Park.

Johnny Cash and the Tennessee Two had not performed in front of a live audience in Memphis other than a church till then. They played both sides of their first record and went over so big they were called back for an encore. They premiered their upcoming single, "Folsom Prison Blues," and the reaction was loud and thrilling.

For Vivian, not so much. She was proud of and happy for her husband, of course, but the delirious reaction of the females in the crowd to Elvis gave her a sense of foreboding she couldn't shake. Johnny was a good husband, but he had admitted to having a girl-friend when he was in Germany supposedly pining for her. He'd be going out on the road now for long stretches. How would he react to having hordes of pretty young girls scream his name and throw them-selves at him? Maybe selling stuff door-to-door wasn't such a bad thing after all. At least then he was home every night.

Bob Neal, impresario of the Country Music Jamboree, managed both Elvis and Cash at the time. But Colonel Tom Parker had already made himself Elvis's "special adviser" and was in the process of luring him away from Sun Records. "Mystery Train" would be the last Presley single produced by Sam Phillips, and it shot to No. 1. It debuted around the same time "Folsom Prison Blues" and its flipside, "So Doggone Lonesome," were recorded.

"Folsom" is a Cash classic, but it was far from that when he and the Tennessee Two introduced it to Phillips in the studio. Perkins couldn't master the guitar parts, and Cash's vocals were uneven. It took them months to get it right.

Cash himself predicted that "So Doggone Lonesome" wouldn't sell more than "three or four copies, because I don't have a steel guitar in the band." He had a lot to learn. Released in December 1955, "Folsom Prison Blues" and "So Doggone Lonesome" became his first Top Ten hits, peaking at No. 4 on the country charts.

On December 9, 1955, a seventeen-year-old Joanne Cash went to see her brother in concert for the first time, at Swifton High School in Jonesboro, Arkansas, about thirty miles from Dyess. But she didn't hear him sing a note that night because, just before he went out on stage, Johnny introduced her to the other star of the show.

"Elvis was the most handsome man I'd ever seen in my life—besides my husband," Joanne laughed. "He was cordial, he was kind. He held and kissed my hand. We talked for almost an hour, and I missed my brother's show. Johnny had some things to say to me on the way back home about that."

Cash and Presley were always friendly with one another, but they were never close pals. They did, however, have interesting backstage patter, according to Cash.

"Oh, yeah, always talked about gospel music . . . well, not always gospel music but girls too," Cash said. "Yeah, Elvis and I at a lot of the shows, we'd sing in the dressing room, and invariably, we'd go to black gospel. And we knew the same songs. We grew up on the same songs."

Superstardom was clearly in the cards for Elvis, and the last thing Johnny wanted in those early days was to look like he was riding on Presley's coattails. Throughout the 1960s and '70s, they swapped occasional notes. When Cash followed a Presley engagement at the Las Vegas Hilton, "The King" would call and wish him good luck. But they never hung out together.

In 1956, Cash, Elvis, and Carl Perkins joined the *Louisiana Hayride*, a popular radio show broadcast on Saturday nights from the Municipal Auditorium in Shreveport, Louisiana. Perkins also recorded for Sun, and he became one of Cash's lifelong friends. It was Johnny who inspired and kept after him to write his signature hit "Blue Suede Shoes" during the *Hayride* tours that took them throughout the Mid-South and into Texas and New Mexico between Saturday night broadcasts in Shreveport.

On the *Hayride* tours, Cash got his first real taste of life on the road—and the snares and pitfalls he had fretted about to Sonny James.

Backstage, there was beer and booze aplenty, plus women Cash heard the more experienced performers refer to as "snuff queens." Later, they were called "groupies." He didn't partake, but the always-near occasion of sin at every venue greatly discomfited him.

The day after one *Hayride* broadcast, Cash, Grant, and Perkins headed out from Shreveport to a show in Gladewater, Texas. As they drove west, Johnny noted cars turning into the parking lots of churches along the highway and dolefully said, "That's why I feel so low this morning. I ought to be in church." But there wasn't time. Later, Cash would look back on that as a pivotal event in his life—the day he put his career ahead of God.

When someone really has a relationship with God, they want to be with God's people. That is, in fact, an indicator of true faith in Christ.

The closer we are to God, the closer we'll want to be to His people. The further we are from God, the further we'll want to distance ourselves from His people. If you find yourself feeling uncomfortable around Christians, maybe there's something wrong with you spiritually.

1 John 3:14 says, "If we love our brothers and sisters who are believers, it proves that we have passed from death to life. But a person who has no love is still dead" (NLT).

Johnny was a true believer, albeit a struggling one.

Back in Memphis, Vivian worried. She couldn't get out of her head the memory of all those women clamoring for Elvis. One day when Johnny was home, she decided to voice her concern. "Baby, are you ever tempted by those women on the road?" she asked,

Cash was scanning the newspaper and didn't look up. "What women?" he said idly.

"You know," pressed Vivian, "the ones who scream . . . and proposition you?"

Now he looked up. "You mean those phony, plastic mannequins?" he snorted dismissively. "You don't ever need to worry about me, baby. You're on my mind every minute, day and night. I walk the line for you."

9

I WALK THE LINE

"Sometimes I am two people. Johnny is the nice one and Cash causes all my trouble. They fight."

—JOHNNY CASH

Johnny Cash's most famous song was originally called "Because You're Mine." He'd been working on it since Germany, when a music tape he made with the Landsberg Barbarians got twisted in the recorder, producing an unusual, evocative sound that Cash gradually spun into a slow melody.

The lyrics came easily, almost faster than Cash could write them down; in just twenty minutes, he was finished. It was one of those rare cases, he would say, of a song "begging to be written."

Backstage at a Texas venue, Cash played his new song for Carl Perkins. He and Perkins were the same age, were raised in the church, and both had worked the cotton fields in their youths. They liked to compare scars on their fingers caused by the sharp needles of the cotton bolls.

Cash told Perkins "Because You're Mine" was a declaration of fidelity to his wife (born of the conversation they'd had about the temptations of the road) and of the kind of man he and God wanted him to be. The pair often bounced ideas off one another, and Cash had been a helpful sounding board for Perkins as the latter worked on "Blue Suede Shoes," offering encouragement and suggestions. Now Perkins returned the favor after Cash gave him a run-through of the song.

"You know," Perkins said, " 'I Walk the Line' would be a better title."

Cash went with it. He worked out the arrangements on the road with the Tennessee Two over a period of weeks, and when they returned to Memphis in the spring of '56, Johnny took "I Walk the Line" to Sam Phillips. The Sun Records chief loved it but ventured that the song would be even better with a more upbeat tempo. When Cash demurred on the grounds that it was a personal love song to his wife, Phillips said fine—but how about, as a personal favor, recording one take with a faster, more energetic beat and the trio's signature boom-chicka-boom sound. Then they'd do it the other way and release that version. Cash didn't see any harm in that.

Not long after that, Cash and The Tennessee Two were driving back from a *Louisiana Hayride* gig when "I Walk the Line" came on the radio . . . only it was the up-tempo version supposedly done as a one-off for Sam Phillips, not the dirge-like song Cash had written.

They drove straight to Sun Records and stormed into Phillips's office.

"Wait, guys, wait!" said Phillips, holding up his hands. "I know what you're thinking. If it don't do what I think it's going to do, then I'll pull the record and release the slow ballad."

Cash gritted his teeth and agreed because he knew Phillips was a wily one.

Within weeks, "I Walk the Line" was a huge smash on *Billboard*'s country charts and extended to the pop charts at No. 17, minting Cash as a powerful new crossover artist. The record stayed on the charts for a phenomenal forty-three weeks and sold more than two million copies.

Today, it's revered as a classic and is Cash's signature song. The 2005 movie about his life was, in fact, called *Walk the Line.*

Years later, Cash still preferred his original version. He told Larry King in 2002 that he felt the record wasn't anything special and was shocked it became such a colossal hit.

"It was in my head too long. Didn't think it was that good of a song," Cash said. "I didn't think anybody would like it. I didn't like the arrangement. I didn't like the sound on the record."

Later Cash discovered that Phillips had sold Elvis Presley's contract to RCA Records for $35,000 and used the money to promote "I Walk the Line."

All was forgiven, and Johnny Cash was now Sun Records' number-one artist.

When a fairly sizeable royalty check came in, Cash gave $1,200 to George Bates, his boss at Home Equipment Store, for advances received in his salesman days. Bates cried when Cash made good on his debt. Johnny and Vivian drove to San Antonio to pay back $800 in loans from her folks. They also gave them their '54 Plymouth and bought a Cadillac for themselves.

Next on his agenda was persuading his father and mother to give up the farm in Dyess and move to Memphis. Now Cash could afford to help them buy them a nice home with all the modern conveniences. By then, sisters Reba and Louise also lived in Memphis, so it'd be a real family reunion.

The Cashes moved out of their apartment into a two-bedroom brick house at Sandy Cove Drive in the Berclair district of Memphis. The house was situated in a cul-de-sac in a nice middle-class neighborhood filled with young families like their own. It was definitely a move up.

With the success of "I Walk the Line," Johnny's career kicked into overdrive. There were appearances on the *Grand Ole Opry, The Ed Sullivan Show,* and *The Jackie Gleason Show.* Although it didn't materialize, manager Bob Neal also tried to get Cash a multi-picture movie deal at a major studio like Elvis Presley's. Judging by the effect Presley's movie career had on his music, it was probably a good thing Cash didn't break through in this medium.

Johnny's schedule of performances, interviews, and personal appearances became increasingly hectic and exhausting. The federal interstate highway system initiated by President Eisenhower was in the building process, and driving around the country to all the places Cash needed to be was so arduous that by the time he got to a venue, he usually required a two- to three-hour nap before he took the stage.

"The road is crushing. The road is endless. The road is boring, it is one concrete slab after another," said Cash historian Mark Stielper. "In the 1950s, Cash was driving hundreds of hundreds of miles each week after working several shows a night, and he had to do it again the next night."

One night, Cash was on a bill with "Hillbilly Heartthrob" Faron Young, whose band included Gordon Terry, a prodigy on the fiddle. As he and Terry chatted before the show, Cash said he was so worn out from traveling he didn't know where he'd find the strength to perform.

"I got something that will fix you right up," said Terry. From a pocket, he brought out a handful of cream-colored pills, plucked out one, and held it out to Cash. "Take this, and you won't be tired for long," he said. "You'll get through the night with no problem whatsoever."

After a moment's hesitation, Cash took the pill and swallowed it. That night, he gave a whale of a show.

The medical name for what he took was amphetamine. On the street, they were called "speed," "bennies," or "uppers." They were readily prescribed by doctors for stress, exhaustion, and even weight loss. They took the country by storm over a period of several years.

Cash loved what they did for him. Getting his own supply was no problem. All he had to do was phone up a doctor and say what he wanted and why, and for less than $10, he got one hundred pills that same day. One or two made him feel invincible and even took away the butterflies he had before every performance. Something that made him feel so "personable, outgoing, and energetic" couldn't be bad. Under their influence, he said, "I loved everybody!" He hadn't a doubt in the world—those magic pills were "God-sent."

Hardly. "Hell-sent" was more accurate, as Johnny would later discover.

It's not unlike when Eve offered Adam forbidden fruit in the Garden of Eden. It seemed like a good idea at the time, but the results of that fateful bite would reverberate through humanity for time immemorial. Sin would enter into the human race.

These pills that Johnny initially loved would actually play a part in keeping him away from God because of his guilt. But once you taste that forbidden fruit, it's hard, if not impossible, to turn back the clock.

It wasn't long before a couple pills weren't enough. It's the nature of the beast. Over the years, Cash's amphetamine use steadily increased and nearly destroyed his career and all of his relationships.

For Cash, 1956 was a seismic year in more ways than one.

After he and the Tennessee Two had been playing the *Louisiana Hayride* for six months, they were invited to play the Grand Ole Opry in Nashville. It was a big deal: the Opry was broadcast over radio station WSM every Saturday night from the Ryman Auditorium, "the Mother Church of Country Music." It was Cash's favorite show growing up in Dyess.

On the Opry stage in July 1956, they did three songs. "I Walk the Line" got a standing ovation, and for an encore, they performed it again.

It was a momentous occasion that became even more so backstage when Cash met June Carter. Her aunt, uncle, and mother made American musical history as the Carter Family, performing country, gospel, and southeastern mountain tunes. After the trio's breakup, Mother Maybelle Carter and daughters June, Anita, and Helen continued the family tradition, performing as Mother Maybelle and the Carter Sisters.

June herself had a Top 10 hit in 1949 with a novelty version of "Baby, It's Cold Outside" she had recorded with the comedy duo Homer & Jethro. She married Carl "Mr. Country" Smith in 1952, and they had a daughter, Rebecca Carlene (later known as Carlene Carter). June and Smith divorced in '56 amidst whispers of his infidelity.

"I've always wanted to meet you," Cash told June that night at the Opry.

"I can't remember anything else we talked about, except his eyes," June wrote in the liner notes of Cash's 2000 box set, *Love, God, Murder.* "Those black eyes that shone like agates . . . He had a command of his performance that I had never seen before. Just a guitar and a bass and a gentle kind of presence that made not only me, but whole audiences become his followers."

Cash was ready to follow her, too. Those agate eyes shone especially bright when he looked at June and said, "Someday, I'm going to marry you."

Less than a year after it was recorded as a ringing anthem of faithfulness to his wife, "I Walk the Line" was just another song.

10

GO WEST YOUNG MAN

"I love the road. I love being a gypsy. In some important ways I live for it, and in other ways it keeps me alive. If I couldn't keep traveling the world and singing my songs to real, live people who want to hear them, I think I might just sit myself down in front of a TV and die."

—JOHNNY CASH

Johnny Cash was sitting pretty at the start of 1957. The twenty-four-year-old entertainer had developed a fervent following, had a beautiful wife and family, a nice home in the 'burbs, and was starting to earn a decent living doing what he loved. He was the third best-selling country artist in the country, and his next ten singles after "I Walk the Line" all landed in the Top 10 on *Billboard's* country chart. Four of them—"There You Go," "Ballad of a Teenage Queen," "Guess Things Happen That Way," and "Don't Take Your Guns to Town"—reached the top spot.

And with Elvis Presley soon headed into the U.S. Army, Cash would have the opportunity to climb even higher up the ladder. As his celebrity and income zoomed, Cash's appetites followed exponentially—for food, for women, and for other distractions from the relentless monotony of the road. Under the influence of the amphetamines to which he was becoming addicted, his behavior became increasingly erratic. Johnny always enjoyed a practical joke—substituting shaving cream for whipped cream on somebody's piece of pie was a guaranteed knee-slapper.

There was never a shortage of firecrackers (or gunpowder) on the Cash bus, and one time near the Texas-New Mexico border at dawn, Cash and his two bandmates stuffed a five-pound metal keg full of them and ran off after lighting the long fuse they'd attached to it. The resulting explosion left a large crater in the highway, and when they came back to inspect their handiwork, there was already a crowd gathered around excitedly yammering about the meteor that had just crash-landed from outer space.

Outlandish stunts soon became the norm, like the time Johnny bought five hundred baby chickens and turned them loose in an Omaha hotel. His propensity for obnoxious pranks made him *persona non grata* at more than a few hostelries, as well as with other singers weary of being victimized by it.

For protection and amusement, the boys always brought a shotgun or two along on the road. As they were driving in Alabama one time, Cash spotted a large bird perched on a television antenna atop a farmhouse. He grabbed his blunderbuss and fired—and when the smoke cleared, both the bird and the antenna were kaput. The Cash Gang beat it out of there before the occupant of the farmhouse came out to give them a lesson in marksmanship.

They got a major ordnance upgrade when one of Marshall Grant's friends gave him a ten-gauge signal cannon. They kept it loaded with gravel to shoot at anything that struck their fancy. One sub-zero winter night in Minnesota, the target was a gaudy neon arrow on a sign at the side of the road. Cash got the cannon out and laid along-side it on his belly to get it properly aimed. When he pulled the lanyard, the cannon boomed and the whole sign exploded. The recoil sent the cannon into the right rear fender of their car, and then it careened fifty yards' down the road. Marshall chased it down, and they managed another clean getaway.

Grant and Luther Perkins weren't off-limits themselves. On the road, the trio always tried to book single hotel rooms with three beds to save money. If that couldn't be arranged, they'd get adjoining rooms with a connecting door between them. After one especially long, grueling drive, the hotel they checked into gave them rooms next to each other but with no connecting door. Cash took one room, and Grant and Perkins took the other. The latter had just gone to sleep when an ax blade crashed through the wall above their double bed. They leapt up and looked through the new hole in the wall, and there stood Cash, winding up for another swing.

"Now we have a connecting door," he said.

It wasn't long before Cash was gobbling ten or more uppers every day. When touring in south Texas, there were frequent side trips into Mexico, where a doctor's prescription for what he wanted was unnec-essary and he could buy all the pills he wanted. Vivian sensed they were dangerous from the start. When Cash was home, she'd get up early in the morning and find him sitting there haggard and bleary-eyed after staying up all night furiously writing, singing, and committing songs to tape. She urged him not to take the pills or at least cut back, but he didn't want to hear it and blew her off.

The pills, everyone agreed, changed his behavior, but Johnny's basic good nature continued to shine through when not under the influence. He committed random acts of kindness, often giving money to strangers in need. Hearing about a fan who traveled a long way to see him perform and who had neither provisions nor a place to stay, Johnny staked him to a hotel room and gave him meal money. Or when he would catch someone in a grocery store who was short on money, Cash would pay their bill. Such things endeared him to family and friends, but unfortunately also made ignoring the telltale signs of his addiction easier for them.

Johnny was living what the Apostle Paul talked about in his letter to the believers in Rome when he wrote, "It happens so regularly that it's predictable. The moment I decide to do good, sin is there to trip me up. I truly delight in God's commands, but it's pretty obvious that not all of me joins in that delight. Parts of me covertly rebel, and just when I least expect it, they take charge" (Romans 7:21-23 MSG).

In the fall of '57, Johnny, Vivian, and daughters Rosanne and Kathy moved to a 3,300-square-foot ranch-style home on Walnut Grove Place on the quiet eastern Gold Coast of Memphis, not far from the residences of George Bates and Sam Phillips—Cash's two bosses in the Bluff City. Not long after that, Vivian was pregnant again.

It was a giant, breathtaking step—actually, a rocket-ship ride—up from where they'd started out just a few years earlier; but Cash didn't spend much time reflecting on and reveling in that. His eyes were fixed on the western horizon.

Cash and the Tennessee Two had spent four weeks touring in and around California earlier that year. That was arranged by Johnny's new hard-charging manager Stewart Carnall, a Los Angeles-based businessman with strong connections in the entertainment field. The huge, sprawling City of Angels was a whole new world, way more cosmopolitan than Memphis and even Nashville, abounding with all kinds of opportunities—musical and otherwise—for good-looking, talented, ambitious, and fun-loving young fellows like Johnny Cash.

He and Sam Phillips had not been clicking lately. Cash—and several other Sun artists, as well—suspected the Sun Records owner was shorting him on royalties, and he resented the attention Phillips devoted to Jerry Lee Lewis, whose dual hits "Whole Lotta Shakin' Going On" and "Great Balls of Fire" were scorching *Billboard's* country and pop charts in 1957 and practically minting money for Phillips.

Cash's list of grievances also included Phillips' adamant resistance to letting him record a gospel album and the fact that Phillips never bought him a Cadillac.

"He gave Carl Perkins one when Carl sold a million copies of 'Blue Suede Shoes,'" Johnny wrote in his 1997 autobiography *Cash*, "but I never got one when 'I Walk the Line' became such a huge hit . . . I still think I should have that Cadillac."

Herein lies the dichotomy of John R. Cash.

Most rock or country stars would want the Cadillac, more money, more everything else. The only reason some do gospel records in country music is when their career is flagging and they need a boost. They can always fall back on that built-in church audience. But for Johnny Cash, his career was just taking off, and the outlaw persona he would be known for was beginning to take shape.

But it's interesting to me that Johnny wanted to do gospel songs all along. It was not something token; it came from his heart.

Despite giving into the enticements that superstardom offered, Johnny still believed—and he was still struggling.

It didn't help one day when Cash dropped by Sun unannounced to invite Phillips to lunch and was told that the boss was too busy even to come out and say hello.

So when Columbia Records producer Don Law sounded Cash out in August 1957 at a party in California about switching labels when his contract with Sun expired the following year, Johnny listened.

Law offered a $50,000 signing bonus plus 5 percent of the retail price of a record. Phillips was giving him just 3 percent. Columbia had way more promotional muscle than a small independent outfit like Sun—and Cash would have a green light to record his precious album of gospel music.

That last part cinched it for Cash, and he signed an option with Columbia immediately.

Sam Phillips was furious and took it quite personally. For the remaining months Cash remained contractually yoked to Sun,

Phillips kept him busy in the studio cutting records Cash didn't want to make but couldn't legally get out of doing. Some were Hank Williams covers that Phillips later released as an album called *Johnny Cash Sings Hank Williams.*

Phillips squeezed the last drop out of his departing artist, and with the large backlog of recordings he stockpiled, he was still putting out Cash product well into 1961.

At least Cash's tenure at Sun ended with a bang. One of the last songs Phillips forced him to record was Charlie Rich's "The Ways of a Woman in Love." It reached No. 2 on the country chart.

When he was finally free and clear of Sun Records in July 1958, Cash decided to put Memphis in his rearview mirror as well. Stu Carnall had been beckoning from Los Angeles, yacking about potential film and television opportunities he could get for Cash. Around September 1, after the wrap of Cash's first recording sessions for Columbia in Nashville, he, Vivian, and the kids (Cindy, their third daughter, was born on July 29) pulled up stakes for the Golden State. They moved into an apartment on Coldwater Canyon Avenue in Studio City, just blocks from Republic and Universal studios.

Vivian was still unpacking when her husband headed back out on the road.

11

SAY GOODBYE TO HOLLYWOOD

"My first wife put up with me for years after I
was hooked, but I'd go home and try to put all
the blame for it on her, and then I'd get into
my jeep or camper truck and head for the
mountains. And I'd get so stoned every time I'd
leave I'd wreck whatever I was driving."

—JOHNNY CASH

The King was gone . . . on U.S. Army duty in Germany for two years.
The Killer's career went over a cliff when Jerry Lee Lewis
married his thirteen-year-old cousin.

The Father of Rockabilly bled all over his blue suede shoes in a
horrific car accident. Carl Perkins survived, but woke up in obscurity.

It was as if life was a football game and Fate was blocking out
everyone standing between Johnny Cash and the end zone.

At the end of the 1950s, all he had to do was keep doing what he did best: writing songs and churning out hits. Though he was now wholly dependent on amphetamines, Cash could still deliver the goods, and did so in his first album for Columbia.

The Fabulous Johnny Cash was a sensational debut effort and ranks among the best of his albums ever produced by the label. It was a best seller with two Top Ten singles: "Don't Take Your Guns to Town" (Cash's fourth No. 1 country single, which held that spot for six weeks) and "Frankie's Man, Johnny" (No. 9 on the country charts). Recorded simultaneously over a two-month period with the album *Hymns by Johnny Cash* (1959), the twenty-nine-minute LP builds on Cash's basic, square sound and is noticeably more polished than his Sun records.

The album also features five tracks written by Cash and back-up vocals by the Jordanaires, who became available when Elvis became unavailable.

Not only a smash in the country and western realm, *The Fabulous Johnny Cash* crossed over to the *Billboard* pop album charts, landing in the Top 20 and staying there for several months—a virtually unheard-of feat for a country artist.

As a result, Cash was playing to much larger crowds. He had graduated from nightclubs and rowdy bars to larger and classier venues, and he hired W.S. "Fluke" Holland in August 1960. The former air-conditioning repairman from Jackson, Tennessee, had worked with Cash when he manned the drums during the famed December 4, 1956 recording session with Elvis Presley, Jerry Lee Lewis, and Carl Perkins on *Million Dollar Quartet*.

Holland worked out so well that the Tennessee Two was later renamed the Tennessee Three. Their sound was much bigger and improved, and bigger paydays lay ahead.

What better time for a spending spree?

It started with the purchase of a $75,000 four-bedroom ranch house with a swimming pool and separate maid's quarters on

Havenhurst Avenue in Encino. The previous owner, Johnny Carson, had moved to New York to start his new nightly talk show on NBC.

In the front yard of his new house, Cash planted and carefully tended several rows of cottonseed from Dyess to remind himself where he came from. Otherwise, he did his best to forget by buying anything he wanted. There were cross-country shopping expeditions with Vivian to fill their new closets and jewelry cases. Johnny was on tour when Vivian's birthday came around, but he arranged for a new pink Cadillac El Dorado to be delivered to her. He spent lavishly on the kids as well. Every homecoming from the road was like Christmas, with Cash dispensing gifts he'd bought for everyone.

The Cashes had three pets—an Irish setter, a monkey, and a parrot. The latter two were named Homer and Jethro, after the Grand Ole Opry comics. Vivian joked that Homer had Johnny's personality. Jethro was the family's unofficial greeter, screeching "Shoot, come in!" when the doorbell rang.

With powerhouse Columbia Records leading the charge for him, other opportunities Cash sought came to pass. He became a featured performer on the Los Angeles-based *Town Hall Party*, a popular weekly television show broadcast on Saturday nights, and he acted on TV's *Wagon Train* and *The Rebel*. This led to the starring role in *Five Minutes to Live*, a low-budget 1961 crime drama later re-released as *Door-to-Door Maniac* and now considered a film noir cult classic. Billed as "a lusty, romantic, guitar-singing powerhouse," Cash would never be confused with Laurence Olivier; but he gave a more credible performance than expected.

Everything was coming up roses (with a smattering of cotton).

Until November 5, 1960.

At five o'clock in the morning, the phone rang in the Cashes' room at the Hermitage Hotel in Nashville. They were in town for a Columbia Records convention. Vivian answered and was told that singer Johnny Horton had been killed in a car crash.

Horton (whose "Battle of New Orleans" won the Grammy for best Country Western recording that year) had been Cash's close friend since they appeared together on the *Louisiana Hayride*. Horton, his wife Billie Jean and the Cashes frequently traveled together and visited each other's homes. The two Johnnys hunted and fished together. In many ways, Horton was the kind of man Cash desperately wanted to be: he rarely drank, never did drugs, and always had a smile on his face and an encouraging word. And Horton never openly passed judgment on Cash's own behavior or let it affect their friendship.

After Vivian hung up the phone, she sat on the bed wondering how to break the news to her sleeping husband. Then came a loud knock on the door. She got up and opened it, and Memphis disc jockey Dewey Phillips barged past her into the room and shouted at Cash, "Hey, man, did you hear Johnny Horton died?"

Cash jolted awake, and Vivian cringed as Phillips blustered, "He got killed by a drunk driver, man! He's dead!"

Cash put his head in his hands and started to moan. He was crushed.

After concluding an engagement at the famous Skyline Club in Austin, Texas—the same club where Hank Williams had given his final performance seven years earlier—Horton and two others had piled into his Cadillac and headed for Shreveport. On Highway 79 near Milano, Texas, Horton's car was struck head-on by a truck whose driver later pleaded guilty to driving while intoxicated. Horton died on the way to the hospital.

Cash's first thought was of Billie Jean. She had been married to Hank Williams when he died of a drug- and alcohol-induced heart attack on New Year's Day in 1953. She and Johnny Horton married nine months later.

Cash tried phoning her but couldn't get through. His intention was to get on the first available flight to Shreveport until Marshall Grant reminded him about a studio session that afternoon at which Cash was to lay down some tracks for *Five Minutes to Live*. He was also booked to perform both at the Columbia Record convention and for his first Grand Ole Opry appearance in more than a year. Shreveport would have to wait.

Johnny's anguish over Horton's death could not be assuaged. It was like losing a brother. In fact, Vivian later said that, as was the case after Jack Cash died, Johnny tortured himself wondering if he could have prevented what happened to Johnny Horton. A week before he died, Horton had called Cash's home in Encino and then tried to reach him several times after that. Cash didn't take or return Horton's calls. Some believe he was most likely on one of his drug binges.

When Cash finally got to Shreveport, he took over the job of making the funeral arrangements for his friend. At Billie Jean's request, he gave the eulogy at the service. The whole time, Johnny was encamped at the Hortons' house instead of a hotel, and the suspicions among the mourners raised about that went up even higher when Cash and Billie Jean spent most of their time at the post-funeral reception sitting together on a swing in the backyard rather than consorting inside with the guests.

Cash had promised Johnny Horton that, if anything ever happened to him, he would look after Billie Jean. With her sultry good looks, that was easy to do, and in fulfilling his pledge to his dead friend, Cash—whose wife back in California was expecting their fourth child—went overboard. He took Billie Jean on a three-week trip to New York City, ostensibly to check on royalties she had coming from her husband's hit records. And if they were slow to pay, Cash promised to float her until her ship came in.

The two stayed at a hotel near Central Park, went to clothing stores, Broadway shows, and cozy night spots, and what was supposed to be a business trip ended up a whirlwind, madcap courtship culminating in mutual expressions of love—and a marriage proposal from the already-married Cash.

Johnny had clearly taken leave of his senses, making drug-fueled and sinful choices.

Had Billie Jean said yes to the proposal, Cash's career would've instantly crashed and burned. But she put on the brakes instead, telling Johnny he should think about it while fulfilling several concert dates in Germany. Unquestionably, it was his reliance on uppers that gave her pause about considering a future with him. Her time with Hank Williams, whom she once deemed "the king of the dope," had given her plenty of insight into the psyche of an addict. She knew that the pills would ultimately destroy Cash, and she didn't want to wake up one day next to a dead man.

Her willing participation in a relationship with a married man notwithstanding, Billie Jean had some grounding in reality—at least as far as Johnny's impulsive nature went.

The Germany tour was largely a bust because the combination of his grief about Horton and his yearning for Billie Jean drove Cash to his cache of pills more than ever. Upon his return, Johnny called her almost daily for weeks, and she finally told him she was embarking on her own singing career and didn't want any distractions. He offered to help get that off the ground for her, but she firmly declined. It was simply too soon after Horton's death, and she wanted to pursue a career of her own, she told Cash.

In '61, Billie Jean actually cracked the Country Top 40 with a single called "Ocean of Tears." Embittered by her choice of music over him, Cash channeled his feelings into a song called "Sing It Pretty, Sue" that appeared on a 1962 album.

With the emotional tumult at a crescendo, Cash decided that only one thing would pull him out of his funk. Actually, two. The first was those magic pills, and more of them. The second was uprooting himself and his family yet again and vacating their Encino digs for a more rural setting.

12

THE BLACK HOLE

"You know, I used to sing 'Were You There
When They Crucified My Lord?' while I was
stoned on amphetamines. I used to sing all
those gospel songs, but I never really felt them.
And maybe I was a little ashamed of myself
at the time because of the hypocrisy of it all:
there I was, singing the praises of the Lord and
singing about the beauty and the peace you
can find in Him—and I was stoned."

—JOHNNY CASH

Johnny Cash thought that changing playgrounds, playmates, and
playthings might give him the happiness and fulfillment that suddenly seemed to be eluding him. It was the classic addict's pipedream.

In the fall of 1961, he moved Vivian and the kids (daughter Tara
was just a few weeks old) from Encino sixty miles north to Casitas

Springs, California, a few miles outside of Ventura. Cash said the Los Angeles smog had wreaked havoc on his throat and sinuses, though considering the poison he was ingesting day and night, the smog was the least of his worries.

Their new sprawling house sat on fifteen acres on a hillside in the bedroom community. He also moved his parents from Memphis to nearby Ojai and bought them a trailer park (called "Trailer Rancho") to manage.

He also called for his sister Reba to move to California to begin managing his fan club, answer correspondence, and start up a newsletter called *The Legend*. Niece Kelly Hancock said her famous uncle was a kindly father figure whom she adored and clung to during her formative years.

"I spent a good deal of time at John and Vivian's house, hanging out with my cousins and swimming in their indoor pool," Hancock said. "I had the greatest respect for Vivian, and I loved her dearly. She didn't have it easy because he would leave for weeks at a time and she was left with the responsibilities of running a home and family."

As for John, she said he was kind and patient and acted in a fatherly way towards her.

"He was so much better with children than adults. He met us on our level and made it a point to spend time with me, make me feel as if I were important," Hancock said. "I trusted him, and he took care of me whenever I was with him. I couldn't wait to see him when he came to the house."

Cash wasn't as tender with his manager, Stewart Carnall, whom he had to fire. His frequent drinking partner and party companion as well as his manager, Carnall spent as much time at the racetrack as the office and was increasingly unavailable when Cash tried to get ahold of him. When Johnny found out that Carnall was AWOL from an important contract parley, he gave him the boot and hired Canadian businessman and promoter Saul Holiff to direct his business affairs.

Needless to say, the general house cleaning didn't include ditching the pills Cash had stockpiled all over the place. Sonny James had once urged him to pray, but Cash wasn't doing much of that anymore. Instead, he sought solace in pills and alcohol, though perhaps numbness is a better word for what he was after. In addition to his drug habit, after he moved to California, Cash took up where he'd left off in Germany with beer, and added vodka and wine to his list of favorite beverages.

"I found you can cultivate a taste for anything as long as you keep tasting," he wryly noted.

The pills and booze made him twitchier than ever. Friends noticed and whispered about the incessant nervousness that manifested itself in odd tics, gyrations, facial expressions, and eyes that sometimes blinked as if Cash was doing Morse Code again.

Vivian and the kids were often awakened in the middle of the night by his pacing and banging around the house. He chain-smoked cigarettes and downed endless cups of coffee. Sometimes, he just up and left, getting in his car and driving recklessly and pointlessly for hours through the streets, hills, and deserts of southern California.

On one pill-and-booze-fueled escapade, Cash drove his jeep at breakneck speed up the side of a mountain, zigzagging around mesquite and manzanita and careening wildly till he reached the summit. He stopped there and considered his situation. It was pitch black out, and there was no visible route back down. After pouring the contents of two cans of beer down his gullet, Cash asked himself, "What have I got to lose?" He started the jeep and, without even turning on its headlights, started back down. As it picked up momentum, the vehicle bounced off rocks and bushes, and Cash had to fight for control of the steering wheel. It got much harder when he plunged through a grove of manzanita. Now it was a struggle just to stay in the jeep as thick branches slapped and whipped his face.

By the grace of God, he made it to the bottom in one piece. Then Cash sat there for several minutes, shaking uncontrollably. He had sweated through his clothes and literally scared himself sober.

Looking back much later on that episode and the torment that caused it, Cash acknowledged his big mistake was that he didn't turn it over to God instead of clinging to his "man pride." When Vivian and others expressed worry about his health and behavior and begged him to get clean and sober, Johnny would assure himself, "You're not so bad" and keep doing as he pleased.

Johnny was following an all-too-familiar trajectory that has been the ruin of many a man and woman who climbed the mountain of fame. Once arriving, however, they found there was nothing there. The stories of rock, pop, and country music stars who ended up with substance abuse problems and worse are endless, and they will probably continue to the end of time.

The difference between John R. Cash and the rest is that he knew better. And so did June, who was also raised as a Christian.

In my 2017 spiritual biography called *Steve McQueen: The Salvation of an American Icon*, I noted how McQueen had virtually no family to speak of and was physically abandoned by his father and emotionally abandoned by his mother. Sadly, she was too preoccupied with her drinking and other pursuits to spend any time with the tow-headed little boy she had given birth to. McQueen had to grow up fast and learn to fend for himself. Over time, he became a classic hedonist.

He had all the things many men aspire to—fast cars and motorcycles, even faster women, drugs, alcohol, and all the other predictable vices. But after he reached the peak of his fame, Steve went on a search.

He had not found what he craved in his success as an actor, despite the fact that he was at one point the No. 1 movie star in the world.

Nor did he find it in the global fame and adulation that was lavished on him.

Steve McQueen found the answers he was looking for—not on a soundstage in Hollywood or in the seat of a racecar—but in the balcony of a church in Ventura, California, where he heard the good news that there was a God in Heaven Who loved him.

McQueen became a Christian and grew spiritually after that.

Tragically, he found out he had cancer some months later, and, though he fought it with his newfound faith, he died in a Mexico clinic.

But he died clutching Billy Graham's personal Bible, which the famed evangelist gave to McQueen before his trip to Juarez, Mexico, to undergo surgery to remove cancerous tumors.

And because he died believing in Jesus, I have no doubt that Steve McQueen is in Heaven right now.

His was a classic conversion story.

As the Bible says, "He went from darkness to light."

Johnny Cash's story has some similarities to Steve's, but it has even more differences.

Cash came from an intact, albeit dysfunctional, home with a distant, often harsh father. But his mother loved him deeply and instilled in him a faith in Jesus Christ that the young boy embraced.

Cash was raised in the church and knew right from wrong.

In contrast to Steve McQueen, Cash went from darkness to light—back to darkness and back to light again, and he continued this cycle throughout his life.

It was inevitable that the drugs and drinking would start to affect Cash's performances. Some nights he'd be stellar, and the next time, Marshall Grant would have to whisper the lyrics of their biggest hits into Cash's ear because he was too wasted to remember them. Other times, he wouldn't even show up at all. Once Grant and Perkins drove from Memphis to Alberta, Canada, a distance of two thousand miles, to join Cash for a two-show gig—only to be informed upon arrival that Johnny wasn't coming. They drove straight back to Memphis, the pointless round trip taking five days, for which they received nothing—not even an explanation or apology from Cash.

Johnny's vocals suffered as the drying agents in the amphetamines—plus cigarettes and alcohol—brought on chronic laryngitis. At his first Carnegie Hall concert in New York City, what should've been a personal and professional milestone for Cash, he could barely talk above a whisper, much less sing. As he started to croak out his first number, there was laughter in the audience as some thought he was joking. It quickly became apparent he wasn't, and the water Cash downed in great gulps failed to help matters. His hour-long set was a disaster, and Columbia ditched plans to release a recording of the concert as an album.

He was on the road 80 percent of the time now and performed close to three hundred shows a year. When a tour ended, it wasn't unusual for Cash to drop completely out of sight, not showing up at home for weeks or even months at a time. The drugs had driven a deep wedge between him and Vivian, and now Cash felt no compunction about dabbling in the "snuff queens" so readily available on the road.

That was one thing, as far as Vivian was concerned; she didn't like it, but those women didn't really mean anything to Johnny. But it was different in late 1961 when she heard that June Carter was joining Cash on tour.

Vivian never forgot their first meeting three years before at a music industry party in Nashville.

"Look," said June, thrusting her left hand into Vivian's face to show off a massive diamond ring from her second marriage. "With every husband, my diamond gets bigger!" At the time, June was married to Edwin "Rip" Nix, a Nashville police officer. Despite having a child together, it didn't last. Vivian's intuition told her that June Carter was trouble, and Lord knows she didn't need any more of that.

Her beautiful home was a veritable drug store. Vivian found pills stashed everywhere—even in Johnny's socks. As fast as she flushed them down the toilet, Cash would replenish his larder.

"Almost overnight, they took control of Johnny, and nothing was the same after that," Vivian wrote in her 2007 book *I Walked the Line: My Life with Johnny.*

Predictably, Cash's behavior led to his debut on a new public stage.

At 3:30 on a November morning in 1961, Nashville Police Inspector W. J. Donohoo and two traffic officers spotted a couple of men outside a club near the city's Printers Alley. One was vigorously kicking away at the front door of the club. When the policemen stopped to find out what was going on, the disheveled man doing the kicking said he had been refused entry there and so was taking matters into his own hands (or feet). At that time of morning, the club wasn't even open for business, and the men were taken to police headquarters, where the fellow who'd done the kicking told them he was an actor. After four hours in jail, each paid a $5 bond and was released.

The headline over the account of the incident in the next day's edition of *The Nashville Banner* screamed, "Johnny Cash Arrested Here on Drunk Charge."

Two weeks later in California, Cash made news again when Ventura police clocked him going 90 mph on the Ojai Freeway at one o'clock in the morning. When they managed to pull him over six miles later, Cash told them, "I just wanted to find out if I could outrun a police car." He couldn't and was cited for speeding and not having his driver's license on him.

New manager Saul Holiff doubtless wondered what he had gotten himself into after an incident in Vancouver, British Columbia. Cash was appearing at the famous Cave Supper Club, and it turned out that performing elsewhere in town then were Buck Owens, Wanda Jackson—and Billie Jean Horton. Cash tracked Billie Jean down at her hotel room late one night and pleaded with her for another chance. He was so blotto on pills and booze there was no reasoning with him, and she told him to leave. On his way out of the hotel, Cash took out his anger on every chandelier in swinging distance, resulting in a lobby full of broken crystal and a massive bill for damages for Holiff to pay.

Busted chandeliers could easily be fixed. The wreckage of Johnny Cash's life . . . not so much.

13

ONE MAN,
TWO PERSONALITIES

"When we fell in love, she [June Carter] took it
upon herself to be responsible for me staying
alive. I didn't think I was killing myself, but
you're on the suicide track when you're doing
what I was doing. Amphetamines and alcohol
will make you crazy, boy!"

—JOHNNY CASH

Johnny Cash had been captivated by June Carter since he heard her
sing on the radio when he was a teenager. His first look at her was
from a seat in the balcony of the Ryman Auditorium. He was eighteen, and he had traveled to the Grand Ole Opry with his Dyess High
School senior class. That night, she sang with the Carter Family and
did a comedy act with Ernest Tubb.

"She was great. She was gorgeous. She was a star," Cash said. "I was smitten, seriously so."

So seriously that when they finally met backstage at the Opry in 1956, Cash blurted out that they would be married someday.

June, her sisters, and Mother Maybelle joined Johnny's tour in late January 1962, and now that Cash and June were around each other all the time, Cash was more enchanted than ever. She was as fun as she was beautiful. She charmed him, brought him out of himself, even mother-henned him, ironing his clothes, keeping after Cash to eat right, get more sleep, and take better care of himself. He sure looked haggard and hollowed out. Then, after a show in Macon, Georgia, she found Cash with a handful of Dexamyl pills, and it was all clear.

June had been through that trip once before when she toured with Hank Williams in the early '50s. She sat Cash down and talked about what it was like to watch a man beloved by millions, with the world at his feet, slowly kill himself. Johnny listened and nodded in understanding—but then just kept right on doing what he wanted. On the road, June took to hiding his pills and even trying to intercept deliveries of them, but Cash always found a way to get high. It was maddening.

But not maddening enough to keep her from falling for Cash as hard as he had fallen for her. Within months, they were involved in a full-blown love affair. They tried to practice discretion, and when, inevitably, word of their carryings-on found its way to Vivian, Johnny flat-out lied about it, telling his wife it was all baseless gossip. Vivian's suspicions were hardly allayed when she ran into June backstage at a show in Bakersfield, California. Vivian was with friends and looked gorgeous in a new, expensive outfit topped by a pristine white leather coat, but June seemed to go out of her way to embarrass her by asking, in an exaggerated fashion, "Vivian, what is that on your coat that looks like . . . dirt?" As Vivian's face reddened, June broke into derisive laughter. Vivian was humiliated.

Any doubt about what was going on with Johnny and June disappeared after the "First Giant Folk Western Bluegrass Music Spectacular" at the Hollywood Bowl on June 15, 1962. The sold-out event featured performances by Cash, Marty Robbins, Patsy Cline, George Jones, Roger Miller, Flatt and Scruggs, Mother Maybelle and the Carter Family, Tompall, the Glaser Brothers, and Johnny Western.

With the Carnegie Hall fiasco still fresh in his mind, Cash made sure to show up in decent shape, and he gave a strong performance. Afterwards, Vivian led the girls and Carrie and Ray Cash to the parking area to say goodbye to Johnny, who was leaving for Phoenix right away for a show the next night. When Cash joined them, he seemed nervous and distracted and kept looking around. Then June appeared, and Cash deserted his family as if they were a gaggle of autograph seekers, hurrying to June and ushering her into a waiting Cadillac.

Recalled Johnny Western, Cash's longtime friend who was behind the wheel of the Caddy that night: "As soon as Vivian saw June get into that car and sit next to Johnny in the backseat, it was a lightbulb moment for her. Maybe it was the way he looked at June or she at him. Maybe it was the way they sat together so close in the backseat and seemed so comfortable. I'll never forget the look of pure anguish on poor Vivian's face. I can't help but think that her woman's intuition kicked in and she instinctively knew what was going on."

Johnny and Vivian always tried to shield the kids from their strife, but there was no sweeping this under the rug. It was a line of demarcation for the couple, and, for the next year, Cash was largely absent from Casitas Springs. He missed the girls' birthdays and Christmas, and Vivian didn't even hear from him on their wedding anniversary.

One of Johnny's refuges was a rural cabin owned by Floyd Gressett, a Texas-born preacher who presided over the nondenominational Avenue Community Church in Ventura, California. Gressett and Cash shared an interest in hunting and fishing, and sometimes Cash used the cabin in Cuyama Valley, ninety miles north of Ventura, to work on music.

It didn't take Gressett long to find out about Cash's addiction. In fact, he once discovered Johnny half-dead from starvation during a heavy drug binge and helped nurse him back to health. Despite Cash's problems and shortcomings, Gressett found much to like about him and never lectured or judged him.

The pastor acted as the Good Samaritan did in the story Jesus told, tending to the need of a hurting man. Gressett showed Johnny Cash God's love in a tangible way, which the singer desperately needed.

Reflecting in 1975 on that awful period in his life, Cash said, "I know that the hand of God was never off me, no matter what condition I was in, for there is no other way to explain my escaping the many, many accidents I had." By his own estimation, he had wrecked virtually every car he ever owned, totaled two jeeps and a camper, and overturned two tractors and a bulldozer. He sank two boats in separate incidents, and he once leaped from a truck just before it went over a six-hundred-foot cliff.

After long, frenzied drug binges, when Cash finally crashed, just before he drifted off into unconsciousness, he sometimes heard a quiet voice say, "I am your God. I am still here. And I am still waiting. I still love you."

I had a similar experience after I came to faith at the age of seventeen. I had been smoking pot every day and taking LSD on the weekends. My life was in a downward spiral when I stumbled across a gathering of Christians having a Bible study on the front lawn of my high school campus. I heard a preacher say that there was a God in Heaven who loved me so much that He sent His own Son to die on the cross for my sins. Unlike Cash, I had not been raised in a home of faith. After praying for Christ to come into my life and forgive me of my sins on my high school campus on Friday, I continued with my plans to smoke some pot and drop acid that weekend. As I packed my pipe with marijuana, I heard that same voice I had heard hours earlier when the preacher spoke. It was the voice of God.

"You don't need that anymore!" I sensed Him saying.

I threw that pipe as far as I could and said, "God, I cannot do this on my own. But if you are really in my life, you are going to have to help me be free from drugs."

God came through for me.

He also would have come through for Cash.

But the Lord does not force His way into our lives.

As Jesus said to a man who needed healing, "Do you want to be made whole?" (John 5:6 NKJV)

Why would Jesus ask a question like that?

Because not everyone wants to change.

Not every drug addict or alcoholic wants to leave that life behind. Some actually find a form of comfort in that darkness.

God was ready to change Cash's life, but Johnny was not quite ready for the Lord to do that.

So the struggle continued.

Cash often vowed to change, to go back to church, and to be the kind of man his brother Jack would have been and would want him to be. But he always relapsed. His heart's desire for righteousness was overruled by his body's craving for amphetamines. It was a true Jekyll-and-Hyde existence.

"John's behavior was really puzzling," wrote Marshall Grant in his 2006 book *I Was There When It Happened*. "He was a tremendous person, one of the finest people I've ever known in my life. But when he was taking those pills, it was almost as if he had a split personality. He'd be fine one day when he was straight, but if he popped some of those pills, the next day he'd be just the opposite."

Another factor in Cash's mounting anxiety as the '60s unspooled was that he hadn't had a hit record for a while. After *The Fabulous Johnny Cash*, he made *Songs of the Soil* in 1959 and also the gospel album he had for so long ached to do, *Hymns by Johnny Cash*. He prolifically wrote songs on concept albums about the Old West, trains, Native Americans, the working man, and the oppressed. On the records, he narrated some of the lyrics instead of singing them.

The songs were personally meaningful and artistically satisfying to him, but they didn't set the charts on fire. That last bit didn't sit so well with his record label, either.

Columbia execs told Cash that because his last efforts had done so poorly, he would not get paid for his next record so the company could recoup some of its investment. And if the new one tanked, they warned, he was finished at Columbia when his contract expired at the end of the year.

His next single dawdled only three weeks on the country charts. It was called "Busted," which seemed appropriate.

"Artists prefer not to be starving artists, so when his back was against the wall and Cash was pretty much out of options, 'Ring of Fire' saved his career," said Cash historian Mark Stielper. "Anything that happened later in his career was because of 'Ring of Fire.'"

Originally titled "(Love's) Ring of Fire," the song was co-written by June Carter and Merle Kilgore. June said she got the title from a phrase in a book of Elizabethan poetry. The song itself was about her torrid relationship with Cash. It was originally recorded by June's sister Anita, but when it went nowhere, Cash claimed the song for himself in a last-ditch effort to save his career.

Legend has it that it was in a dream Cash heard "(Love's) Ring of Fire" open with a blast of mariachi horns. That would be a sure-fire attention-grabber, he decided when awake, and he went with it. He also pared the title down to "Ring of Fire."

Cash needed no less than a home run, and he knocked "Ring of Fire" out of the park. Released in April 1963, the song zoomed to No. 1 on the country charts and parked there for seven weeks. It was the biggest single of Johnny Cash's career to date. To capitalize on his new momentum, two months later, Columbia issued an album called *Ring of Fire: The Best of Johnny Cash*, a mish-mash of B-sides, oddities, and unreleased tunes that had sat in the vault collecting dust. It was the first No. 1 when *Billboard* debuted its Country Album Chart in January 1964. It also reached No. 26 on the pop LP charts, selling more than 500,000 copies and earning him his first Gold record.

"Ring of Fire" was not such a hit with Vivian, especially when she found out that Cash was giving June Carter half his royalties. Pressed for an explanation, he told her June needed the money and he felt sorry for her. Vivian countered that June clearly lacked for nothing since Johnny had been lavishing all kinds of extravagant gifts on her, including expensive jewelry, clothes, electronics, and items for June's children. Vivian had the receipts Johnny had unsuccessfully tried to hide to prove it.

Cash was out of the woods professionally, but in his personal life, he remained up a creek without a paddle.

14

EL PASO TIMES

"All mood-altering drugs carry a demon called Deception. You think, *If this is so bad, why does it feel so good?* I used to tell myself, 'God created this; it's got to be the greatest thing in the world.' But it's like the old saying about the wino: he starts by drinking out of the bottle, and then the bottle starts drinking out of him. The person starts by taking the drugs, but then the drugs start taking the person. That's what happened to me."

—JOHNNY CASH

The rousing success of "Ring of Fire" put Cash in the catbird seat with Columbia Records. He got a new five-year contract that came with a $500,000 advance, and Columbia agreed to take out six full-page ads a year in the music trade publications exalting Johnny's future releases and status as a multi-genre superstar. The time had come to market Cash as a contemporary artist, not just a country, folk, Nashville, or rock act. He had transcended such easy categorization.

Musically speaking, Cash was in fact entering a period of great fecundity and creativity. Always least effective when aiming for a deliberate hit, he now let his instincts and imagination roam free in a series of concept albums and musical offerings more ambitious than anything the country had seen.

Of course, the ante was upped when folk turned electric and the British invasion hit U.S. shores. Artists like the Beatles, the Rolling Stones, Bob Dylan, and Joan Baez were changing the musical landscape, influencing other artists as well as popular culture. Cash seemed to be the only one of his stature paying attention. He played at the Newport Folk Festival in Rhode Island in 1964 and went to clubs in New York's Greenwich Village to hear Dylan, Baez, and other "folkies." They all became friends and members of a mutual admiration society—especially Cash and Dylan.

Cash experienced both commercial and artistic success with *Blood, Sweat and Tears, Bitter Tears: Ballads of the American Indian; I Walk the Line; Johnny Cash Sings Ballads of the True West;* and *Orange Blossom Special.* Demonstrating Cash's virtuosity with elements of country, folk, Americana, and pop, they all became top sellers on the country charts. There were also plenty of Top Ten singles that kept Cash in heavy rotation on radio stations: "The Matador" (No. 2); "Understand Your Man" (No. 1); "The Ballad of Ira Hayes" (No. 3); "It Ain't Me, Babe" (No. 4); and "Orange Blossom Special" (No. 3).

I was twelve years old at this point but very aware that the golden age of rock and pop music was upon us. Led initially by the Beatles and other British invaders like the Rolling Stones, the Dave Clark Five, Herman's Hermits, the Kinks, and many others, the whole sound of music was changing.

I was very aware of Johnny Cash as well. He was a favorite of the older generation but also an artist I personally related to and appreciated more than others like Frank Sinatra or Dean Martin.

Johnny Cash always seemed to transcend time, generations, and genres.

Somehow, he did all that while his personal life floundered more than ever. By 1964, Cash's affair with June Carter was an open secret in the industry, and as Cash's addiction to pills and his behavior spiraled out of control, even that relationship sometimes devolved into open warfare. In Albuquerque one morning, Cash holed up in his hotel room and refused to heed the pleas of his entourage to get up so they could proceed to El Paso for the next show. What finally got him moving was when June stormed into his room and shouted, "Lay there, star!" She thought for sure her days on the Cash tour were done, but at the airport, a contrite Johnny presented her with a Native American peace pipe he bought in the souvenir shop.

It was a tenuous peace. After a Cash drug binge in Toronto, June told him she couldn't take it anymore and was leaving. He got angry, and a major fight ensued. June finally returned to her room to take a shower. While she was doing so, Cash stole in, gathered up all her clothes and took them back to his room. Wearing just a towel, June had to pound on his door and beg for her things.

They made up, as they always did—even after the time June overheard Johnny tell Vivian over the phone that he loved her and reacted by smashing everything she could get her hands on. The fact was that, by then, there was no love left between Cash and his wife. He had asked Vivian for a divorce several times—even offered her a settlement of a half-million dollars; but because the Catholic Church in which she'd been raised didn't countenance divorce, Vivian refused, though she and the kids were mortified by the notoriety and shame that reflected on them as Johnny's behavior knew no bounds.

The fact is, Vivian had scriptural grounds for divorce from Johnny.

The Bible teaches that when one partner is unfaithful to another, as Johnny was to Vivian, the faithful partner has the option of terminating the marriage (Matthew 5:32, 19:9 NIV).

But Vivian held on anyway in hopes that Johnny would perhaps, like the Prodigal Son, come to his senses and return home to her and the children.

Sadly, that was not going to happen.

Vivian attempted to save their marriage by asking to go out on the road with Johnny more often. At first, he'd come up with a handy excuse or explanation about how impractical that would be; later, he didn't even bother to respond to her. Vivian once reached June on the phone to ask her—not so nicely—to leave her husband alone. The call ended up with an abrupt click on the other end.

Another time, Vivian caught up with June backstage after a show. It was, she recalled in her 2007 book, "an ugly, tense five minutes of angry words, posturing, and June punctuating her position with five devastating words that rendered me speechless: 'Vivian, he *will* be mine.'"

Sometimes June must've wondered if he was worth the trouble. In Nashville, Cash wrecked her Cadillac, broke his nose, and lost his front teeth driving head-on into a utility pole. He claimed a wet roadway was the cause of the accident. Cash was taken to Vanderbilt Hospital, where, surprisingly, he refused a shot of morphine for the pain and had his nose set. Another surprise was that the policeman heading up the investigation of the crash was Officer Rip Nix—June's husband. No charges were filed, and the incident didn't make the paper; but Officer Nix's wife undoubtedly got an earful at home.

There was no excusing his behavior the night Cash ignored a "No Trespassing" sign and drove his camper full speed through the front gate of the Naval Air Weapons Station in the Mojave Desert. Cash recklessly sped several miles down a heavily cratered dirt road until pulled over by military police. "I fully expected to see you blow up before I could get to you," said the officer in charge. Cash had trespassed on an ordinance testing site; there were experimental landmines planted everywhere.

Cash was let go with a warning that time, but it was different in June 1965 when he was on a fishing trip in the Los Padres National

Forest, a 1.8 million-acre preserve home to numerous federally protected species. Hopped up on pills and alcohol, Cash stalled his brother-in-law's Chevy camper in the sand on the edge of creek, and as he repeatedly revved his engine in a futile effort to free it, the heat from the exhaust pipe set a patch of grass on fire. The blaze spread rapidly and ended up scorching 508 acres and driving off forty-nine endangered condors before an emergency crew of 450 firefighters could put it out.

Don Hancock was married to Cash's sister Reba at the time. "We saw the smoke and heard the news on the radio," he recalled. "Reba and I received a troublesome call from Vivian. She was frantic and upset. The Ventura County Sheriff's Office had called to inform her that they had arrested Johnny and said he had actually started the fire."

The authorities instructed Vivian to come fetch Cash at Los Padres and take him home. Instead, Hancock and Reba went in a 1946 Army Jeep that belonged to Cash. They met a park ranger at the entrance to the National Forest and followed him for five miles over a road so rutted and primitive it took them a half hour to reach their destination.

When they arrived where Cash was being held, Hancock recalled, "The sheriff got Johnny out of the vehicle and released him to our care. Johnny was very disheveled, dirty, and both of his hands were burned. He had tried to put out the fire with a blanket from the camper bed, and he burned his hands in doing so."

The drive to Johnny's house was even more harrowing than the one into Los Padres because Cash insisted on taking the wheel. "He was erratic," recalled Hancock. "He would speed up, then slow down, weaving back and forth into oncoming traffic."

Hancock safely got Johnny out of Los Padres National Forest, but Cash wasn't out of the woods by any means.

The Department of the Interior filed suit against Cash for $125,127 to cover the damages to Los Padres. When asked in court to account for his behavior, he was sullen and uncooperative, insisting, "No. My truck did it, and it's dead, so you can't question it." Eventually, he agreed to pay $82,000. Because the camper Cash used that night belonged to Don Hancock, the latter's insurance company had to fork over $8,000 in the settlement.

That wasn't Cash's biggest problem with the federal government that year. The Food and Drug Administration had finally tightened up requirements for prescription amphetamines, making it more difficult for addicts like Johnny to legally score all the pills they wanted from amenable physicians. After a show in Dallas on October 2, 1965, Cash flew to El Paso, Texas, and from there took a taxi across the Rio Grande River into Juarez, Mexico. In a seedy bar, he met up with a dealer who sold him 668 Dexedrine and 475 Equanil tablets. Before re-crossing the border, Cash hid the stash inside a guitar.

I find it interesting that Juarez is where actor Steve McQueen would take his last breath before he went to Heaven. For Johnny, Juarez is where he discovered hell on earth.

At El Paso International Airport, he boarded a plane for Los Angeles but had barely settled into his seat when two men came up and identified themselves as federal customs agents. They escorted Cash off the plane and into a room in the terminal where Cash learned that the man he had done business with in Juarez was under surveillance as a possible heroin dealer. Cash denied buying heroin, but when his belongings were searched, the cache of illegal pills was discovered in the guitar, and he was placed under arrest.

The next day, a photograph of Cash in handcuffs and dark sunglasses appeared in newspapers across the country. The cat was finally out of the bag.

15

END OF THE LINE

"Everyone was plotting against me.
If I saw a police car, I'd duck down a side street,
then drive like mad through residential areas,
narrowly missing innocent pedestrians. Why I
didn't kill anyone, I don't know—
or maybe I do know."

—JOHNNY CASH

His hit records, money, and fame didn't get Johnny Cash special accommodations at the El Paso city jail. The worst dump he'd ever stayed in on the road was better than the cramped cell he now occupied. The toilet didn't flush; his bunk was a ratty blanket tossed over hard bed springs. The overhead light remained on 24/7, making it impossible to ignore the mad scurrying of cockroaches everywhere.

Cash heard occasional laughter and loud cursing coming from neighboring cells. Somewhere, an inmate cried hysterically, and another frantically beseeched God for mercy. Cash tried to pray himself, but he was too wired and distracted by the constant din. Finally, he crashed, and as he slept, word of his arrest traveled to newspapers and radio and TV stations around the world.

His breakfast the next day was a bowl of black-eyed peas and a piece of bread. Three times Cash was brought out of his cell to take phone calls from concerned friends and associates. After the third one, he told the guard he was no longer available to callers and sank down on his bunk, utterly despondent. He had ruined his life and let down family and friends. He imagined his daughters hearing about what happened and crying, and he started to weep himself.

"I don't ever want out of this cell again," he sobbed. "I just want to stay here alone and pray that God will forgive me—and then let me die."

The most miserable man or woman around is the one who knows the will of God and does not do it. Johnny was that man.

He sang so often of people living lives of crime that many thought he was a serious criminal himself. But now Johnny was seeing what a life behind bars, albeit a short one, was really like. He fell into a state of deep despondency.

King David, after his fall into sin, was guilty of crimes far worse than Cash. David not only committed adultery, but he also played a role in the murder of an innocent man—the husband of the woman he had the affair with.

Describing how he felt at this time, David wrote:

When I kept it all inside,
my bones turned to powder,
my words became daylong groans.
The pressure never let up;
all the juices of my life dried up.
Psalm 32:3-4 (MSG)

Johnny Cash could have written those very words at this stage of his life.

His old belligerence returned as Cash, wearing a black suit and white shirt, was marched to a bond hearing arranged by local lawyer Woodrow Bean, who'd been hired by Marshall Grant. Seeing a phalanx of photographers and reporters recording the scene, Cash angrily swore at one and threatened to kick another. But he was appropriately somber in the courtroom as U.S. Commissioner Colbert Coldwell read the indictment charging him with "willfully smuggling and concealing drugs after importation."

Coldwell set Cash's arraignment for December 28, released him on a $1,500 bond, and ordered him not to leave the United States.

He went home to Casitas Springs with his tail firmly tucked between his legs. Vivian and the kids welcomed him with open, loving arms, and Cash came clean about his addiction. He vowed to kick it. For the first time in his life, he said, he felt real shame.

Shame has its place in a person's life. It means your conscience is working.

"Are they ashamed of their disgusting actions? Not at all—they don't even know how to blush!" (Jeremiah 6:15 NLT)

But Johnny had not gone that far—yet.

Six weeks later, he returned to El Paso to face the music. Vivian accompanied him. Cash pleaded guilty to possession of illegal drugs, a misdemeanor that carried a maximum fine of $1,000, one year in prison, or both. The district judge deferred sentencing indefinitely, pending a report from Cash's probation officer, and Cash was free to resume his touring without restriction.

Plenty of concert dates had been cancelled in the immediate wake of his arrest, but it didn't take long for Cash to pick up right where he'd left off.

Unfortunately, this also applied to his abuse of amphetamines.

The following March, Cash set out for a string of concert dates in Canada and New York State, including a three-night stand at Toronto's prestigious O'Keefe Centre for the Performing Arts. No country artist had ever played there before, and manager Saul Holiff left no stone unturned to promote the engagement. He even got Cash to sit down with reporters and take questions about El Paso. He was contrite, humble, and made a good impression.

"It was my first conviction of any kind," Cash said. "Of course, I can't goof up like that again."

But for all of Cash's public talk of having put drugs behind him, Holiff knew it wasn't so. His behavior at the Four Seasons Hotel—running around naked in the hallway, pounding on doors in the middle of the night—told a different story.

All three O'Keefe Centre shows were sold out, and Holiff held his breath each time Johnny took the stage. One time, he came out and faced the wrong way, and at the final show, Tex Ritter, the cowboy singer who was a supporting act on the bill, had to push Cash out on stage. Johnny wasn't even wearing shoes, just socks. But somehow that and his addled condition didn't keep him from giving a performance that wowed fans and critics.

Saul Holiff sank into his bed later that night relieved and exhausted. Then the phone rang.

"There's something wrong with Johnny," said June Carter breathlessly when he answered.

They were supposed to be in Rochester, New York, the next day for afternoon and evening shows. Abe Hamza, the Rochester promoter, was a large, menacing, cigar-smoking Godfather type who'd warned Holiff he would personally break both his legs if he failed to deliver Cash.

Saul flew out of bed, out of the hotel, and to Cash's motor home in the parking lot. A crowd of performers and others milled around the entrance of the vehicle when he arrived, each face he saw looking grim. When Holiff pressed his way inside the motor home, there lay his star on the floor, unconscious. Saul knelt, grabbed Cash's wrist and checked for a pulse. Nothing. Someone else put an ear to Cash's chest and reported the same result.

Holiff joined the others back outside, and as Cash lay apparently dead or dying, a raucous debate ensued about what to do. Wellesley Hospital was nearby, said someone, but somebody else pointed out that Toronto General had a better reputation. American hospitals were best, said another—but if they made a pell-mell dash for one and got searched at the border, Lord only knew what contraband would be found in the motor home, and they'd all take a fall for it.

Unable to shake the image of a glowering Abe Hamza out of his head, Holiff decided to head straight for Rochester, three-plus hours away, and hope for the best. June and Marshall Grant rolled Cash in a blanket and off they went. The border crossing was blessedly uneventful, and they made it to the Rochester Memorial Auditorium at 2:30 the following afternoon. Holiff went back to check on Cash and almost went into cardiac arrest himself when he found Johnny sitting up and drinking coffee as if he'd just awoken from a good night's sleep.

"How are you doing?" asked the almost hyperventilating manager.

"Why are you asking me how I'm doing?" responded Cash in genuine puzzlement. "What do you think I'm doing? I'm going to go out and give a show."

He did two sensational shows that day. Even Abe Hamza smiled.

Johnny was really skating on thin ice. God would graciously give him another chance, but he would return to his old ways again.

The concerted PR effort to present Cash to the public as a regular, fun-loving guy whose worst days were behind him included the recording of *Everybody Loves a Nut*, a thirty-minute album of goofy novelty tunes complete with a cartoon cover. A single on it called "The One on the Right is on the Left" reached No. 2 on the country singles chart, but the album tanked overall. Today, it's actually considered something of a classic and beloved by a whole new legion of fans. Cash had a skewed view of it years later.

"I think that came out of amphetamines," Cash said. "It was part of my craziness at that time, and it happened to find its way onto the tape. I thought some of the songs were funny. And I thought it might show that I did have a sense of humor. But there were no great songs on that album, that's for sure."

In May 1966, the craziness continued. That's when Cash went on a tour of the United Kingdom and Europe. Bob Dylan was touring overseas at the same time. They met and partied at Dylan's hotel in Cardiff, Wales. Cash was booked at the prestigious Olympia Theatre in Paris, but when Saul Holiff went to meet him at Heathrow Airport in London for the flight to Paris, Cash was a no-show. Holiff was so furious he immediately tendered his resignation as Cash's manager and spent a week walking around Hyde Park to recover his equilibrium. Six weeks later, he and Cash reconciled.

Back in California, Vivian Cash was in bad shape herself. The overwhelming emotional stress and strain of the past few months had worn her down to a mere ninety-five pounds, and when she went to see a doctor, he was blunt.

"You need to do *something*," he said. "If you don't, somebody *else* will be raising your girls."

That cut it for Vivian. In June, when Cash returned from Europe, instead of coming home, he camped at the Nashville home of Columbia Records executive Gene Ferguson. It was no coincidence Ferguson's abode was close to June Carter's house.

Vivian got herself a lawyer, and on June 30, she filed for divorce, charging Cash with extreme mental cruelty. She was wracked by guilt and misgivings and even called Cash in Nashville to ask if there was any chance of them reconciling. He was high and incoherent, and Vivian heard June in the background telling Johnny to hang up the phone.

"No," he managed to say. "It's too late."

Vivian was awarded the Casitas Springs house and some other property, alimony of $1,000 a month, child support of $1,600 a month, and 50 percent of royalties on all songs Cash wrote and recorded up to 1966.

What she didn't get was closure. That would come much later.

Decades later.

16

FREE MAN FREEFALL

"Over a period of time, you get to realizing that
the amphetamines are slowly burning you up . . .
then you get paranoid, you think everybody is out
to do you in. You don't trust anybody—even the ones
who love you the most."

—JOHNNY CASH

The end of his twelve-year marriage to Vivian might have seemed like the opportunity for a fresh beginning to Johnny Cash, but he didn't exactly start off on the right foot by moving in with Waylon Jennings.

Cash rented a one-bedroom apartment at the Fontaine Royale Apartments off Gallatin Road in Madison, Tennessee. It was close to the home of Mother Maybelle and Pop Carter, who had become like another set of parents to him. His place was also close to June's home on Gibson Drive, although he made it a point not to be seen there publicly.

Cash and Jennings became roommates that August because the latter was at loose ends and needed a place to crash.

"When we shared the apartment together, we weren't poor," Cash recalled. "I could have afforded a better apartment. I could have afforded an apartment without having to room with Waylon, but I thought it would be fun, which it was."

They weren't exactly the Odd Couple. Two Oscar Madisons was more like it. Theirs was a cramped and disorderly bachelor pad. Two king-sized beds took up most of the space in the bedroom, an ever-growing mountain of dirty dishes rose in the kitchen, and Cash and Jennings hid their supply of drugs in separate places. June and Mother Maybelle came by once a week to cook them a country breakfast and shovel the place out, but it was a losing battle. Luckily, disparate touring schedules kept Cash and Jennings from being home much at the same time.

In early '67, Cash and June released the duet "Jackson," which reached No. 2 on the country charts and won the Grammy the following year for Best Country Single. The tune was the centerpiece of a bunch of other hastily arranged songs for their first album together, which reached the No. 5 spot. The album was titled *Carryin' On with Johnny Cash and June Carter*, which likely caused more than a few guffaws on Music Row.

Financially, Cash should've been sitting pretty. But his money went out as fast as it came in. The divorce had cost him big time, and in addition to that, former manager Stewart Carnall was suing Cash for back royalties, and he was paying lawyers to negotiate a settlement with the federal government for the damage caused by the fire he'd inadvertently started in the California wildlife sanctuary.

Even with all that hanging over his head, Cash didn't pinch pennies. Deciding that he needed a home of his own where he could relax, write, entertain, and showcase his expanding collection of books and records, he went to noted Nashville architect and builder Braxton Dixon and asked to see available lots on which he might build his dream house. Dixon happened to be in the process of building a unique, one-of-a-kind house for himself overlooking Old Hickory Lake in Hendersonville, about twenty miles north of Nashville, and he took Cash to have a look at it to get some ideas for his own place.

Dixon's house was built of stone and hand-hewn timber he had collected from more than a dozen old barns and houses—some more than two hundred years old. The rafters were made of skinned tree trunks, and three of the outside walls were glass. It was unusual and impressive, and as soon as he saw it, Cash wanted it. He loved the lake and the roughness of the stones and wood. It filled him with a sense of peace and space. He imagined it as a place where he could straighten out his life and get re-acquainted with the trees, flowers, grass, and other natural things that had lulled and inspired him as a boy.

What Cash was really longing for was that simple, childlike faith he once possessed as a boy in Arkansas. But his mind was so blurred from drugs and other bad choices, he really did not know which way was up. So he became obsessed with this house that somehow connected him to simpler days, like fishing with his brother Jack and talking about life.

Dixon told him the place wasn't for sale, but Cash wouldn't be deterred. After a long back-and-forth they settled on a price of $150,000 (more than $1.1 million in today's dollars), shook hands, and sealed the transaction over a beer.

That was the easy part. The fact was that Cash didn't even have enough for the down payment Dixon wanted, and he only managed to come up with it when a Columbia Records executive stepped forward to guarantee a loan for him.

When Cash wailed about his financial predicament to Saul Holiff and asked for a reduction in the amount in commissions his manager charged against his earnings, Holiff didn't hesitate to remind him where the blame for his money woes lay. He noted Cash's recent purchases of a new Cadillac, a new tour bus, expensive antique furniture, the $70,000 annual expense of having Carl Perkins and the Carter Family on his road show, and the singer's refusal to make investments that would reduce his whopping yearly income tax bill. Holiff went on to point out that Cash had missed $40,000 worth of dates that year and that he was on the hook to Vivian's attorney for $6,500.

The kind-hearted manager did agree to cut his own commissions by 5 percent—which qualified him for sainthood considering Cash's unrestrained drug use and unrelenting unreliability, which damaged both his and Holiff's credibility. By then, Holiff was having so much trouble securing bookings for Cash he tried to line up lucrative county and state fair appearances for him—a considerable step down from the O'Keefe Centre for the Performing Arts—and even then only succeeded in adding just four dates thanks to Johnny's well-known penchant for blowing off shows. When Holiff confronted him about the situation in person, Cash got angry and smashed an expensive guitar against the wall.

Johnny could have been enjoying a successful career at this point, but he had effectively sabotaged it time and time again, even breaking a prized possession.

When people are under the influence of drugs, they do not think rationally. The Bible warns, "Watch out! Don't let your hearts be dulled by carousing and drunkenness, and by the worries of this life" (Luke 21:34 NLT).

That is exactly what happens.

Our hearts and minds are dulled by bad influences. Simply put, sin makes you stupid.

And even the great Johnny Cash was not immune to its magnetic pull.

Cash moved into the house on Old Hickory Lake in April 1967, before construction was even completed. There was no electricity or furniture. He invited a few of his musical friends and June over and had them stand in the living room and sing "How Great Thou Art."

June was divorced from Rip Nix by then, and Cash wanted them to live in his grand new house as man and wife. She told him not until he got himself straightened out.

But that was something he couldn't do on his own, even in front of kin.

Johnny invited family members to join him in Hendersonville on May 20, even though only the kitchen and bedroom had been finished. His parents were reluctant to fly by themselves all the way from California, so Cash traveled cross-country to meet them at the Los Angeles airport and accompany them on a flight to Nashville. Such a touching gesture was tarnished, however, when Cash, who'd not slept in three days, fortified himself with a hand-ful of drugs and as a result was higher than the airplane when it headed east.

During a brief layover in Memphis, Cash got out of his seat and keeled over face-first in the aisle. Too stoned to stand up, he had to be carried off the plane. Roy Cash still lived in Memphis, and he took Johnny to a motel and kept an eye on him overnight. The next morning, the groggy Cash boarded a plane for Nashville. When it arrived there, he was met at the gate by his parents and his brother Tommy, who worked for Johnny on various projects in Nashville.

Ray and Carrie looked worried. Tommy looked mad and wasted no time laying into his brother:

"Is your show about over with for today?" Tommy asked sarcastically. The comment stung.

Johnny took a swing at him, and as the brothers started to mix it up right there in the airport, Ray Cash stepped in and said sharply, "You want to fight in front of your mother? If either one hits, I'll hit you." They separated, and Tommy walked off.

The next day, Johnny apologized to him and gave Tommy, who was a collector, a prized Indianhead coin to smooth things over. Tommy thanked him, and the two put it past them. Cash later realized he was in the wrong.

"It was the worst thing I could ever do," Cash recollected, "to throw a punch at my own brother in front of a bunch of people."

Tommy Cash, who was eight years younger than his famous brother, once said, "Johnny's as complex as anything God or man put on this earth. He's a man of uncommon characteristics, mentally or physically. Even if you're his brother or his wife or his mother, you never know him completely. I've felt myself at times trembling because of my inadequacy around him. And then there's times I feel completely at ease."

The peace in the house on Old Hickory Lake was only temporary. The day after that, Johnny decided to have a big family dinner, a venture complicated by the fact that there was no food in the place. He placed a frantic call to June, who dropped everything, went out and bought enough to feed an army, took it to Cash's, and commenced to cooking—a task made so difficult by the drug-addled Cash's constant tantrums and interruptions that June fled in tears. She returned after a while and finished preparations for the big wing-ding.

Cash was so out of it by then he was convinced his brother Jack would be joining them and insisted that a place be set for him at the table.

After everyone went to bed that night, Cash roamed around the house for hours. Then he left in his car and didn't return till daylight. He gulped down a batch of pills and lay down on the floor behind the fireplace. As he drifted off, he heard his parents and Roy whispering about him.

When Johnny awoke hours later, he was alone in his dream house. His parents and siblings were gone. Later, Roy told him they didn't expect to see him alive again.

17

THE CAVE

"The times I was so down and out of it were
also the times when I felt the presence of God,
or whatever you want to call it in whatever
religion you might follow. I felt that presence."

—JOHNNY CASH

Anyone who saw Johnny Cash in late 1967 would have agreed with his brother Roy: he wasn't long for this world. Because his diet now consisted mostly of amphetamines, he had wasted away to a gaunt 150 pounds—almost skeletal for a man his size. Contrary to what his family and friends thought, he didn't actually have a death wish; but he was fatalistic about his condition and addiction and figured it didn't really make much difference anymore what happened to him.

For all intents and purposes, he had given up.

The love of June Carter was the only bright spot in his life, but his drug consumption was driving her away, too. Throughout their hotter-than-a-pepper-sprout relationship, Cash repeatedly asked her to marry him. June always said only when he got clean, and that prospect was farther away than ever.

Many times, Cash had said he would get treatment after a tour or some other date in the future but didn't. If he was determined to kill himself, June finally decided, she couldn't stick around and watch. She told Cash that after their tour of Michigan in October ended, it was over between them.

It was a mule kick to the gut. He had given up his marriage, kids, and half his estate with the idea that marrying June would make it all worthwhile. Her rejection plummeted him lower emotionally than he ever thought possible. He didn't sleep for days. He ate amphetamines like a kid digging into his Trick-or-Treat haul, and when the tremors came, they had him climbing the walls, so he switched to barbiturates to calm himself down. He felt he had wasted his life, drifting so far from God and every bright and stabilizing influence that all hope was lost.

The glamor of sin was gone, and in its place were the harsh and bitter results.

The Bible warns about the effects of sin in our life, telling us it produces death. Johnny was feeling the full force of that at this low point in his life.

It talks about enjoying "the fleeting pleasures of sin" (Hebrews 11:25 NLT). Johnny had experienced all of those. The problem, of course, is the so-called pleasures are relatively short while the repercussions are deadly and sometimes last for a lifetime. Now he was getting a taste of that, too—and it was bitter.

Cash's own accounts of when and how he finally got the strength to buck the monkey off his back differed over the years. In one account, it was after he was arrested in Lafayette, Georgia. In another, much more dramatic version, it was when he descended into the bowels of a cave in Tennessee with the intention of killing himself after he got into it with his mother Carrie.

"I had turned my back on my own mother. She had given up on me and had driven back to California and had a slight heart attack on the way," Cash told South Dakota TV host Glenn Jorgenson. "At that time, it didn't bother me in the least because there's one thing about someone addicted to pills or alcohol. They're very selfish."

Cash said June had a bad feeling about his state of mind and went looking for him at a friend's home in Chattanooga.

"June found out where I was and came to my friend's house in Chattanooga looking for me," Cash said. "I found out she was coming, so I went to the cave."

Nickajack Cave, thirty miles from Chattanooga, was an underground warren where Cash had previously searched for Indian arrowheads and inscriptions left by Confederate soldiers. The story goes that Cash decided to crawl into the cave and keep going until his flashlight flickered out (so he wouldn't be able to find his way back out if he lost his nerve) then lie there and die. Cash claimed that, after three hours, he had descended a mile into the cave. That's when his flashlight died, and he hoped to follow suit.

"I lay down to die in the total darkness," he recalled, beseeching God to take him away.

But all of a sudden, he said, he was suffused with a powerful, peaceful sensation, a comforting warmth. Then he heard the voice of God tell him to get up and get out of here—He wasn't ready for Cash to die just yet.

Cash said it took hours of crawling in the dark to find his way out and that when he emerged from the mouth of Nickajack Cave, he collapsed. When he awoke, June Carter and his friend were there. He promised them he was finally going to hand it over to the Lord.

It was time to crawl out of the cave.

Another incident in Lafayette, Georgia, occurred on November 2, 1967. Cash was visiting a friend there, went out by himself that evening, and got lost. In an effort to get directions back to his friend's house, he knocked on the door of an elderly woman who lived alone, and she called the police on him. Deputy Bob Jeff responded and in patting Cash down, discovered prescription drugs on him (which were legal). He took Cash to jail, and he spent the night in a cell.

The next morning, Sheriff Ralph Jones awakened Cash and took him into his office. Cash was sick and despondent and expected the lawman to come down on him hard. But instead Jones opened a drawer, took out the money and pills taken off Cash the night before, held them out, and said: "I'm going to give your money and your dope back because you know better than most people that God gave you free will to do with yourself whatever you want to do."

Cash could throw the pills away or go ahead and take them and kill himself, said Sheriff Jones, adding, "Whichever one you want to do, Mr. Cash, will be all right with me."

Johnny was dumbfounded. What was going on here?

As sorrowfully as if he were talking to his own wayward son, Jones explained to Cash that he and his wife had been Johnny Cash fans for over a decade—and had every record he had ever made, in fact.

"We love you," he said. "We've always loved you. We've watched you on television, listened for you on the radio. We've got your album of hymns. We're probably the best two fans you've ever had."

The night before, continued the sheriff, upon finding out that the great Johnny Cash was in his jail and why, he went home to his wife and told her. Jones said he actually felt like resigning right there and then because it was so heartbreaking to see how far a man who meant so much to them and others had fallen.

Then Jones told Johnny to take his money and pills and go.

"Just remember—you've got the free will to either kill yourself or save your life."

Indeed, Cash, like all of us, had free will.

God will not force His way or will in our lives.

He will set the choices before us and even give us the strength to follow through once we have made them. But the Lord will not choose for us; that is up to us. God says, "I call heaven and earth as witnesses today against you, that I have set before you life and death, blessing and cursing; therefore choose life, that both you and your descendants may live" (Deuteronomy 30:19 NKJV).

I love how this passage lays the choice before us, but the Lord tells us what the correct response is. He says, "Therefore, choose life that both you and your descendants may live!"

It would be like a teacher in a classroom doing a pop quiz and then giving us the correct answer to the test.

Johnny had been choosing the death and cursing part.

Now it was time for a change.

Cash looked at the aggrieved lawman for a while and then broke eye contact. Then he took the handful of dollar bills and the pills and walked out. His friend and fellow musician Richard McGibony, who had come to make bail for Cash, was waiting in his car. Before he got in, Cash threw the pills away. He vowed to McGibony that he was done for good with them. All he needed in his life was God.

And June. Two days later, Cash was at her front door, and on November 5, they went together to services at First Baptist Church in Hendersonville. Rev. Courtney Wilson preached that morning on the gospel story of the woman at the well.

While resting at Jacob's well in Sychar, Jesus meets a Samaritan woman there to draw water. Jesus engages her in a conversation, and offers what He refers to as "living water." The woman is confused, and Jesus tells her that anyone who drinks from the water in the well will eventually become thirsty again but whoever drinks from the water He gives them will never thirst.

You could write the words, "Whoever drinks the water of this world will thirst again" over many "wells" in life.

The wells of fame, material things, sex, drugs, booze—the list goes on.

Johnny had drunk from some of those more than others, all with the same effect. He was empty and thirsty spiritually. Rev. Wilson's message had connected. Now it was time to make some choices.

Cash later told Rev. Wilson that his sermon made him thirsty for the "living water." It would replenish his wasted body and spirit, and no more would he defile either with drugs—at least for a while.

18

CLEANUP TIME

"Most everybody had written me off. Oh yeah,
they all acted like they were proud for me
when I straightened up. Some of them are still
mad about it, though. I didn't go ahead and die
so they'd have a legend to sing about and
put me in Hillbilly Heaven."

—JOHNNY CASH

Declaring he was ready to kick his addiction to amphetamines was one thing. Actually doing it was another, and to help Johnny Cash with the herculean task facing him, June Carter enlisted the help of Nat T. Winston, a psychiatrist and Tennessee State Commissioner of Health. Back in the '50s, when Mother Maybelle Carter starred in her own television show in Johnson City, Tennessee, Winston was a frequent guest, picking the banjo and jamming with Maybelle.

Dr. Winston was alarmed when he saw Cash for the first time at the house in Hendersonville. Johnny was down to 150 pounds and was thrashing around in the throes of withdrawal on his round bed in the master bedroom. Dr. Winston grasped the magnitude of the challenge he faced when June told him that the singer was gulping down up to twenty-five ten-milligram uppers at a clip, three and four times a day, and at least twenty tranquilizers, plus Equanil when he was coming down or wanted to sleep. By his own estimate, Cash said he ingested close to a hundred pills a day during this period.

While Cash said he was earnest about getting clean, he adamantly refused to go to the hospital or a facility. Winston knew that if he forced the issue, Cash would simply check himself out a few days later. Instead, Winston mapped out an intense schedule of regular one-on-one counseling sessions. That would be the easy part. The hard part would be interdicting the steady supply of pills smuggled in to Cash by dealers and friends and rooting out all the caches of drugs secreted in the cavernous house.

Sometimes Cash beat them to it. One day, he raided one of his pill stashes, got high, climbed on his tractor, and trundled along the bluff overlooking the lake. He got too close to the edge, and the tractor overturned. Cash plunged into the lake with the tractor tumbling in after him. It was November, and Cash had on a long leather coat. He might have drowned in the freezing water had not Braxton Dixon, the developer who sold Cash his house, happened to be looking at an adjacent property at the time, seen what happened, and come running. As it was, he was almost hypothermic when Dixon and June got him back to the house and into bed.

When Cash awoke at around four in the morning, he found Dr. Winston in a chair next to his bed. The psychiatrist gently but firmly laid it on the line: "I've never known of anyone as far gone as you are to really whip it. Only you can do it, and it would be a lot easier if you let God help you."

Cash knew he was right. God had been waiting all this time for him to come back. June and Dr. Winston would do all they could for him, but unless Cash himself summoned the fortitude and discipline required, the battle would never be won. For that, he needed God's help more than ever. He had to ask for and depend on it.

"Get set for the fight of your life," Winston told Cash as he rose to leave.

The world had seen the meteoric rise of the Arkansas boy who picked cotton to the No. 1 country singer in the world. Many had also seen his fall, though few knew how far down he actually went.

The time had come for the redemption of Johnny Cash.

But we cannot redeem ourselves.

Only God can do it.

The word "redeem" is used many times in Scripture, especially in the New Testament. It literally means "to buy out of a slave market."

In New Testament times, many people served the Roman empire as slaves after their country was conquered by the Roman military machine. They were for sale by the thousands. One could go to a slave market and purchase a slave, and the purchase was made by the highest bidder.

Scripture uses this image of redemption to speak of what Jesus Christ does for a sinner when they believe. He "redeems" them.

Johnny was not in a slave market per se, but he was a slave to drugs, among other things. Only Jesus Christ could redeem him, and the singer knew that. A lot of other people did, too, and that's why they prayed for him.

If God did not come through for Johnny, he would surely become another sad entertainment casualty like so many others who preceded and followed him into the white-hot spotlight of fame.

Downstairs, the psychiatrist told June they'd never get anywhere if someone wasn't there at the house 24/7 to keep an eye on Cash and also stand guard at the front door to make sure nobody got in with more pills. June, Maybelle, and Pop Carter moved in the next day and slept in sleeping bags on the lower floor. Braxton Dixon and his wife Anna volunteered to take a few night shifts, and Anna proved her mettle when a determined caller tried to bull his way past her into the house; she chased him away with a butcher knife.

The singer was not the easiest patient Dr. Winston had ever treated, and Winston had seen and dealt with a lot of difficult people in his day. Unable to sit still for one-on-one sessions like most patients, Cash had the psychiatrist accompany him on long walks after nightfall, or they would jump into Cash's Jeep for long rides and talk about Johnny's past. It quickly became clear to Dr. Winston that the death of Jack Cash was the single most impactful event in his patient's life.

Cash would speak of this time as being like "forty days in the wilderness," but his actual detox span was closer to ten days. Undoubtedly, it seemed like forty. Every day was an ordeal as his body reacted to the shock of going without the chemical stimulants that had altered his nervous system for years. Winston had seen patients suffer from seizures and die and worried that the same could happen to Cash, who often shook, spasmed, cramped up, and broke out in cold sweats.

Nights were the worst. When he was finally too exhausted not to sleep, the same nightmare came over and over. A glass ball was in Cash's stomach and steadily expanded until it was so big he floated off his bed through the roof of his house. Then the ball exploded into a million minute slivers of glass that penetrated his body and entered his bloodstream. Cash felt the shards cutting and tearing through his heart, his limbs, his face, and brain. The pain was so excruciating it woke him up. Then he'd fight his way back to sleep and have the same awful dream again.

But he persevered, leaning hard on God, June, and Dr. Winston, and made so much progress it was decided Cash would be able to keep a promise made months before to perform at a November 18 concert to raise money for the Henderson High School band's trip to the Orange Bowl in Miami on January 2, 1968.

Johnny took the stage that night with more butterflies than he'd ever felt before. He was tentative at first but gained confidence as the show went on and began to feel so good he even laughed, joked, and bantered between numbers. He performed for a whole hour—and, as he felt the presence of God with him, closed the show with "Were You There When They Crucified My Lord?"

It was a powerful and befitting song to end his set with.

The song describes what it would have been like to stand at the foot of the cross of Jesus Christ. Then it transitions to the empty tomb, asking the question, "Were you there?" The chorus is, "Sometimes it causes me to tremble, tremble, tremble, tremble, tremble."

Cash had done more than his share of trembling of late, most if from the suffering he endured as he withdrew from drugs. But it was a different kind of trembling the author of the song describes— trembling sparked by awe of what Jesus did for humanity.

Johnny was getting back to his gospel roots, but, more importantly, back to God Himself.

The redemption had started.

The crowd whooped and cheered, and when Cash looked off-stage, there stood June with tears of joy streaming down her cheeks. He shot her a thumbs-up. He hadn't done a show straight in many years and felt "about six feet off the floor."

"I felt Him with me," Cash later recalled. "I was more alive than I'd ever been before. I knew I was again holding onto the Man I was singing about in that song, and I knew He was still holding me."

It sounds like a boffo Hollywood ending, and Cash himself would write in his autobiography that he'd come out on the other side of hell free and clear.

Not quite. But unquestionably, he was healthier; the home cooking of June and Maybelle had packed thirty pounds onto his no-longer-gaunt frame. When Cash performed at the Shrine Auditorium in Los Angeles on November 28, he looked and sounded stronger than he had in ages, and received a rave review from a major newspaper. His friend Carl Perkins was so awed and inspired by the transformation that on the spot, he swore off alcohol and tossed his bottle of bourbon into the ocean. He didn't take another drink for years.

Johnny's recovery hit a bump in the road on December 22—the day his divorce from Vivian became final. It was what he wanted, but the reality and finality of it hit him so hard that Cash resorted to pills to get through what he called "the worst day of my life."

Contrary to the 2005 Tinsel Town version of his life, there would be more of them. But there would be more of the stellar ones, too, and one of the most stellar of all came a month later when Cash gave the concert performance of his life—at a place he first heard of when he was in the Air Force in Germany.

19

FOLSOM

"You know, there's three different types
of Christians. There's preaching Christians,
church-playing Christians, and there's practicing
Christians—and I'm trying very hard to be a
practicing Christian. If you take the words of Jesus
literally and apply them to your everyday life, you
discover that the greatest fulfillment you'll ever
find really does lie in giving. And that's why I do
things like prison concerts."

—JOHNNY CASH

Johnny Cash and the Tennessee Two played their first prison concert at the Texas State Penitentiary in Huntsville in 1957. The prison
held an annual rodeo ("The Wildest Show Behind Bars") for inmates
and had a musical act as intermission entertainment. The rodeos,
which were open to the public, took place every Sunday in October
and grew so popular they became a major source of income for the

prison as well as an outlet for the entertainment of prisoners and employees alike.

Cash, Marshall Grant, and Luther Perkins had just set up in the middle of the outdoor stage and launched into "Folsom Prison Blues" when there was a sudden thunderstorm. The drenched trio proceeded as best as they could, and the inmates responded in kind.

"We all got soaking wet, but we all had a great time," Cash said.

The prisoners' raucous, unstinting appreciation moved Cash, and he never forgot it.

He didn't hesitate to accept an invitation to perform at California's San Quentin State Prison on New Year's Day, 1959. It was a great show, and Cash was asked back the following year. Word got around about Cash and his unique rapport with convict audiences, and soon he became the most popular entertainer on the "prison circuit."

Cash didn't do the prison shows for publicity or to impress anybody with his *noblesse oblige*. Nor did he do them for money—most of the time he performed for free. He did them because all his life Johnny cared about and rooted for the underdogs, the forgotten men, the strugglers, the downcast—because he saw himself in them. He was genuinely touched by the inmates' response—they'd stomp their feet, bang the tables, yell, whistle, and make as much noise as humanly possible. It was a way for them to let off steam, and he was happy to provide that outlet.

Niece Kelly Hancock said her uncle's heart was in the right place.

"He had an affinity for these men because he felt like they had no voice," she said. "Once he obtained a platform, he could speak for them and give them a voice. It was about forgiveness, too. He felt it was our duty to forgive and help them because we are all God's children. He would always say jokingly, 'Just look at what I've done.'"

Cash often declared at his prison shows in the 1970s he was there for several reasons. "We're here because the inmate population petitioned us to come. We're here because we love the applause you give us in prison. And I'm here because I'm a Christian."

"Because I'm a Christian." That was no small thing for a man of Cash's stature to openly declare—and before an audience of prisoners, to boot—that he was an unashamed follower of Jesus Christ.

Cash, being a "man's man," connected with the incarcerated.

Like the men in front of him, Cash himself knew what it was like to be in jail, to stand in handcuffs awaiting sentencing, and to feel the wrenching guilt of breaking the hearts of his loved ones. He identified with those who thought the system and life itself was rigged against them. That didn't mean Cash excused, justified, or rationalized the crimes of the inmates he entertained. He knew most deserved to be in prison. But that didn't mean they should be forgotten and forever denied a touch of humanity. He knew their pain and could have easily joined their ranks given the life he had been living up to this point. But by God's grace, he was there as an entertainer, not an inmate. And he was there to give them a show.

A touch of humanity is what Johnny's prison concerts aimed to deliver and did. The almost rapturous vibes he and the convicts exchanged and the energy they infused in him induced a buzz better than any pill ever had.

Johnny Western, who served as the emcee at Cash's show over several decades, including prison shows, observed firsthand a magical connection between Cash and the inmates.

"I saw three-time murderers brought to tears because Johnny Cash came to perform for them," he said. "They greatly appreciated him because he made them forget they were in prison for a little while."

The concert he recorded at Folsom Prison in early 1968 wasn't Cash's first one there. In November 1966, Rev. Floyd Gressett passed along to Cash a request for a Folsom concert from inmate Earl Green, then serving a life sentence for bashing a man's skull in with a baseball bat. Cash agreed, and his unpublicized show brought down the house, as usual.

The success of his prison concerts had given Cash the notion that recording one of them live would make a great album. In 1965, he planned to record a show at the Kansas State Reformatory, but according to Cash historian Mark Stielper, prison authorities vetoed the project because the singer was erratic and unreliable. A no-show could have caused them major problems, so they took a pass.

At Folsom, Johnny mentioned his idea to the prison's entertainment director and was told he was more than welcome to come back and do it anytime he wanted. He was ready after a recording hiatus.

Cash's last album, *From Sea to Shining Sea*, was another concept album released that March. It didn't yield any singles, but the songwriting was evocative, blending country, folk, and Americana. The only other time he entered the recording studio that year was to cut the single "Rosanna's Going Wild," a cover of the Carter Sisters' version that reached No. 2 on the country charts.

The anticipation of the Folsom concert got his juices going again.

Cash wanted not only to reestablish his creative side but also document where he was as an artist at that moment in time. He wanted an album whose passion and energy detonated every time the phonograph needle touched the vinyl. That would require a performance that transported both artist and audience beyond their own restraints— corporeal and otherwise.

The Columbia Records brass had never gotten behind Cash's dream of a live prison album, but in 1967, producer Don Law, who had overseen Cash's projects since Johnny came aboard the label, turned sixty-five and was put out to pasture. His replacement, Bob Johnston, had produced some of Bob Dylan's (*Highway 61 Revisited*) and Simon & Garfunkel's (*Sounds of Silence*) finest work—and he couldn't wait to do the same for Johnny Cash. Johnston thought Cash had been mishandled by Columbia and made it a priority to rectify that—first by helping Cash to define his artistic vision and then enabling him to realize it.

When Cash broached the idea of recording a live prison album with Johnston, the producer immediately picked up the phone and put in a call to San Quentin. Unable to reach the warden, Johnston next called Folsom, and in no time, two performances were scheduled there for January 13, 1968.

The day before the big event, Cash and June checked into the El Rancho Hotel in Sacramento, where they were presently joined by the Tennessee Three and the two other acts on the Folsom show—the Statler Brothers and Carl Perkins (who now played with Cash's band and also performed his own hits). Also present were Ray Cash and Rev. Floyd Gressett, who had helped facilitate the concert.

The importance Johnny placed on the concert was clear when he called a rare rehearsal in the hotel's banquet hall. He had selected the songs they'd play with deliberate care. Almost half were about prison, crime, loneliness, and despair—themes Cash knew would resonate with the Folsom inmates.

A last-minute addition to the playlist was "Greystone Chapel," a spiritual tune about the grace of God written by Glen Sherley, who was doing five years to life at Folsom for armed robbery. Sherley had given a cassette of his song to the prison recreation director, who passed it on to Gressett, who gave it to Cash, who loved it.

Before the rehearsal broke up around midnight, a surprise visitor dropped over to convey best wishes on behalf of the State of California. Republicans were holding a $500-a-plate dinner for Governor Ronald Reagan at the El Rancho, and Reagan made it a point to say hello and shake Cash's hand in the hotel's Fiesta Room.

Early the next morning, Cash and his troupe made the twenty-five-mile drive east to Folsom. Built in 1890, it was California's second oldest prison, housing some of the state's most hardened criminals. Five massive cellblocks held over 3,500 inmates.

Two weeks earlier, a Folsom guard was held at knifepoint by some convicts, and the prison was still on high alert. Cash was informed that the show would be halted for good if a single inmate in the audience so much as left his seat. He was plenty nervous already, and it wasn't entirely a case of pre-show jitters. At the hotel, Cash had swallowed a couple of pills to take off the edge—and then, when the bus entered the prison grounds and passed a large sign informing visitors they were subject to being searched, he gulped down the ones he'd brought with him. Producer Bob Johnston watched Cash rifle through his pockets to make sure none were left.

In the dining hall where the first show was to start at 9:40, approximately a thousand inmates dressed in matching denim shirts and pants sat at small white tables. Armed guards patrolled along overhead walkways, and the entire hall was lit by bright fluorescent lights that, unlike those at traditional venues, would not be dimmed when the show started.

Conditions were far from ideal for live recording. The dining hall's high, pitched roof and thick stone walls did not make for an acoustically friendly environment. Technicians used five separate machines—running simultaneously in a mobile unit parked out in the prison yard—to record the concert. Bob Johnston spent weeks afterwards removing the echo from the tapes.

Out of such adversity came one of the most storied performances in music history. Cash took control of the room as soon as he opened the show with the greeting, "Hello, I'm Johnny Cash"—which subsequently became his signature line. Then, appropriately, he launched into "Folsom Prison Blues," and the place went nuts. Throughout the seventeen songs that followed—each interspersed with raw, rowdy humor, authentic banter, and fun novelty tunes—the captive audience cheered as if everyone in it was getting a pardon.

Cash closed the show with "Greystone Chapel" to the surprise and delight of Glen Sherley in the front row. He shook Sherley's hand when he finished, and the songwriting convict later joined him backstage for a few minutes of conversation. (Sherley was released from prison in 1971, and when Cash testified before a Congressional panel on prison reform, Sherley accompanied him. Sherley later toured with Cash, but his pathological and potentially violent behavior led to his dismissal from the troupe. Sadly, he committed suicide in 1978. Cash paid for his burial.)

Between the two shows (the second one started at 12:40 p.m.), Cash prayed in the prison chapel. Photographer Jim Marshall was on hand to document the concerts. He took a poignant picture of Cash kneeling at the altar, focused on a golden cross and a painting of Jesus at the Last Supper.

This was a glimpse into the dichotomy of John R. Cash.

Gulping pills to deal with his pressure and stress—and praying not long afterwards. It was a struggle that would continue through most of his life.

Just because a person puts their faith in Christ does not mean they will not be tempted in life. They have a choice as to what to do each and every day. Johnny made some good choices, and he made more than a few bad ones.

Contrary to what many may think, being a Christian does not make a bad person "good."

If anything, we realize that that none of us are "good" as far as meeting God's standards go—for that would require absolute perfection.

There are many people who never abuse drugs or alcohol and are faithful to their spouses for a lifetime. But those people need to still admit they are sinners and put their faith in Jesus, as Johnny did.

Heaven is not a place reserved for "good" people, as many think.

Heaven is a place for *forgiven* people. And Johnny Cash knew that as well as anyone.

Throughout both Folsom shows, the inmates were boisterous but well-behaved, and the day was deemed a great success by everyone involved. The best review of all came as Cash's bus headed back to the motel. That's when Ray Cash gave his son a rare compliment, telling him that it was a job well done.

When *At Folsom Prison* was released a few months later in May 1968, *Time* magazine called it "one of the most original and compelling pop albums of the year." It also received huzzahs from FM and underground rock radio, the *Village Voice*, and *Rolling Stone* magazine.

"Cash, more than any other contemporary [country] performer, is meaningful in a rock and roll context," wrote *Rolling Stone* editor Jann Wenner, citing Cash as a rock pioneer because of his work at Sun Records. Wenner's endorsement was an enormous critical and commercial boost because the rock audience was beginning to control the national sales charts and dominate the popular culture.

At Folsom Prison hit No. 1 on the country chart and climbed to No. 13 on the pop side. It remained on the country charts for ninety-two weeks and in the *Billboard* Top 200 for 124 weeks, selling three million units. Today it is revered as a classic—arguably one of the greatest country albums of all time—and considered a landmark work in music history. Fifty years after the concert that produced it, *At Folsom Prison* was inducted into the Grammy Hall of Fame. And the Library of Congress added it to the National Recording Registry in 2003.

The whole project was a classic illustration of a verse that Johnny knew well.

That verse is Romans 8:28, which promises that God "will cause all things to work together for good to those that love Him" (NKJV).

For all of Johnny's bad choices and run-ins with the law, it caused him to have empathy for others who had done the same.

Compassion has been defined as "pity plus action."

Johnny felt this compassion for these incarcerated men and wanted to make a difference in their lives. Visiting them in prison also made a difference in his life.

One of the reasons this album resonated as it did is because it was not contrived. It was a genuine love letter from Johnny Cash to the men of Folsom—and ultimately to the world.

There are many who have never darkened the doorway of a prison facility but may be in a prison of some other kind—a cell of loneliness, isolation, addiction, or despondency.

And Johnny Cash, with his life experience and its ups and downs, connected with them. You can't fake that.

Already a seminal year for Cash, 1968 would get even better. On February 29, "Jackson" won the Grammy for "Best Country Performance, Duo or Group," and the day after that, the best country duo finally tied the knot.

20

———

GOOD TIMES, BAD TIMES

"What I really enjoy is the Bible. I love to set
myself a test, give myself something to study.
I find a passage I don't quite understand and
chase it down in the concordance and the
chain references until I learn what it means,
or at least what the best-versed scholars have
been able to interpret it as meaning."

—JOHNNY CASH

The slump was over, and Johnny Cash's life and career were on the upswing. Johnny had learned that good things happened when he stopped doing bad things. While he wasn't 100 percent clean, Cash had his wits about him—and a full appreciation of how close he'd come to the abyss.

His sobriety was a work in progress, but his house was finally finished, and that winter, Cash's daughters came for their first visit.

Being reunited with them was glorious. One night after they'd gone to bed, Cash went to his room and looked out the window at snow gently drifting down. Having the girls there and the picture postcard scene outside suddenly imbued him with a serenity he hadn't felt since he couldn't remember when. He sank to his knees to thank God for everything good in his life and for sparing him from the bad end he'd come so close to for so long. Cash also acknowledged that he still had far to go and entreated, "Don't give up on me, Lord. I can't make it without You."

God had kept His promise to Johnny. God set "death and life" (Deuteronomy 30:19 NKJV) before the singer as he does with all of us. Cash chose life, and he did so not a moment too soon.

It comes as a surprise to some that the hope of the follower of Jesus is not just life after death in Heaven. Of course, that would be more than enough, but the Lord also offers a dimension of life during this life. Medical science seeks to add years to our life, but Jesus Christ offers life to our years. Jesus promised an abundant, fulfilling, rich life if we will walk closely with Him. Johnny was doing that now, and instead of feeling hemmed in, he felt like he had been set free. I'm sure he wondered why he had not done it sooner.

In February 1968, in front of five thousand witnesses at a hockey arena they were playing in London, Ontario, and right after they finished singing "Jackson," Cash proposed to June Carter again. He figured she couldn't say no in front of all those people—and he was right. On March 1, they were married by Rev. Leslie Chapman at the First Methodist Church in Franklin, Tennessee.

It was a small, low-key ceremony; photos showed Cash in a black tuxedo and the bride in a light-colored, scalloped, knee-length dress. Old friend and "Ring of Fire" co-writer Merle Kilgore was Cash's best man, and June's friend Mickey Dale Brooks was her maid of honor. June's daughters Rosey and Carlene served as bridesmaids. Others in attendance included the Tennessee Three and their respective wives, as well as a sprinkling of family and friends.

162

During the ceremony, Mother Maybelle's friend George Morgan sang "I Love You Truly" and "Because." June cried during both songs. Kilgore enlisted the help of a local radio station owner to have the nuptials taped on a reel-to-reel recording.

Hundreds of relatives, friends, and music industry types came to an alcohol-free reception at the lakeside house later that afternoon to celebrate Nashville's newest glamour couple. After a few days' rest, the newlyweds went back out on the road.

Music had brought them into each other's lives, and what cemented their bond now was their interest in exploring and nourishing their mutual Christian faith. Johnny and June had long discussions about Jesus and his teachings. They attended a Baptist church in Hendersonville between tours, and Johnny delved into spiritual matters more than ever.

"The times I was so down and out of it were also the times I felt the presence of God," he told an interviewer. "I felt that presence, that positive power saying to me, 'I'm still here, Cash, to draw on whenever you're ready to straighten up and come back to the life.'"

Johnny was tuned in spiritually now instead of having his mind dulled and his heart hard due to bad decisions fueled by drugs.

The Bible tells the story about the Prophet Elijah who had been discouraged and had found a cave to hide in. It was not unlike Johnny's cave experience.

And there the prophet heard the "still small voice" of God (1 Kings 19:12 NKJV).

Johnny was hearing that voice now and wanted to do what the Lord directed him to do. It was a new day for John R. Cash.

The Cashes became interested in Jewish history, especially as it related to the Bible. They studied Josephus, the Jewish historian, and read *The History and Decline of the Roman Empire*, *The Robe*, *Ben Hur*, *Quo Vadis*, *Spartacus*, and all the books by Taylor Caldwell, Edward Gibbin, and Thomas B. Costain that had as their setting the time of Christ.

After a tour of Britain in May, Johnny and June went on a belated honeymoon to Israel. Israel is not a vacation destination *per se*. There are far more beautiful and romantic places to visit. But there is simply no place on earth like it for the Christian or the Jew. The reason for that, of course, is the rich biblical history that happened on a tiny piece of real estate in what is often called "The Holy Land."

Barely larger than New Jersey, the land of Israel is literally a place where prophets spoke and Scripture was written. It was also the place where Jesus Himself walked. Johnny and June were irresistibly drawn to it as countless thousands of Christians are from around the world. He took along a camera and tape recorder to collect impressions, soundscapes, and narrations of the things they witnessed, and he used them in an album called *The Holy Land*. It was not exactly the follow-up the Columbia suits wanted for *At Folsom Prison*, but Cash was an artist in bloom and would not be denied. As a compromise, Columbia released the album during the holidays. It got a boost from "Daddy Sang Bass," a catchy single written by Carl Perkins that garnered Cash another No. 1 country hit and camped on the charts for six weeks while *The Holy Land* reached No. 6 on the country album charts. The suits were not disappointed.

In the Middle East, the Cashes visited many places sacred to Jews, Christians, and Muslims, and historic sites they knew from the Bible, including Nazareth, the town where Jesus grew up, the area around the Sea of Galilee where His early ministry took place, and Via Dolorosa, the path where Jesus walked to His crucifixion. Of course, the actual streets Christ walked on are about thirty feet below the streets of today, as each successive nation to conquer Jerusalem built over the previous one. The result is layers of history. But when one walks these streets, it is not hard to imagine what it might have been like two thousand years ago. Just to be in the general vicinity is a moving thing. Many have had their lives changed after a trip to Israel. At a jewelry shop, Johnny and June bought each other rings engraved with "Me to my love and my love to me" in Hebrew.

Upon their return to the States, Cash and the Tennessee Three went to Los Angeles for a guest appearance on *The Summer Smothers Brothers Show*, a comedy/variety CBS summer replacement series hosted by Glen Campbell. That appearance proved so popular Campbell soon got his own music/variety show on CBS, *The Glen Campbell Good Time Hour*. In its first year, the show pulled a whopping Nielsen rating of 22.5, and, not surprisingly, network programmers started looking at other country artists with the talent and charisma to carry their own weekly show. Guess which one stood out?

In late July 1968, Cash went into the studio to lay down the tracks for *The Holy Land*, a mixture of Cash originals, narrations, and gospel tunes. It turned out to be the last time he worked with original Tennessee Two lead guitarist Luther Perkins.

Perkins was a chain-smoker who had a cigarette in his hand most of the time—even when he lay down in bed to go to sleep. Sometimes he would drift off before stubbing the butt out in an ashtray and would be jolted awake when the cigarette burned down to his fingers. Unfortunately, it didn't work that way on August 3. After going fishing and working on the roof of his new house not far from Cash's, Perkins went to relax in his den and fell asleep in his chair with a burning cigarette in his hand. The smoldering butt ignited a fire that soon engulfed the den and kitchen. Firefighters found Perkins unconscious, and he was rushed to Vanderbilt University Hospital with smoke inhalation and third-degree burns over half of his body. He died two days later.

Cash and Marshall Grant were among the pallbearers at the August 7 funeral in Hendersonville. When Perkins' casket was lowered into the grave, Cash was heard to say, "Thank you, Luther."

As was the case when his brother and Johnny Horton died, Cash's grief over the loss of Luther Perkins was suffused with overwhelming guilt. Luther had called him the night of the fire and asked Cash to come over and talk. But it was late, and Johnny decided to wait till morning to see what his friend wanted.

Decades later, Dr. Nat Winston recalled being told by Cash that nothing affected him more than the deaths of Jack Cash and Luther Perkins. "A part of me died with Luther," he said.

The unexpected loss of a beloved comrade is always tragic. The death of Luther Perkins was especially so—and on top of that, it amounted to a textbook definition of a crying shame, for Johnny Cash was about to head off down a road seemingly paved with bricks of gold.

21

COUNTRY SUPERSTAR

"I don't know what's in store for me,
but I know there are things I'm going to do
that I haven't touched on yet. I don't know what
they are, but I feel it."

—JOHNNY CASH

Johnny Cash's general sobriety and rising profile led to opportunities he'd never had before. He had clawed and fought his way to the top of the entertainment ladder. For the first time in his life, he was looking forward instead of back over his shoulder. His rough-and-tumble childhood left emotional scars, but it also provided him with the hunger and raw determination to become a star.

Suddenly, every professional wish or fantasy he ever dared to imagine had been granted a hundredfold—and some he had never imagined. His concert fees more than doubled; he was the subject of a documentary, *Johnny Cash: The Man, His World, His Music*; he sold out Carnegie Hall and the London Palladium; and more offers were coming in for concerts and TV appearances than Saul Holiff could handle.

Equally important and especially impressive was that even as Cash's star shot into the stratosphere, he took time to make amends for past transgressions. Concert dates he had blown off in the throes of his addiction were rescheduled; promoters who'd lost money on him received restitution. He openly expressed his gratitude to people and acknowledged the efforts of others that helped him achieve his personal and professional attainments.

On New Year's Eve 1963, Cash had started an annual tradition—writing a letter to himself that chronicled the plusses and minuses of the year just ending and listing the things to look forward to in the coming one.

His December 31, 1968, letter said:

"I feel that this year, 1968, has been, in many ways, the best year of my thirty-six years of life. It has been a sober, serious year. Also probably the busiest year of my life, as well as the most fulfilling."

The list of high points included Cash's marriage to June, the concert at Folsom, touring England and Scotland, his and June's visit to Israel for *The Holy Land*, fishing in Old Hickory Lake, a visit to Wounded Knee—and the propitious discovery of Bob Wootton at a rally for Arkansas Governor Winthrop Rockefeller that September. Wootton was a longtime Cash fan and a guitarist who volunteered to fill in with Cash's short-handed band at the rally. He did such a bang-up job Johnny promptly hired him as successor to Luther Perkins in The Tennessee Three.

On the look-forward-to list for 1969 was another milestone: Granada Television in the United Kingdom wanted to get Cash back to Folsom Prison to film a second gig there for a documentary.

Cash's interest in revisiting Folsom then was nil because it would be a step backwards artistically, and who knew if lightning would strike again. How about San Quentin instead? suggested manager

Saul Holiff. Cash and Granada went for it, and the big event was set for February 24. Granada producer Geoffrey Cannon, director Michael Darrow, and a film crew arrived at the maximum-security prison outside of San Francisco ahead of time to film prison scenes and interview inmates.

The San Quentin playlist included plenty of new material, including "Starkville City Jail," a song about the night in 1966 that Cash spent in a cell in Starkville, Mississippi, after a concert at Mississippi State University. He and the band went to a friend's house for a late dinner, but Cash got antsy and started back for the hotel by himself. He never made it.

"I was just walking down the sidewalk, looking for a cigarette machine in a gas station," he told writer Christopher S. Wren. "I was grabbing flowers as I walked, picking a daisy here, a dandelion there. Somebody phoned the police. The police car came and pulled alongside. The police got out and grabbed me by the arm and said, 'Get in!' I asked what for. 'Just shut up and sit down,' they said. They took me to the police station. I don't know what for."

Cash was marched to a cell in the Starkville jail, his demands to know why he was under arrest ignored. He was still upset in the morning and vented his anger by kicking the cell door so hard he broke his left big toe and sprained his ankle, though he didn't realize it until his adrenaline wore off. When finally brought before the chief of police and asked why he had been roaming the streets at 2 a.m. and picking flowers, Cash said he was just going for cigarettes. The chief apologized and personally drove Johnny back to his motel. As they said goodbye, the chief presented Cash with a going-away present: a $36 ticket for being drunk and disorderly.

Another new song premiered at the prison: "San Quentin" was written two days before the concert at the request of Michael Darrow.

Three days before that, at a party on Old Hickory Lake, Cash received the lyrics to a song called "A Boy Named Sue" by Shel

Silverstein. The Cash house was the epicenter of the music world that night. Graham Nash premiered "Marrakesh Express," Bob Dylan unveiled "Lay Lady Lay," Kris Kristofferson presented "Me and Bobby McGee," and Joni Mitchell debuted "Both Sides Now."

"A Boy Named Sue" told the story of a ne'er-do-well father who gave his son a girl's name to make him "grow up quick and grow up mean" and never step aside for anyone. The song was so new to Cash he had to read the lyrics off a sheet of paper, but the San Quentin crowd hung on every word and gave the singer a standing ovation. Released as the first single of the *At San Quentin* album, it rose to No. 1 on the *Billboard* country singles chart and No. 2 on the pop charts, behind the Rolling Stones' "Honky Tonk Women." It was Cash's highest-charting crossover single ever, and later netted him a Grammy for Best Male Country Vocal Performance.

The Granada Television documentary was screened in Britain in April 1969. It was crucial in pushing the album and single in Britain and building buzz in the States.

It also showed off Cash at his charismatic best, and not long afterward, the American Broadcasting Company came calling with an offer to host his own summer replacement television show, airing in the prime time slot of the popular variety show *Hollywood Palace* during its hiatus from June through September.

Saul Holiff had two conditions for production company Columbia Screen Gems: that the show be taped at Nashville's Ryman Auditorium and that Canadian Stan Jacobson, who'd made a 1967 Canadian Broadcasting Company special about Cash, be named producer of the hour-long variety show. ABC network brass agreed to both. Considered the weakest of the three major American TV networks, ABC was desperate for a hit.

It got one.

I remember watching Johnny's show as a teen. Somehow, he transcended time and culture. I regarded Bing Crosby, Frank Sinatra, and Dean Martin as my "parents' music." But Johnny did not neatly fit into that category. Actually, I don't know that he fits in with any particular musical genre. He was his own category.

Toward the end of his life, in my opinion, John R. Cash saved the best for last.

His voice did not have the range of his earlier days, and his black bouffant hair had turned to grey. But somehow, he remained cool.

I think a whole new generation discovered Johnny because he was one of a kind. He was authentic.

On the eve of the TV show, Cash talked his sister Reba and her husband, Don Hancock, into moving back to Hendersonville in March 1969. They brought with them their seven-year-old son, Tim, and five-year-old daughter, Kelly. Kelly, who would later play a major role in her uncle's life, worked alongside him and her mother at the House of Cash for most of her adult life.

"John sensed the show was going to take his career to another level and felt he needed my mother to move to Tennessee and manage his music publishing company," Hancock said. "The following year, he purchased a building in Hendersonville, which became the House of Cash. There Reba could oversee all his daily business affairs."

The Johnny Cash Show went into production in April and made its national network debut on June 7. The schedule was brutal, with rehearsals taking place Monday through Wednesday, with Thursdays set aside for tapings. Cash kept his weekends open for concerts. He later reflected that this period was perhaps the most physically taxing of his career.

Initially, ABC insisted on padding the lineup with old-school guest stars such as Bob Hope, Burl Ives, Kirk Douglas, Lorne Greene, and Peggy Lee, which rankled Cash to some degree.

"They [ABC] got to where they wanted to book anybody who had a name that meant something for ratings, whether they had talent or whether I could relate to them or not," Cash said. "I'm not going to name names, but there were people who came in from Hollywood that I was uncomfortable working with because the network wanted them for their ratings. And I thought that was silly and cruel to do that to an artist."

But that all changed as the show scored well in the ratings and, after its summer-long trial run, was added to ABC's regular-season schedule. By then, Cash had more creative control to indulge his own personal taste. His aim was to keep the show fresh by featuring acts most viewers didn't see much on TV, offering an eclectic mix of musical genres and some of the biggest rock, folk, jazz, gospel, and country acts of the day.

The premier showcased the talents of Joni Mitchell, Cajun fiddler Doug Kershaw, and Bob Dylan, who Cash worked with earlier in the year on his landmark album *Nashville Skyline*. On subsequent shows appeared a variety of musical icons and newbies that included Neil Young, Derek & the Dominoes, James Taylor, Creedence Clearwater Revival, Merle Haggard, Charley Pride, Stevie Wonder, Mama Cass, Gordon Lightfoot, Jerry Lee Lewis, and Louis Armstrong.

Cash opened each episode with his customary greeting since Folsom: "Hello, I'm Johnny Cash." Other regular performers included June Carter Cash and the Carter Family, The Statler Brothers, Carl Perkins, and the Tennessee Three. Cash pushed for and got a "Country Gold" segment that showcased such legends as Bill Monroe and his Blue Grass Boys, Marty Robbins, Tom T. Hall, Chet Atkins, Loretta Lynn, and Tammy Wynette.

One of the most popular segments was called "Ride This Train," in which Cash, usually dressed in period costume, covered the history of America in medley form.

The show usually closed with a gospel song—a musical touch Cash insisted on. Here was Johnny, at the peak of his powers and fame, giving a prominent place to a song about his faith. This was no small thing.

Everything about the show was an extension of Cash's personality, even (or especially) when he pushed the envelope. He repeatedly mentioned his Christian faith, knowing that it rankled the network brass; he had famed evangelist Billy Graham on to preach a sermon; he refused to have the word "stoned" bleeped when he performed "Sunday Morning Coming Down"; he fought to have folk singer and outspoken pacifist Pete Seeger on the show. Cash also premiered the song "Man in Black," his social commentary anthem that let everyone know his worldview and where he stood when it came to his fellow man. The show became a platform for Cash's commitment to social justice, addressing race, war, poverty, and any issue that didn't sit well with him. Nothing seemed to be off limits.

Cash called the first TV show he did at The Ryman one of the proudest moments of his career. Even before the cameras started rolling, he got a standing ovation. The last time he'd been at the Grand Ole Opry four years earlier, he'd earned a ban for smashing the footlights with the microphone stand in an amphetamine rage. Now the man who'd personally banned Cash warmly welcomed him back.

It was a new Johnny Cash for sure. Gone was the greasy-haired outlaw who thumbed his nose at authority and got busted multiple times. Now he dressed much sharper for the show but made it work for him: Cash sported tuxedo jackets, pinch-waist frock coats, riverboat gambler vests, ruffled shirts, bow ties, and black button boots. His luxurious mane of black hair was artfully piled high and blow-dried. Cash's inlaid Martin D-45 bearing a mother-of-pearl nameplate, usually strapped over his shoulder, helped him to cut a striking figure.

The bad guy who stomped out lights, used profanity, crashed cars, and smuggled drugs had morphed into an upstanding middle-aged family man who revered his wife, praised the Lord, and rigorously upheld middle American values.

Stan Jacobson, the show's director, called Cash "the voice of America." His craggy face now graced the covers of *Parade*, *Look*, *Vogue*, *New York Times Magazine*, *TV Guide*, and *Life*, which called him "The Rough-Cut King of Country Music."

Cash's respectability and iconic stature gave him access to the most powerful people in the industry and throughout the world, including evangelist Billy Graham and President Richard Nixon.

The weekly national TV exposure also did wonders for his music career. *At San Quentin* topped the country and pop charts, was nominated for Album of the Year at the Grammys, and eventually matched the three million-plus sales of *At Folsom Prison*. All told, Cash sold more than six million records in 1969, besting the Beatles, Elvis Presley, the Rolling Stones, Jimi Hendrix, Janis Joplin, Led Zeppelin and every other musical act in the world. It wasn't even close.

He capped off the year by headlining sold-out shows at Toronto's Maple Leaf Gardens and Madison Square Garden in New York City—the first country artist ever to do so.

The one-time sharecropper was walking in mighty tall cotton.

22

BROTHER BILLY AND TRICKY DICK

"I think the dignity of the office of President
of the United States should be maintained
and respected no matter who is our president.
He is our president, and we the people
have elected him whether you or I voted
for him or not."

—JOHNNY CASH

These were the great years.

Cash had always been a man on a mission, looking to build his fame and gild his image while maintaining a dignified composure. Mission accomplished. He had carefully and successfully crafted his public image to fit the hero he wanted to be, and now the world had a new icon—The Man in Black.

He represented the poor, the downtrodden, the underrepresented, the marginalized, the disenfranchised, the incarcerated, the voiceless. Cash wore black as a statement against the status quo, the hypocritical houses of God, and against "people whose minds are closed to others' ideas."

That message resonated with a lot of people in the late 1960s and early '70s. I was certainly one of them.

Johnny walked a thin line. He was simultaneously "counter-culture" and "status quo."

To conservative middle America, he was "one of them."

At the same time, to my generation in full rebellion mode, he was also "one of us."

I can't think of an artist of any generation that has managed to pull this off. But Johnny Cash did.

Cash was recognized—and mobbed—wherever he went. He was applauded in hotel lobbies, tour buses jammed the streets of his Old Hickory Lake neighborhood, and the network was flooded with thousands of letters a week requesting autographs, signed 8 x 10s and other mementos of their hero.

The Johnny Cash Show consistently drew up to fifteen million viewers a week, giving Cash a platform rarely afforded to entertainers.

"Everybody in the entertainment industry wanted to come on our show," said Joe Byrne, executive producer of the show for ABC. "Johnny Cash was a magnet to other performers, and they not only respected him personally but also his talent."

One of Cash's greatest admirers reached millions through a special platform of his own, and in late '69, "America's Evangelist" Billy Graham called "The Man in Black," Johnny Cash. Billy asked if he might travel to Hendersonville from his home in Asheville, North Carolina, to consult Cash on several matters, including problems Graham was having connecting with his teenaged son Franklin (a situation hardly uncommon between fathers and sons in the "Age of Aquarius").

Ray and Carrie Cash, Johnny's parents. The two couldn't have been more opposite and yet had seven children together and were married for 65 years. *Courtesy of Arkansas State University.*

Unidentified woman and two children at the entrance of Dyess, Arkansas, circa mid-1930s. *Courtesy of Arkansas State University.*

The Cash family home in 1936, Dyess, Arkansas. The boy in front of the house is believed to be Jack Cash. *Courtesy of Arkansas State University.*

The Dyess Colony circle, 1937. It included an administration building, a co-op and a movie theater. On most Saturday afternoons, young J.R. Cash could be found there visiting friends, buying goods, or taking in a movie. *Courtesy of Arkansas State University.*

The Cash family on the front porch of their home in 1943. The picture includes Sam, the family dog; young J.R. is the only one not in it, and it is believed he's the one who snapped the photo. From left to right: Carrie Cash, Joanne Cash, Wandene Cash (Roy's wife), Ray Cash, Roy Cash, Reba Cash, Tommy Cash, and Roy Cash, Jr. *Courtesy of Arkansas State University.*

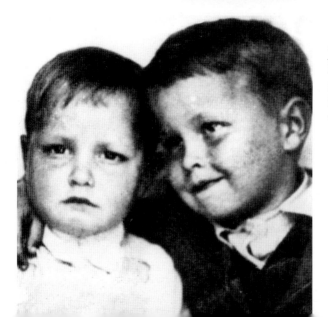

J.R. Cash (left) and his older brother Jack (right) in 1936. J.R. was four at the time and Jack was six. *Photofest.*

The Three Musketeers – J.R. Cash (bottom); A J Henson (middle); and J.E. Huff (top) were thick as thieves and best of friends growing up in Dyess, Arkansas. *Courtesy of A J Henson.*

A teenaged Jack Cash, shortly before his tragic death in a sawmill accident. *Courtesy of Arkansas State University.*

The Dyess school complex where J.R. Cash received his education from kindergarten all the way through high school. *Courtesy of Arkansas State University.*

The school shop and agricultural building where Jack Cash suffered his fatal injury. *Courtesy of Arkansas State University.*

Cash family photo from 1949. Back row, from left: Roy, Carrie, Louise, Ray, Reba, and J.R. Front row: Tommy and Joanne. *Courtesy of Joanne Cash Yates.*

Airman J.R. Cash (center) posing with Joanne (left) and Tommy (right) in the front yard of their Dyess, Arkansas, home before a tour of duty in Germany, circa 1950. *Courtesy of Joanne Cash Yates.*

The Million Dollar Quartet was comprised of Sun Records artists Jerry Lee Lewis, Carl Perkins, Elvis Presley, and Johnny Cash. The four gathered for a jam session on December 4, 1956. The result was a classic album. *Photofest.*

Reba and Johnny Cash in the recording studio, August 1959. *Courtesy of Kelly Hancock.*

A late 1950s publicity photo showcasing Johnny Cash as an actor. *Courtesy of Johnny Western.*

Contact sheet of Johnny Cash and Johnny Western at Columbia Studios in New York City, 1960. *Courtesy of Johnny Western.*

Johnny Cash, First National Bank of North Minnesota President John Nutting, W.S. Holland, Marshall Grant, June Carter, Johnny Western, and Luther Perkins, 1963. Cash took an excursion from the road to see the pistol (in June's hands) that Jessie James used to rob the First National Bank of North Minnesota. The pistol became a prized possession of the institution and was kept in a vault. *Courtesy of Johnny Western.*

Johnny Cash was arrested in October 1965 when U.S. Customs agents found hundreds of pep pills and tranquilizers in his luggage. Cash, who was returning by plane from a trip to Juarez, Mexico, spent a night in the El Paso County Jail, and later pleaded guilty to a misdemeanor. Cash paid a $1,000 fine and received a thirty-day suspended sentence. *Courtesy of El Paso County Jail.*

This picture, snapped by Carrie Cash, was taken backstage before a Cash concert sometime in the 1960s. *Courtesy of Joanne Cash Yates.*

Singer Al Homburg of Cumberland, Maryland, taking a photo with Johnny Cash on a regional tour in the mid-1960s. *Courtesy of Al Homburg.*

Aerial view shows rambling home of Johnny Cash and June Carter on the shore of Old Hickory Lake in Hendersonville, Tennessee. The grounds included a tennis court, guest house, swimming pool, and lots of lush greenery. *Associated Press.*

Johnny Cash at Folsom Prison with June Carter looking on. This January 1968 concert was the start of Cash's astounding career comeback. *Photofest.*

From 1969 to 1971, no one in show business was more white-hot than the Man in Black. *The Johnny Cash Show* was a popular television series and showcased a wide variety of musical talent. During those years Cash also kept up a busy touring and recording schedule. *Photofest.*

The Nixons and the Cashes. This April 17, 1970 photo was snapped in the East Room of the White House when Johnny Cash played to approximately 225 people, many of them influential senators and congressmen and members of President Nixon's cabinet. *Courtesy of the Richard Nixon Presidential Library and Museum, NARA.*

Johnny Cash and his four daughters on a June 1970 visit to the St. Anastasia Roman Catholic Church in Inglewood, California. The Cash family had to leave the church after fifteen minutes because the young churchgoers got too excited. The daughters are, from left, Kathy, 13, Tara, 8, Rosanne, 15, and Cindy, 11. *Associated Press.*

Johnny Cash and his brothers Tommy (far left) and Roy (far right) flank their sister Joanne and brother-in-law Harry Yates after their December 27, 1971 marriage at Evangel Temple in Nashville, Tennessee. *Courtesy of Joanne Cash Yates.*

Cash made *A Gunfight*, a 1971 Western starring opposite Kirk Douglas, during his career resurgence. The film was financed by the Jicarilla Apache Tribe, who wanted to back Cash for his support of various Native American causes. *Publicity still courtesy of Paramount Pictures.*

Johnny Cash and June Carter Cash with their son John Carter at a sneak peek of *The Gospel Road* in Nashville, Tennessee. Cash sank $500,000 of his own money into the 1973 film. He called it his proudest work. *Photo by Dale Ernsberger.*

Discussing prison reform with President Richard M. Nixon in the White House Oval Office, July 26, 1972. *Courtesy of the Richard Nixon Presidential Library and Museum, NARA.*

Johnny Cash shaking hands with Christian International President Bill Hamon inside the House of Cash after receiving his Associate of Theology degree, May 1977. *Courtesy of Bill Hamon.*

John Cash's diploma from Christian International. He earned his Associate of Theology in March 1977. *Courtesy of Bill Hamon.*

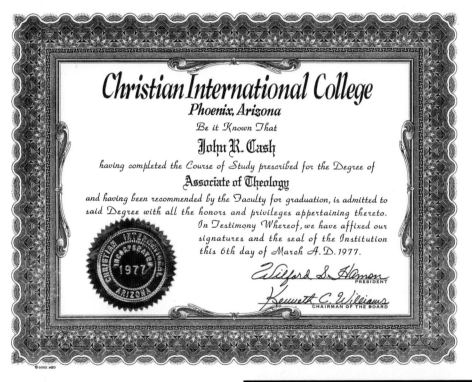

Reunited on stage with Johnny Western at a 1978 concert in Flagstaff, Arizona. *Courtesy of Johnny Western.*

Ray and Carrie Cash outside their home in Hendersonville, Tennessee, in the late 1970s. They literally lived across the street from their famous son. *Courtesy of Joanne Cash Yates.*

The front entrance of Cash's Bon Aqua residence in Bon Aqua, Tennessee. The two-story farmhouse was built in 1847 by a retired veteran of the Mexican War. It became Cash's special sanctuary where he read and studied, wrote songs, and took long walks on the 107-acre farm to reflect in peace. *Courtesy of Kelly Hancock.*

The Carter Family making an appearance on *Johnny Cash Christmas 1983*, which aired on CBS. Helen and Anita Carter (seated, from left) and Joe Carter, June Carter Cash, and Janette Carter. *Publicity still courtesy of CBS Television.*

The Highwaymen formed in 1984 and gave Cash's career a much-needed shot in the arm during a creative and commercial lull. The group produced three studio albums, a live album/DVD and a made-for-TV movie. From left to right: Kris Kristofferson, Johnny Cash, Waylon Jennings, and Willie Nelson. *Publicity still courtesy of Columbia.*

The Cash children in Kingsland, Arkansas, in front of the church where their mother Carrie attended, circa late 1980s. From left to right: Louise Cash Garrett, Reba Cash Hancock, Johnny Cash, Joanne Cash Yates, and Tommy Cash. *Courtesy of Joanne Cash Yates.*

In 1986, Cash starred in the CBS TV remake of *Stagecoach*. He portrayed Sheriff Wilcox. *Photofest.*

The Cash children in front of The Cove, a music and dinner theater venue in Hendersonville, Tennessee, circa early 1990s. *Courtesy of Kelly Hancock.*

Johnny Cash and Joanne Cash Yates after singing a duet at Notre Dame University, 1991. *Courtesy of Joanne Cash Yates.*

Fortieth anniversary of the Dyess High School class of 1950. *Courtesy of A J Henson.*

Cash with Dennis Agajanian accompanying him on guitar at a tribute for Billy Graham, circa early 1990s. *Courtesy of Dennis Agajanian.*

Carrie and Johnny Cash sitting at the piano inside the House of Cash. *Courtesy of Joanne Cash Yates.*

Pastor Harry Yates, Joanne Cash Yates, and Johnny Cash at a 1994 Christmas party at the Old Hickory Lake property. *Courtesy of Joanne Cash Yates.*

A lion in winter. Johnny Cash and his Martin guitar in the 1990s at the start of his amazing final comeback. *Photofest.*

Franklin and I have been friends for over twenty-five years. He told me he was in full rebellion mode at that point in his life, drinking and smoking and getting into quite a bit of trouble. Even a man like Billy, along with his sweet wife Ruth, could not tame their son. Franklin said his parents were outstanding examples to him; that was never the problem. He just wanted to live his own life, not theirs.

But Billy took notice of the fact that Franklin listened to Johnny's music and saw it as a way to build a bridge to his prodigal son.

On December 7, Billy Graham sat down to Sunday dinner with Johnny and June and Cash's parents, who'd recently moved into a house across the street from their son's residence. The conversation was wide-ranging, lighting on topics as diverse as the Vietnam War and Cash's recent Madison Square Garden concert.

Cash and Billy took an instant liking to one another, and at the end of the evening, Cash said, "If there's ever anything I can do to help you, anytime, I wish you'd let me know."

Graham mentioned a crusade he would be conducting in May at the University of Tennessee. He wondered if Cash would be interested in performing one of his gospel songs there and maybe even saying a few words about his faith in Jesus Christ. Johnny readily assented.

"I'd like to tell 'em some things I haven't said much about before," he said, "about how I grew up in the Baptist church in Arkansas and about some of the troubles I've had to overcome to get where I've gotten . . . and Who I owe it to."

It was the start of a firm, enduring friendship between America's favorite entertainer and America's favorite preacher.

"He's a good man. He is what he appears to be," Cash once said. "Billy's a friend like Waylon's a friend. We don't talk about the Bible or religion all that much. We talk about life."

Tom Phillips is the vice president of the Billy Graham Evangelistic Association, and he has served with that organization for several decades. Graham and Cash, he said, "were Southern boys, and their culture was all about relationships. Everything was built around relationships.

"They were southern men who were from a culture of courtesy and respect. They both had a calling of evangelism on their hearts, that each person has an opportunity to have a personal relationship with Jesus Christ as Lord and Savior . . . they were so connected."

At every opportunity over the ensuing years, Cash and Billy prayed together, vacationed together, and confided in each other. They discussed their lives, their problems, their hopes and fears, and bucked each other up. Ruth Graham once told me that June Carter gave her a fur coat, but she felt self-conscious wearing it and put it away for safekeeping. When Billy expressed concerns about the younger generation butting heads with the establishment, Johnny counseled him to reach out to youthful dissenters seeking a better way to deal with the immemorial problems of injustice, poverty, and despair. They often talked politics—a subject both were well versed in. Graham had known and ministered to every president since Harry Truman; Cash eventually met several commanders in chief.

In their conversations, neither man held anything back.

"I've always been able to share my secrets and problems with Billy, and I've benefitted greatly from his support and advice," Cash wrote in his autobiography. "Even during my worst times, when I've fallen back into using pills of one sort or another, he's maintained his friendship with me and given me his ear and his advice, always based solidly on the Bible."

This is no surprise to me.

Having gotten to know Billy personally and having served on his board of directors for over twenty-five years, I can attest to the fact that Billy was a very good listener. In fact, when you were with him, the last thing he wanted to talk about was himself. He always wanted to know about you.

On many occasions, I pumped him for details of meetings he had with famous people, ranging from presidents and other world leaders to celebrities ranging from Bob Hope to Bono to Johnny Cash. Billy would share the occasional anecdote, but for the most part, he was a closed book. If you said something to him in confidence, it would remain in confidence—a very admirable trait that did not go unappreciated by Johnny Cash.

"America's Pastor," as Billy Graham was known, was also a confidant of the thirty-seventh President of the United States. He and Richard M. Nixon had been friends since 1950, and after Nixon moved into the White House in 1969, Billy was a frequent guest there. He and President Nixon often prayed and read the Bible together; Billy advised President Nixon about spiritual matters. In 1970, Nixon became the first president to participate in a Billy Graham Crusade, speaking to a crowd of eighty thousand in Knoxville, Tennessee.

At one of their parleys, Billy mentioned his friend Johnny Cash and the influence the singer had on young people through his popular television show, his music, and most especially through his powerful testimony regarding his own personal trials and the salvation he credited to God. Not long afterwards, Cash received an invitation to perform for the President and First Lady Pat Nixon at the "Evening at the White House" concert series in the East Room on April 17, 1970.

Cash accepted with great pride and excitement. One of the first things he did was tell his father, whose approval still meant more to him than anything, and make sure that Ray and the entire Cash family (with the exception of Carrie, who did not like to fly) would be there when he performed for the president of the United States.

It was already an especially happy time for Johnny and June. Their son John Carter Cash was born on March 3. (Nine months earlier, the Cashes had vacationed in the Virgin Islands, and on their way home, Cash said to June, "Let's name him John Carter Cash." She laughed and said, "Who says I'm pregnant?" The Man in Black was apparently prescient, along with all his other powers.)

Cash's road to 1600 Pennsylvania Avenue was not pothole-free. His acceptance of President Nixon's offer to entertain there was roundly lambasted by young liberal activists who accused Cash of selling out his principles and independence to curry the favor of the Republican president they loathed mostly because of the seemingly endless war in Vietnam.

But Cash wasn't endorsing Nixon and his policies. He had never even voted in an election. As Billy Graham had done for both Democratic and Republican presidents, Johnny was going to the White House at the invitation of the commander in chief. His acceptance was based on patriotism, not politics.

It has been my privilege to visit the White House on a number of occasions. I can tell you, it is not something one takes lightly.

The history of "the people's house" is a lot to take in. As you walk down the hallways and look at the presidential portraits hung on the hallowed walls, you are struck by the fact that decisions that affect the globe are made in this building.

I have had the privilege of joining with other pastors and praying for the President in the Oval Office. It's surprisingly small and is indeed in the shape of an oval. But when you stand in that room, you know it is not something to take for granted.

I understand Johnny's willingness to go as a guest of the President, despite Nixon's unpopularity. I would personally go to the White House regardless of who the sitting president is at the moment. Billy Graham certainly did, and he was very influential with many of the Oval Office's occupants, including Eisenhower, Johnson, Reagan, Clinton, and both Bushes.

Billy thought he had more influence on President Nixon than he actually did, unfortunately.

President Nixon's winning '68 campaign was said to be based on a "Southern Strategy," but that didn't mean he knew anything about country music. Three days before Cash was to perform at the White House, he received word through a secretary that the

president was especially anxious for him to sing "Okie from Muskogee" and "Welfare Cadillac" at the event.

Trouble was, neither was a Cash song. "Okie from Muskogee"
was Merle Haggard's signature hit, and "Welfare Cadillac" was by
Guy Drake. When Cash sent word back to the White House that
there wasn't enough time to learn and get the tunes down pat, he
was told to sing whatever he wanted. Nevertheless, the Washington
press corps found out about the Nixon request and tried to spin it
as an attempt to co-opt the Man in Black for the Nixon administration's own anti-protest, anti-welfare purposes.

The president poked fun at the supposed controversy in his
opening remarks at the gala in the East Room. "I'm not an expert
on [Cash's] music," he acknowledged. "I understand he owns a
Cadillac, but he won't sing about Cadillacs . . . One thing I've
learned about Johnny Cash is that you don't tell him what to sing."

All that was instantly forgotten when Cash started his performance. He wore a black frock coat and trousers, winged
collar, frilly shirt and sleeves and bow tie—all of his own design.
That Mount Rushmore visage and baritone voice commanded
the undivided attention of the 225 people in attendance, many
of them influential senators, congressmen, and members of the
Nixon cabinet.

The president got a huge kick out of "A Boy Named Sue," and
before Cash launched into "Five Feet High and Rising," about the
Great Flood of '37, he looked over at Ray Cash and said, "Daddy,
you remember this." The loudest applause was for a new song
called "What is Truth," which Cash wrote after his initial meeting
with Billy Graham. The lyrics touched on the nation's cultural and
generational divide and the "world waking to a new-born day."
The song elicited prolonged applause from the crowd.

At the concert's conclusion, Johnny thanked President and Mrs.
Nixon for their invitation and said, "We pray, Mr. President, that
you can end this war in Vietnam sooner than you hope or think it

can be done, and we hope and pray that our boys will be back home, and there will soon be peace in our mountains and valleys."

No one dissented, and the Nixons led a very enthusiastic standing ovation at the end of the show.

Later, President and Mrs. Nixon gave the Cashes a tour of the upstairs living quarters at the White House, and the president insisted on having a photograph taken with Ray Cash when he introduced himself in the receiving line. There was no mistaking the look of unabashed pride on Ray's face as he posed with Nixon. In his traditional letter to himself the following December 31, Cash would write that the White House performance was his best of the entire year and that God had surely been with him that night.

He had truly reached the top of the mountain. But as Cash's new fan Richard Milhous Nixon himself would soon find out, the trouble with mountains is there's an upside and a downside.

23

A COG IN THE WHEEL

"Public life is unbelievable . . .
Being a 'star' means so many things
and all of them opposite normalcy. If your
face is familiar, you are stared at, pointed at,
laughed at, whispered at, yelled at,
and followed. People say lots of things
about you that they wouldn't say if they
knew you heard. Everything you do well is
taken for granted. Any mistake is a
matter for great attention."

—JOHNNY CASH

From 1969 to 1971, no one in show business was more white-hot than the Man in Black. Johnny Cash hosted a popular television series and kept up a busy touring and recording schedule. And in the summer of '71, he made his first appearance on the silver screen in almost a decade, co-starring with macho legend Kirk Douglas in the motion picture *A Gunfight*, an offbeat Western drama about two famous, aged, and broke gunfighters who sell tickets to their fast-draw showdown in a bullring. The most interesting thing about the film, shot in New Mexico and Spain during *The Johnny Cash Show's* summer recess, is that it was financed to the tune of $2 million by the Jicarilla Apaches of Dulce, New Mexico, one of the most progressive Indian tribes in the world with investments in oil, gas, lumber, and electronics. Cash's goodwill toward Native Americans over the years was a major reason why they invested in him and the picture.

The eighty-eight-minute movie was no box-office bonanza, and most critics were unimpressed, though *Variety* called *A Gunfight* "a fine depiction in discreet allegorical form of the darker sides of human nature."

With so many irons in the fire, it seemed to some as though Cash had lost his edge when it came to making music. Even so, there was such a great desire for new Cash songs that even the *World of Johnny Cash* album—an uneven compilation of prior album tracks, covers, and minor hits—was certified gold and reached No. 2 on the country album charts. His next album, *The Johnny Cash Show*, was a collection of his live performances on the TV show—surprisingly, not even the best ones. But the label was shrewd enough to tack on Cash's cover of Kris Kristofferson's "Sunday Mornin' Coming Down," which helped the LP turn gold and score another top spot on the country album charts in May 1970. It was a golden period during which he could do no wrong.

The TV show was the flagship of Cash's public endeavors, and through it, he reached multi-millions of old and young, black and white, and urban and rural viewers. Billy Graham once told Johnny, "God has given you your own pulpit. You can reach more people in one TV show than in fifty Crusades."

By the time ABC renewed the show for a third season, Cash was receiving around 100,000 letters a year. Every now and then, one of them wondered if he was actually a practicing Christian. On the surface, it seems like an odd thing to question about a man who featured gospel music and hymns on his show and professed his faith in a variety of public forums. But in many ways, Cash seemed a puzzling contradiction: he had proudly served in the military but didn't beat the drums for the war in Vietnam; he professed a skepticism about politics but befriended some of the most powerful people in the country; he was unabashedly patriotic but fought to have noted pacifist Pete Seeger on his show; he never tried marijuana but didn't denounce it, either, and warned people to be careful only because it was considered illegal.

According to executive producer Joe Byrne, the pungent waft of reefer was familiar on the set of *The Johnny Cash Show*, and if alcohol was the guests' preferred poison, there was plenty of that, too. Byrne recalled the time country singer-songwriter Joe South guested on the show and was blotto when it came time to perform his hit single "Games People Play."

"He fell off the stage, dusted himself off, and got back to the microphone and started singing . . . the crowd went nuts," Byrne said. "That's why I taped the rehearsals and the live spots—in case something went awry."

Fact was, Cash himself was not completely drug-free, though his use of amphetamines was a pittance of what it once was and didn't noticeably alter his behavior or cognition.

He had the adulation of millions, but when stray questions about his faith and character came to his attention, Cash decided to answer them as forcefully as possible. He wrote out a statement he intended to read on the November 18 episode of *The Johnny Cash Show*. It said:

"All my life, I have believed that there are two powerful forces: the force of good, and the force of evil, the force of right and the force of wrong, or, if you will, the force of God and the force of the devil. Well, now, the force of God is naturally the Number One most powerful force although the Number Two most powerful force, the devil, takes over every once in a while. And he can make it pretty rough on you when he tries to take over. I know.

"In my time, I fought him. I fought back. I clawed. I kicked him. When I didn't have the strength, I gnawed him. Well, here lately, I think we've made the devil pretty mad because on our show we've been mentioning God's name. We've been talking about Jesus, Moses, Elijah the prophet, even Paul and Silas and John the Baptist. Well, this probably made the devil pretty mad all right, and he may be coming after me again, but I'll be ready for him. In the meantime, while he's coming, I'd like to get in more licks for Number One."

When Cash showed his proclamation beforehand to producer Stan Jacobson, the latter cautioned him not read it on the show because it was too blunt and, frankly, quite unnecessary. Cash would not be deterred, and when the show taped, he read his statement as an introduction to the gospel number "I Saw a Man." Before the show aired, Jacobson went to Cash and urged him to delete his ringing profession of faith. Cash told him that if it was cut from the show, they would not be on speaking terms.

It stayed.

Johnny spoke these words from his heart. There was no teleprompter, just raw conviction. He had no apprehension or fear. If anyone knew that God was real, it was John R. Cash. He would not be standing on that stage if it were not for Jesus.

In his song, he sang, "I heard my savior say, He said if I be lifted I will draw all men to Me." This is a reference to a statement Jesus made about that fact that if He was "lifted up," meaning when He died on the cross, He would draw people to himself.

Then Johnny, looking into the camera, sang, "I touched the hem of His garment that fell round Him there. My life, my heart I gave, my soul was in His care."

And it was.

That's not to say Johnny did not still have his struggles—because he did.

But he was going a new direction in life.

More professions of faith soon followed. Cash proudly declared himself a Christian on one episode; on another, he brought together the best of African-American (Mahalia Jackson, the Staple Singers, Edwin Hawkins) and Southern (Blackwood Brothers, Oak Ridge Boys) gospel artists for a musical happening unusual in those days before Christian-specific cable networks. Most stunning of all was when Cash had Billy Graham on the same show to deliver a sermon.

No one had ever heard or seen anything like it on network television.

It's possible that the viewing public was more interested in being entertained than evangelized, or, as Stan Jacobson worried, that people were turned off by Cash's perceived support of President Nixon and his tendency to take himself too seriously. For whatever reason, *The Johnny Cash Show's* ratings took a big dip after the Season Three opener. For all intents and purposes, the show was starting to run out of steam and ideas by the third season—which was not unusual for a variety show, according to executive producer Joe Byrne.

In a last-ditch effort to spice up the format and punch up ratings, they introduced specifically themed programs: comedy, youth, the Wild West, country music, even the circus. It didn't help. Rated seventeenth in the 1969-'70 Nielsen Ratings, *The Johnny Cash Show* didn't break the top twenty during the 1970-'71 season.

The show's death knell came with the implementation of the Federal Communication Commission's "Prime Time Access Rule" that eliminated a half-hour of primetime programming from all three networks' nightly schedules starting in September 1971. Cash's show was one of many with strong rural followings that were canceled by networks in what was known as the "rural purge."

While the third season finished airing in the States, Cash flew to Australia in March 1971 for a tour. On arrival, reporters asked why *The Johnny Cash Show* had been canceled. Having decided to pull the plug after fifty-eight episodes, ABC executives had somehow neglected to notify the star. Johnny was infuriated—he had spoken to a network pooh-bah on the very eve of his departure and was led to believe a fourth season was in the offing. But his anger was supplanted by relief that the decision to end the show had been made for him. Cash had felt increasingly restless and wanted to embark on other projects that had more meaning for him. He was weary of the television grind, the battles and compromises with network bureaucrats, and especially of the heavy weekend travel schedule necessary to support his touring company of twenty people.

"It was all right for the first year," Cash would later reflect to a reporter about his experience as star of his own television show. "But I soon came to realize that to the networks I was just another piece of the merchandise, a cog in the wheel, and when the wheel starts squeaking and wobbling, they'd replace me with another cog. Besides that, I began to feel as if every part of my personal life was being merchandised and exploited; I felt as if they were stealing my soul."

History has been more than kind to the show, and it was prescient. There were more than seventy people on *The Johnny Cash Show* in either the Rock and Roll Hall of Fame or the Country Music Hall of Fame.

"It was an all-star revue every single week, but we didn't appreciate what we had," said Cash historian Mark Stielper. "The country people saw all those rock people on the show and said, 'What's Johnny Cash doing?' The rock people said, 'He's one of us.' He was always trying to walk that line, not always successfully, but that's what he did. We can now look back and say he straddled the line despite being constantly pushed and pulled from either side."

With *The Johnny Cash Show* now history, Johnny and June turned their attention to a much bigger production intended for a much bigger screen—with an even bigger star.

24

LET'S TALK ABOUT JESUS

"That's one thing that people like me
have to learn to do, that after you've
straightened up and stopped all that, and you
know that God forgave you, then the big sin
would be not to forgive yourself. So I'm not
ashamed of all that rot that I did. I don't like to
think about it. Some of it I've erased from my
mind, so I don't think about it, and some of it
I refuse to admit that I remember."

—JOHNNY CASH

The cancellation of *The Johnny Cash Show* marked the end of an era
in many ways. It was Johnny Cash's most fruitful professional
period, the apex of his global fame, and the time of his most prodigious and commercial output as an artist.

More importantly, it was also the true beginning of his spiritual life,
engendered by a genuine desire to seek God and get right with Him.

To be sure, by then Cash was an old hand at petitioning God and hailing Him as the author of his salvation. But the fact is that he usually ran to God when a crisis was at hand and he needed rescuing, the same as the rest of us mere mortals. Also like some of us, Johnny was a natural backslider who kept God's number on speed-dial for emergencies but otherwise sought direction and fulfillment through earthly channels.

A lot of people live this way.

But God is so gracious. He both hears and answers our prayers when we call on Him. But the most miserable place for a person to live is in a compromised life.

Johnny had been in that ditch far too long.

This time, it was different. Cash was actually on top of his game and not on his heels. His show was cancelled, but he was a huge international star, and his concerts were sellouts. His movie career had been revived, his marriage to June was blissful, and the birth of his longed-for son John Carter Cash rejuvenated him. Earning a reputed $3 million a year, Cash lived in a custom-built, luxurious 10,000-square-foot home on a 146-acre tract. He had purchased a nearby home across the street for his parents and visited them daily when off the road. He wanted for nothing during this period of his life—except maybe peace of mind.

Ever since he left Dyess, Cash's attendance at church was sporadic. On the road, he would sometimes creep into the back of a church on a Sunday morning; at home, he'd visit different churches in Hendersonville and Madison, hoping to find one that felt comfortable. The trouble was that when word got out Cash was regularly attending a particular church, wannabe songwriters and singers would show up there in droves and slip him demo tapes or ask for introductions to record labels and executives.

Cash once recalled that, while out on the road on a string of one-nighters, he stopped in a small Ohio church on his way to Wheeling, West Virginia, for a Sunday night service. As soon as he walked in, all heads turned towards him, and the congregation started buzzing. All Cash wanted to do was sit in the back, worship the Lord, hear a good message, and quietly leave when it was over. But that wasn't going to happen this night because the pastor lacked the sensitivity to understand where Cash was coming from and what he needed.

"The preacher recognized me and asked me to stand. I bowed and sat down," Cash recalled. "Then he asked me to sing. I declined due to a lack of accompaniment."

Somewhat stymied, the pastor asked, "Well, how about sharing a testimony with us?'"

To "give one's testimony" means to tell your story about how you came to put your faith in Christ. Frankly, Cash was still working that out.

His need for privacy during worship all changed when he bumped into Jimmie Snow in 1969.

Cash and Snow had a shared history that dated back to 1956 when he was a performer on the same circuit as Elvis Presley. The son of legendary country singer Hank Snow, Jimmie carved out a career for himself and had a record deal with RCA. But his career quickly derailed thanks to an addiction to alcohol and amphetamines.

Snow and Cash had fallen down the same rabbit hole.

"John and I were both basically shy, withdrawn, and a bit backwards, so I'd cover it as best as I could because it was very difficult for me to walk out on that stage," Snow said. "To sing? No problem. But to ad lib? Big problem. The pills and the drinking would bring me out of my shell, and I think Johnny may have done it for the same reasons."

In November 1957, the twenty-two-year-old Snow experienced a life-transforming encounter with Jesus Christ and gave up his show business career to become a full-time preacher for the Assemblies of God.

Cash and Snow renewed acquaintances at the Saigon airport, which was a mere Quonset hut. They had come to Vietnam separately to entertain American troops. Cash suffered a major relapse there and was in bad shape emotionally and physically. It's quite possible that some of the harrowing scenes he had witnessed while there had pushed him over the edge.

"I think about the time that June and I went to Vietnam in 1969 and saw the burning flesh," Cash later recalled. "The boys coming in from the helicopters on stretchers . . . the flesh falling off from the napalm on their bodies. You never forget the smell of that."

Bumping into Snow was a Godsend to him.

Clearly, this was a divine appointment for Johnny and Jimmie.

Timing is everything when it comes to spiritual matters.

Johnny was finally ready to get even more serious about his faith.

Cash knew Snow was pastor of his own church, Evangel Temple, on Dickerson Road in Madison, Tennessee. "I need to talk to you," Cash said. He wrote down his home phone number and asked Snow to call when they were both back stateside.

Snow called a few weeks later, and Johnny invited him to the house at Old Hickory Lake. When Snow arrived, they got in Cash's jeep and drove to a secluded log cabin Cash had built back in the woods as a place to relax, write songs, or just be alone. Cash brought along a Bible and said, "Let's talk about Jesus."

Recalled Snow, "I'd spent several years at that point as an evangelist, and I learned to read people pretty good. He said he had allowed himself to get into some pretty far-out things, including his problem with pills. He confided in me because of the kinds of things I'd done when I hardly drew a sober breath for several years. He said, 'I've got some things I want to do for God, and I need to get to a good place in my life.'"

They prayed together in the cabin, and Snow urged Cash to come to his church and make a public stand for God. Johnny was noncommittal then, but over the next few months, he and Snow got together several times, including on the set of *The Johnny Cash Show*. It was strictly friendly, and at no time did Snow ever try to force or push Cash to attend services at his church.

He did eventually approach it from a different direction—music. "Why don't you come visit us some time at the church and bring your guitar and knock off a few songs for us?" Snow asked offhandedly.

"I thought you'd never ask," Cash said.

Evangel Temple had made a name for itself in Music City, USA, as a place where singers and entertainers could worship and play the kind of music they grew up on—gospel and hymns. Snow's master plan was to have a profound Christian impact on the country music scene by giving artists a haven on Sundays and to minister to their hearts through music. His earliest musical recruits included songwriters Larry Lee, Wayne Walker, Connie Smith, Eddie and Pam Miller, engineer Ronnie Light, steel guitarist Sonny Garrish, and a then-unknown singer-songwriter named Larry Gatlin.

Johnny's sister Joanne had started singing in the church choir. Her own Road-to-Damascus experience was as compelling as Johnny's. In 1969, Joanne went through a bitter divorce in Houston and moved back to the Nashville area. After a family reunion in Kingsland, Arkansas, Johnny rented a six-seat single engine plane for the trip back to Nashville. Everything was fine until there was a hailstorm the likes of which no one aboard had ever experienced.

"Twenty minutes in a hailstorm seems like an eternity, and my sister kept pushing my head down, thinking we were going to crash," recalled Joanne. "I cried out to God—'God, if You save me, I'll give You all the rest of the days of my life.' After a while, we crossed over a line of sunshine and landed the plane. When we got out, Johnny's face was shocked white. I couldn't speak. I was so scared and thankful to be alive. We walked around the plane and it looked like it had been beaten with a hammer. The next day was Sunday, and I was in church."

More than one person has made that promise to God and then failed to follow through. Louis Zamperini, whose life story is told in the amazing book *Unbroken*, crashed his plane in the ocean during WWII due to mechanical difficulties.

He was stranded on a life raft for forty-seven days, adrift at sea.

He prayed, "God, if you spare my life, I'll serve You for the rest of my life!"

God did spare Louis, but Louis did not act on that promise he made to God until years later at a Billy Graham Crusade during one of the evangelist's altar calls.

Soon, it would be Johnny's turn.

At Evangel Temple, Joanne, a longtime drug addict and alcoholic, walked to the altar, dropped to her knees, and gave her life to Jesus in front of Rev. Snow and Assistant Pastor Harry Yates (who became her husband a year later).

"After I asked Jesus to come into my heart, we prayed, and I felt this heat come up my body to the end of my fingertips," Joanne said. "I knew I was born again. I knew I was saved. I knew I was gonna go to Heaven. I knew I would get to see Jack again. I was just elated . . . I then started praying for Johnny."

When Joanne told her mother what happened that day, Johnny was there and just listened. He didn't say anything until two weeks later when he met Joanne in the driveway of their folks' house.

"You really got it, didn't you, Baby?" Cash asked.

"Yes, John, I did," replied Joanne. "I'm born again—and I'm praying for you."

"You think I need it?" Cash asked.

"Yes, I think you do need it, and all of us are praying for you," Joanne said.

Cash finally took Rev. Jimmie Snow up on his invitation to visit Evangel Temple. He immediately felt comfortable amidst the congregation of about two hundred members, many of whom had, like him, been through harrowing times and come out whole thanks to the grace of God. As Rev. Snow suggested, Cash brought his guitar, and when he was called on to sing, he performed a song he'd written in 1958 called "My Prayer." It felt good. Then Rev. Snow preached a sermon about salvation whose simple eloquence harkened Cash back to his youth. Nobody made a fuss about the big star in their midst, which was refreshing in itself. But he did not take the step to turn his life back over to the Lord—that would take some more time and contemplation.

Over the next few months Cash was kept busy with his show and weekend touring. Meanwhile, June's daughter Rosey began attending Evangel Temple services and found them so moving and enlightening she started lobbying Johnny and June to come with her. They finally did, and it wasn't long before they were regulars.

When John, June, daughters Rosey and Carlene, and son John Carter attended Evangel Temple on May 9, 1971, Cash sat in his usual spot in the very last row. The congregation sang a couple of rousing favorites—"At the Cross" and "Standing on the Promises." Cash loved that the church stuck to the basics, musically—the hymns were the same ones he'd sung in church as a boy. When he looked at the choir, he was struck by their appearance, later recalling, "Their faces were like beacons. They had spirit, and the feeling was infectious. They were beautiful, and they sang like they believed it."

The guest performer that day was twenty-two-year-old Larry Gatlin. He sat on a stool next to the pulpit with his guitar and sang a song he wrote called "Help Me," a cry to the Lord for understanding of "just where I fit into Your master plan." (Cash later included the song in his movie, *The Gospel Road*.)

Cash soaked in the words, envious that the young Gatlin already knew what it had taken him so long to realize—that he couldn't make it without the Lord. How much suffering he could have saved himself over the years had he abandoned the selfish lifestyle he chose to live and instead walked in a consistent relationship with God.

That day, Rev. Snow preached from Acts 16:31—"Believe on the Lord Jesus Christ and thou shalt be saved and thy house" (KJV)—and Cash listened intently. He found himself moved by his friend's almost childlike sincerity. There were no grandiose rhetorical flourishes and affectations.

Snow closed the service with the traditional altar call, urging everyone to "get off the fence with your faith" and make a public stand for Jesus Christ—the same thing he'd said to Cash almost a year before.

An altar call, or invitation, is a moment when whoever is speaking challenges people listening to make a public profession of their faith. The reason for this is to help the person making that commitment to put "feet to their faith" and stand up and be counted. When I extend invitations for people to come to put their faith in Christ, I often quote the words of Jesus, where He said, "Whoever will confess me before others, I will confess him before my Father and the angels" (Matthew 10:32 NKJV).

That moment had come for Johnny.

As others got up and moved down to the altar, Cash recalled the time he made his first altar call at the Baptist church in Dyess when he was twelve years old. He'd spent so many of the twenty-seven years since then in the wilderness. It was time for his wandering to end. Cash got to his feet, drew himself up to his full height, and proclaimed loudly to everyone in the congregation:

"I'm reaffirming my faith. I'll make the stand, and in case I've had any reservations up to now, I pledge that I'm going to try harder to live my life as God wants, and I'd like to ask your prayers and the prayers of these people."

Then the Man in Black led his family to the altar, and they sank to their knees and recited the "Sinner's Prayer."

Rev. Jimmie Snow is still moved by the memory of the day.

"When I pray with someone, I guide them through the 'Sinner's Prayer' to make sure that they surrender all to Christ," he said. "We did this with a number of people around John. He prayed it out loud, and we all heard and saw his tears."

There is no official "Sinner's Prayer" in the Bible, per se.

But I, too, have led many in that same prayer.

It goes along these lines:

196

God, I know that I am a sinner.
I believe that Jesus Christ died on the cross for my sins,
    and I turn from them now.
Come into my life and be my savior and Lord.
I choose to follow You from this day forward.
Thank You for hearing this prayer.
In Jesus's name I pray, amen.

Johnny Cash not only said those words, but he lived by them for the rest of his years. He stumbled many times along the way, but he always maintained the course.

25

THE GOSPEL ROAD

"The devil has plenty of movies these days . . .
I felt like I was obliged to make one for Jesus."

—JOHNNY CASH

Johnny Cash was no longer just a fair-weather follower. He was now a totally committed disciple of Jesus Christ. Soon after he knelt at the altar to pledge himself to the Lord, he and June decided to make Evangel Temple their home church.

Though raised as a Southern Baptist, Johnny felt a deep affinity for Jimmie Snow because of his simply being there when Johnny needed his help.

Plus, he said he "naturally felt good at a service with the bunch of would-be-down-and-outers and losers you see in that congregation . . . There's just enough underdogs and second-lifers over there to make me comfortable—my sister Joanne, for one. I've got a lot in common with them. They understand me."

Niece Kelly Hancock, who also attended Evangel Temple at that time, said she believes that fame nearly destroyed her uncle and finally brought him to his knees.

"Love and fame cannot exist in the same body, and I think John knew that," Hancock said. "Once June came along and steered him in that direction, he got over the stigma of his childhood, and he was able to approach God on his life. And God met him right where he was."

Johnny had finally found a home church.

If a believer wants to grow spiritually, this is simply not an option, even if you are a superstar like Cash.

The church is more than a place to listen to sermons and sing a few songs. It's a spiritual community where one will find a new kind of family—the family of God.

It's a place where you can find fellow believers to pray with, grow with spiritually, and, as the Bible says, "Encourage one another" (Hebrews 10:25 NLT).

The church is a hospital for sinners, not a museum for saints.

Cash's inscription on the first interior page from one of his family Bibles was a strong statement of his faith:

This I believe:
That Jesus Christ is the Son of God.
That he lived and died as a human, but after the third day,
    arose from the dead,
and for many days walked among us.
That in His glorified form He ascended to heaven, where He
    now sits at the right hand of God the Father.

Cash's next statement of faith he intended for the whole world. He wanted to make a film about "the most misquoted, misread, and misunderstood man in history"—Jesus Christ.

He further elaborated: "Lots of people go all their lives thinking Jesus was some kind of pious pushover. He's been portrayed as a sissy, and I'm just not buying that concept of Him. He didn't bawl on that cross; I think if you or I had been up there, we would have squalled and bawled and tried to get down. Not Jesus. He was a real man."

His concept of the movie production was amorphous. He'd travel to Israel, visit locations connected with Christ's life, and let the cameras roll as he delivered a narration, much as he did with *The Holy Land* album. He figured the film would virtually make itself as it went along, and he planned to bankroll the production himself to the tune of $500,000 in order to retain complete artistic control.

He started with a working title—*In the Footsteps of Jesus*. Now he needed a director. Cash had enjoyed working with Robert Elfstrom, who directed the 1969 documentary *Johnny Cash: The Man, His World, His Music* (mostly because Elfstrom had focused on his music and not his drug-riddled past).

He called Elfstrom out of the blue and told him, "I want you to make me a film about Jesus."

"Jesus who?" replied the director, figuring Cash was talking about a Latino musician or entertainer.

When Cash explained he wanted to make a movie about Jesus Christ, Elfstrom started to tap dance. He was a confirmed agnostic himself and at age thirty-one had his doubts that making a religious film was a good career move. But Elfstrom liked Johnny Cash, and it sounded like a fun adventure. He jumped in with both feet and didn't regret it.

The movie was actually the fulfillment of a dream June had in '68, in which Johnny stood on a mountain in Israel, a Bible in his hand, talking to people about Jesus. A few days after they arrived in Galilee, the land where Jesus lived, to begin filming, June excitedly tugged at Johnny's sleeve and said, "There's the mountain I dreamed about where you were standing!"

The project was not entirely seat-of-the-pants. In preparation for it, Cash had extensively studied the Bible and a *Harmony of the Gospels*, which laid out the life of Christ in chronological order. While in

London, he purchased an armload of books on the life of Christ by various writers and theologians. He also spoke to people in all walks of religious life, including a professor of politics at New York's Yashiva University, to prepare himself for the job of authoritatively telling the story of Jesus.

Cash co-wrote the script with Larry Murray, who had put together some of the "Ride This Train" segments on *The Johnny Cash Show*. In a way, "Ride This Train" provided a model for the movie—Cash would tell the story of Jesus's life, death, and resurrection through music and would link the songs with his own narration. He and Murray mustered up an eight-page general outline that left plenty of opportunities for come-what-may in Israel.

Elfstrom went to Israel with Murray in late October 1971 to scout locations. Johnny, June, and John Carter joined them on November 4 with about thirty friends and supporters serving as the film's cast and crew. They checked into a hotel in Tiberias, on the western shore of the Sea of Galilee, about 120 miles north of Jerusalem. In addition to access to the Jordan River, there was an abandoned Palestine refugee village nearby that served as the set of Old Jerusalem.

Rather than use professional actors, some long-haired hippies traveling through Israel at the time were hired as film extras. The major roles in *The Gospel Road: The Story of Jesus*—the film's new title—were filled by members of the Cash entourage. Manager Saul Holiff played Jewish high priest Caiaphas, promoter and booker Lou Robin a Roman soldier, songwriter Larry Lee was John the Baptist. Johnny's sister Reba Cash played Mary, the mother of Jesus, and June played Mary Magdalene. Rev. Jimmie Snow, serving as a religious consultant, also played Pontius Pilate. Director Robert Elfstrom was rewarded for his leap of faith in taking on the project with the role of Jesus Christ (though his long blond hair and blue eyes may have provoked a few double-takes and the question "Jesus who?"). The offbeat casting added to the production's overall feel of a home movie rather than a glossy Hollywood confection.

In addition to his consulting and acting duties, Rev. Jimmie Snow was called on for a special assignment. "John walked up to me early one morning and said that he and June wanted to get baptized in the Jordan River," Snow recalled. After baptizing them, he also baptized June's two daughters. "That was truly one of the highlights of my life," he said.

Elfstrom's approach as a documentary filmmaker made the experience far more relaxed and improvised than a typical feature film. His creative juices must have been flowing because many of the film's ideas came from Cash himself, who often worked in his pajamas alongside Elfstrom late into the night—sometimes until 3:30 a.m.—figuring out the next day's shoot. Cash frequently stepped in as director himself, offering his vision to the actors before the cameras rolled. He called the crew "the most devoted bunch of people that anybody could ever hope to have."

After filming wrapped later that month, Elfstrom spent almost a year in New York assembling and editing the footage. Cash joined him when could take time off the road, dubbing in songs and spoken-word narration. In addition to his own music, Cash enlisted a variety of songwriters to contribute to the double-album movie soundtrack, including Larry Gatlin, Kris Kristofferson, Joe South, John Denver, and Christopher S. Wren (a folk singer-songwriter turned journalist who penned the first serious biography of Cash in 1971).

The final cut of *The Gospel Road* was underwhelming to say the least.

I remember seeing it as a young man, and, though impressed with certain elements of it (mostly Johnny's singing), to me the acting seemed non-existent and failed to connect on many levels. It was far too ambitious a project to undertake with so little preparation.

I don't think I was alone. Many critics found it too folksy, simplistic, and down-home. *TV Guide* called it "well-intentioned, but more than a little odd." Including *Gospel Road* in his 2009 listing of "Top Ten Jesus Films," *Time* magazine critic Richard Corliss wrote,

"As Cash intones the words, 'This is My beloved Son, in Whom I am well pleased,' it's easy to imagine that God must have a Southern accent" and added that the film's "simplicity and good intentions overwhelm" its "weirdness."

But you cannot help but appreciate Johnny's willingness to put it all on the line for his faith. His heart was in the right place, but the production qualities and other elements that make for a successful film—regardless of the subject—were simply not there. It was hard to get over a blonde Jesus that looked more Norwegian than Middle Eastern.

Cash found out the hard way there was little interest in Hollywood for *The Gospel Road*. When he screened it for several agents, distributors, and studio executives, they scratched their heads and said they wouldn't have a clue how to market the film. (Which was pretty much the case for all Christian cinema until director Mel Gibson punched through the ceiling with 2004's *The Passion of the Christ*.)

The Gospel Road premiered on February 14, 1973, in Charlotte, North Carolina, with a big gala that included a local hundred-member marching band and Billy Graham serving as honorary chairman of the event (Georgia Governor Jimmy Carter and his wife Rosalynn were also in attendance). The Cashes were on hand to ensure the movie was properly launched. The following night, Cash screened *The Gospel Road* at the Park Theater, a first-class movie house in Memphis. Tickets sold out almost immediately. Johnny Cash's hometown crowd loved it—but how would it play in other parts of the country where Cash couldn't be there in person to cheerlead for it? And how many showings could he afford without a distributor to help out?

Eventually 20th Century Fox got on board, paying Cash $200,000 for distribution rights. That amount covered less than half of his initial outlay; he was still several hundred thousand in the hole.

The initial plan was to release the film in the South, the so-called "Bible Belt," in hopes it would create strong enough buzz and word-of-mouth for a follow-up general release throughout the rest of the country. But even in the South, the reception was so lukewarm that Fox decided to only screen the film wherever there were requests for it.

To the rescue came two old, dear friends—Billy Graham and Floyd Gressett.

Billy Graham's organization, World Wide Pictures, bought the rights from Fox to show *The Gospel Road* for free in churches across the country. It flickered in thousands of church basements and was widely seen. Billy also had the film translated in several foreign languages and tacked on a personal invitation to viewers to receive Jesus Christ into their lives at the end of the movie that resulted in countless new professions of faith.

Rev. Gressett took a print of *The Gospel Road* and had it screened in almost every penitentiary in America, where it was seen by more than 150,000 inmates. He told Johnny that hundreds of them were moved by it to commit their lives to Christ.

That lifted Cash's spirits to the point he began thinking about following up *The Gospel Road* with a film biography of the Apostle Paul. Ultimately, he decided to publish a written biography instead, called *Man in White*. That option was definitely much cheaper.

The Gospel Road's double album reached No. 12 on the country album charts. The song "Children" stalled at No. 30 on the singles chart. Neither made a deep impression on listening audiences.

Cash paid a heavy price for making *The Gospel Road*. It cost him the attention and support of a large segment of the secular audience, and January 1973 marked the first time in years he didn't have an album on the country charts. It was the start of a long tailspin in his recording career.

But he didn't care and never regretted making *The Gospel Road* because it was his personal witness and his on-the-record faith statement.

"This is my life's proudest work that I wanted to produce, to lay down a story and put it on the screen, have people go and sit and enjoy it, and when they walk out of the theater, feel good about it,"

Cash said. "Not walk out of the theater saying, 'Oh me, I'm a sinner. I've got to run and do something quick, to get right.' It's the kind of thing that will make you think about your religion, but it's a beautiful film."

Johnny Cash gained far more than he lost, including the fulfillment of June's vision of him standing on a mountaintop in Israel, preaching to millions about Jesus.

26

A C-PLUS CHRISTIAN

"I sincerely love people. And I especially
love children. Now that I have six daughters
and a little boy and I'm forty-three years old,
I've learned to appreciate children. So I have
them in mind when I make my records, and I
also have the church people in mind, because
that's part of my life now, too. And I also have
convicts in mind. I try to remember that the
airwaves belong to everybody—anybody can
turn on a radio—so I try not to put
my music into a bag."

—JOHNNY CASH

The old Johnny Cash was dead, supplanted by a strong, whole-hearted, dedicated follower of Christ. The old Cash and the old ways were in Johnny's rearview mirror now. No more wasted days and nights. He wanted to make up for lost time and for his life to make a difference, using the massive platform God had given him.

Cash had always thought of himself as a basically decent man. But he learned from Ephesians 2:8 that, "For by grace you have been saved through faith. And this not of your own doing; it is the gift of God."

Johnny realized to a greater extent the depth of his sin, but even more, he saw the depth of God's love for him, through thick and thin.

Now he wanted to do good for God and others out of gratitude for all that Christ had done for him.

"I don't have a career anymore," he told a journalist. "What I have now is a ministry. Everything I have and everything I do is given completely to Jesus Christ now. I've lived my life for the devil up until now, and from here on, I'm going to live it for the Lord."

Cash wanted to use his high profile and the way he lived his daily life to shine a light for Christ. His desire was for people to know how Jesus had changed his life. He felt the entertainment world was at the very front line of spiritual battles, and he wanted to be sure his image remained above reproach.

When he asked Billy Graham's advice on the subject, Cash related later, "He advised me to keep singing 'Folsom Prison Blues' and 'A Boy Named Sue' and all those other outlaw songs if that's what people wanted to hear, and then when it came time to do a gospel song, give it everything I had. Just put my heart and soul into all my music."

That was excellent advice. It's called "building a bridge" instead of burning one.

There was a lot of goodwill toward Cash in America. He was respected by multiple generations now. Despite his advancing years, young people connected to Johnny. I know as a kid and teen I did.

"Johnny Cash made it cool to be a rogue who loves Christ," said Rick Scott, the former drummer for Alabama who worked for Cash as a songwriter. "I can't think of anyone in popular music who's pulled that off before or since."

The timing was good for evangelistic outreach to youth. In 1971, America was in the midst of what *Time* magazine called "the Jesus

Revolution," the greatest spiritual awakening of the twentieth century. It was mostly led by young Christians—including hippies and long-haired flower children—who were excited about Jesus in a new way, especially when it came to music and worship.

I was one of those kids myself, and I had my life transformed by Jesus. Like Johnny, I struggled with drugs and drinking. I, too, had lost my way. But I was just some unknown kid, not a superstar like Johnny. But the answer for both of us was the same—a relationship with God through Jesus Christ.

I wrote a book in 2018 about this special moment in time called *Jesus Revolution* to elaborate further on my personal story and what was happening in America at that time.

Campus Crusade for Christ (now called Cru), an interdenominational organization committed to evangelism and discipleship for college and high school students, congregated eighty thousand young people from over seventy-five countries to praise Jesus in June 1972. Held in Dallas, Texas, Explo '72 (short for "Spiritual Explosion") attempted to make Christianity relevant to a generation that yearned for more than the status quo, did not trust anyone over thirty, and talked of fulfilling a spiritual yearning in their souls. It was a paradigmatic event in the history of American evangelicalism and one of the signature events of the 1970s Jesus Movement.

The four-day event included evangelism classes, seminars and esteemed guest speakers, and concluded with an outdoor concert attended by more than 150,000 people. Billy Graham, co-sponsor of Explo and the keynote speaker, referred to it as the "religious Woodstock"—a moniker that not only stuck in the media but greatly benefited Campus Crusade. It was also an opportunity for Cash to be a part of the movement because he felt a responsibility for young people to know Christ.

Cash headlined a "Jesus Rock" lineup that included mainstream artists Love Song, Larry Norman, Andrae Crouch and the Disciples, and Randy Matthews. The bill also included Kris Kristofferson and

Rita Coolidge, national artists Cash wanted to introduce to this new music phenomenon.

Decked out in his traditional black, Cash was introduced by Billy Graham to a large and cheering crowd as "the most exciting man in American music today." Cash sang "I See Men as Trees Walking," "A Thing Called Love," and "Supper Time." During his performance, he confessed, "I have tried drugs and a little of everything else, and there is nothing more satisfying than having the kingdom of God building inside of you and growing."

Though closer to my parents' age, younger people still felt that Johnny was "one of us." No matter what Johnny did, through his ups and downs and highs and lows, he was always . . . himself.

His voice had authenticity to it.

We felt that, unlike many other adult figures, we could somehow trust him.

And we did.

Cash took the message of Christ on the road. He made appearances at the Johnny Cash Country & Gospel Festival at the Pocono International Raceway in Pennsylvania in August 1972 and the first All Lutheran Youth Gathering in Houston, Texas, in August 1973. A month later, he headlined SPREE '73 (SPiritual REEmphasis), the British extension of Explo '72. It was also organized by Rev. Billy Graham, and Cash performed at the closing concert at London's Wembley Stadium with Carl Perkins, Cliff Richard, Kevin Gould, and June Carter before a crowd of 30,000-plus.

Johnny and Billy Graham made a powerful tandem for Christ, recalled Tom Phillips of the Billy Graham Evangelistic Association. "The establishment in America at that time was anathema to young people, and even preachers were seen as establishment," he said. "Johnny Cash had a life and the music that young people could relate to, and Billy had the message to deliver. They were a great combination for Jesus."

Johnny Cash even took on Sin City during a seven-night run at the Las Vegas Hilton that paid him $100,000. He reportedly used his concerts to evangelize and made altar calls at the end of the shows. He was forced to issue a disclaimer to a national newspaper, but he emphatically added that "the Holy Spirit dwells in me at all times."

His evangelical leanings and dedication to God was now a growing thread through his life and work.

Rev. Jimmie Snow recalled the time Evangel Temple was in need and Cash stepped up to help. "Our property had been incorrectly surveyed, and we had a barbed-wire fence up between us and the adjoining property. It created a problem with parking on Sundays," Snow said. "I was very upset about it, and we prayed about it."

After services one Sunday, Cash asked Snow about the ugly barbed-wire fence. Snow filled him in and asked Johnny to pray for a solution to the problem. A few weeks later, Cash presented the astonished Snow with the deed to the property next to Evangel Temple. He'd purchased it himself for $43,000, and as he gave the deed to Snow said, "Now let's take that fence down."

He also asked the pastor to keep the transaction strictly between them, which was typical.

"He'd give people cars, he'd pay off mortgages on other people's homes—he did that many, many times—and would always swear me to secrecy," said Rev. Snow.

Cash also prayed with people in the church, recalled Rev. Snow, kneeling down with newcomers to the Lord during altar calls. Most came with pure intentions, but there were exceptions—like the stranger who knelt at the altar and prayed the Sinner's Prayer and then, when Cash knelt alongside him, turned to him with cassette tape in hand and said, "I've got some songs just right for you that I believe could be hits."

Recalled Rev. Snow: "John could have gotten really upset about that, but he just said, 'I don't feel this is the right time or place to discuss that, but I'll give you the phone number at my office and you can call me tomorrow.'" Cash later called the man's insensitive act the greatest violation of his privacy that he had ever experienced.

During the rollout of *The Gospel Road*, a local Youth for Christ chapter based in San Diego reached out to the entertainer for help. Cash and June set up screenings at first-run movie houses to raise money for the organization. Marshall Grant recalled that Cash and June did so for more than a year at considerable expense to themselves.

"All the money—and I mean *all* the money—from screenings of *The Gospel Road* during this period was turned over to Youth for Christ for their use," Grant wrote in his 2006 memoir.

Likewise, when Cash played a prison concert, he never took a dime, and if a fee was offered, he asked prison officials to put the money into programming for inmates instead. He donated $5,000 towards the building of a prison chapel at Cummins, Arkansas. His policy was the same where it concerned the Billy Graham Crusade—he never took a dime, even to cover his expenses.

On July 26, 1972, Cash, along with Glen Sherley and Harlan Sanders (former inmates in his employ) appeared before the U.S. Senate Subcommittee on Prison Reform in Washington, D.C. Cash was candid about his past incarcerations and relayed stories of the worst abuses he heard about during his prison visits.

He proposed separating first-timers and hardened criminals, the reclassification of offenses to keep minor offenders out of prison, a focus on rehabilitation rather than punishment, and counseling to prepare convicts for the outside world to reduce the possibility of them re-offending.

"A first offender needs to know that somebody cares for him and that he is given a fair shake," Cash said. "The purpose behind prison reform should be to have less crime. The prisoner has to be treated like a human being. If he isn't, when he gets out, he won't act like one."

Later that day, Cash met with President Nixon in the White House's Blue Room and asked him to get involved in prison reform. A photo of the two men hit the news wires and made national news.

For all this, Cash often referred to himself a mere "C-plus Christian" because he knew he was less than perfect. He trusted in 2 Corinthians

5:21: "For our sake he made him to be sin who knew no sin, so that in him we might become the righteousness of God" (ESV).

I don't know about grading one's self as a Christian, but from what I can gather, Johnny was doing incredibly well as a follower of Jesus Christ. But like all true believers, he could see he had so far to go. Yet he had come so far—and in a relatively short amount of time.

There was simply no one out there with "street cred" like Johnny who used their platform for their faith. Beatle George Harrison certainly had done the same for the Hare Krishna movement, but no one had ever done it for the Christian faith. In his way, Johnny Cash made Christianity cool for many.

If a man's man like Johnny Cash would follow Jesus, others might consider it as well. You can understand how the devil would set his sights on such a threat.

And he did.

But Johnny was not going to obsess over that. He had already "given the devil his due."

Now it was time to honor the Lord, and—like the man he wrote a book about, the Apostle Paul—say to Jesus, "Lord, what do you want me to do?" (Acts 9:6 NKJV)

The Apostle Paul, formerly the notorious Saul of Tarsus, had once hunted down Christians. Now he was one of them. He wanted his life to count.

He wanted to do as much, if not more, for God's kingdom as he had previously done for Satan's kingdom. And Paul did.

So did John R. Cash.

27

FAIR TO MIDDLING

"There's a decline of morals all around.
The country is just not in the best shape.
Churches are losing members every day.
People are backsliding . . . I'm not saying we
can change the world, but you can't listen
to our show without seeing the strength and
influence of the family unit. When we sing
'Will the Circle Be Unbroken?' that isn't just a
song, it's our life. God and family—the simple
old traditional values that hold a person
together."

—JOHNNY CASH

Johnny Cash's recording career suffered a downturn in the mid-'70s with the release of sub-par material and his open profession of faith. His efforts to evangelize to mainstream concert audiences—even in Las Vegas— had tarnished his reputation as a musical "outlaw" in the minds of some—though in fact it was the most "outlaw" thing Cash had done to date. Acceptable conformity, to some of his detractors, apparently was following the familiar trajectory of "drugs, sex, and rock 'n' roll" (or, in Cash's case, country music) to an early grave, like Hank Williams and a host of others. To these folks, Johnny was now just too mainstream, entertaining presidents and heads of state, hosting TV variety shows, guest starring on popular television shows like *Columbo* and *Little House on the Prairie*, and getting his own star on the Hollywood Walk of Fame. Cash's core audience didn't cotton to their hero all buffed up and sanitized. He was attacked by agnostics and atheists when he came off as too pious and denounced by the religious community when he seemed too worldly.

Fact is, Johnny was just trying to make a living as an entertainer, and these were the doors that were opening to him now.

This criticism did not deter Cash in his newfound faith.

That same determination he had in earlier days to go the wrong way was now channeled in the right direction. And that did not fit the image some wanted upheld of the Johnny of San Quentin Prison days flipping the bird in the now-famous photo by Jim Marshall.

People like to think that was Cash's sentiment for the whole world, but the fact was that Marshall specifically asked Johnny to express what he thought of the prison authorities when he played the show at the penitentiary. The iconic photo followed Johnny the rest of his life and has adorned posters, tees, mugs, and just about everything else since then. It was not who he really was, but it's how some people want to remember him.

There is a similarity in this image of Johnny Cash and that of Steve McQueen, whom I wrote a book about in 2017. McQueen was known as "The King of Cool," and for good reason.

He had it all—massive success, the ultimate car and motorcycle collection, global fame. Steve had a detached way about him that was reflected on the screen and in his life. This was due largely to his extremely difficult childhood with an alcoholic, disconnected mother and a father he never knew. After massive hits like *The Magnificent Seven*, *The Great Escape*, and *Bullitt*, McQueen's legend was firmly established. But what many do not know—and this is why I wrote a book about him—is that Steve McQueen, the No. 1 movie star in the world at that time, walked away from Tinsel Town in search of something more and found it in a relationship with Jesus Christ. In the volumes of material about Steve in books and documentary films, this is often either omitted altogether or marginalized. That's because it does not fit the image many have of McQueen. But facts are pesky things.

The same was true of Johnny Cash. The Man in Black was now a fully committed follower of Jesus Christ, and he wanted the world to know it. But was the world ready for *this* fact?

In 1973, Cash's thirteen-year association with manager Saul Holiff dissolved.

Holiff told promoter Lou Robin (who replaced him) that Cash's career had peaked and would likely be in freefall from there on out. Johnny's latest releases—a duets album with June called *Johnny Cash and His Woman* and another greatest-hits package—failed to dent the Top 30 album charts, which seemed to bear out Holiff's forecast.

In fact, Cash himself had long been looking to ditch Holiff on the grounds that Saul was not showing much interest in his career anymore. The easy-going Robin was doing most of the heavy lifting already, and was less contentious than Holiff, to boot.

The simmering mutual discontent boiled over that July during Cash's engagement in Lake Tahoe, Nevada, when Holiff dropped by the Cashes' bungalow one morning and June lit into him for not joining her and Johnny when they performed at the Billy Graham Crusades.

"Do you have something against Jesus?" she asked. Holiff pointed out that since the Graham organization handled all the arrangements for the Cashes at a Crusade, there was no reason for him to be on hand. June accused him of being only concerned about money. Tempers flared, and Holiff ended up tendering his resignation as Johnny's manager, effective five months thence.

At a November 3 show at London Gardens in Ontario, Canada, Holiff's hometown, Cash paid public tribute to his manager, calling him a "great family man and one of the wisest men I know" and presenting him with two bottles of champagne. A few months later, the Cashes sent Holiff an expensive Patek Phillippe watch in gratitude for his service.

In later years, Cash heaped praise on Holiff, lauding him for saving his career from the doldrums. Holiff and his family were guests at the Cashes' Jamaica retreat, Cinnamon Hill, in 1974. When Cash was honored by President Bill Clinton at the Kennedy Center in Washington, D.C., in 1996, Holiff sent him a congratulatory note. In a return letter, Cash wrote, "It was so nice to hear from you after all these years. We often reminisce about the years we worked together, and always know that we think well of you."

Sometimes people part ways.

Sometimes it's for the best.

Johnny was trying to follow the counsel of Scripture, which says, "Do all that you can to live in peace with everyone" (Romans 12:18 NLT).

That is not the easiest thing to do.

But Saul Holiff was wrong. Johnny's best days were not behind him.

They were, in fact, before him—but that would happen quite a bit later.

As Saul Holiff rode off into the sunset, Cash's relationship with Columbia Records began to erode. A series of albums recorded in the House of Cash studios, in an office building Cash bought in Hendersonville in 1970, showed Cash to be creatively at a standstill. *The Johnny Cash Children's Album, Junkie and the Juicehead Minus Me,* and *John R. Cash* were all weak efforts that tanked right out of the gate.

According to Marshall Grant, it was hard to even get Cash into the studio, which was just a stone's throw from his lake home. That was partly due to his demanding touring schedule, which sapped a lot of his energy. When he did hit the studio, Cash was uninspired, worked at his own pace, and wasn't much for accepting guidance. He did make the Top 20 album list in '74 with *Ragged Old Flag*; and in April '76 reached the top of the country singles chart with "One Piece at a Time," a novelty tune about an automobile built from stolen car parts. That was the last time he reached the top spot in the 1970s. Cash would fare even worse in the following decade.

But he remained a big draw on the road, as evidenced by a record-breaking Billy Graham Crusade in Seattle's Kingdome in March 1976.

"The Kingdome had just opened, and approximately seventy-five thousand people jammed the venue including the floor to see Johnny Cash and June Carter Cash sing as well as hear Billy Graham," said Tom Phillips of the Billy Graham Evangelical Association. "We had an enormous number of various commitments for Christ that evening—many of whom, perhaps, would not have heard Billy Graham's message had it not been for Johnny and June's presence. It's an attendance record that was never broken."

Once a controversial counterculture figure who wasn't afraid to buck the status quo, Cash's concerts had become so family-friendly he was often thanked for having a "clean show." His new image as a flag-draped, traditional-values conservative was just what organizers of America's Bicentennial celebration were looking for when the country celebrated its 200th birthday in 1976 with big public galas and TV specials. Cash hosted a program on NBC that wove the story of the circus into America's history, and he served as grand marshal (with Ray riding shotgun) at the July 4 Bicentennial Parade in Washington, D.C. Afterward, Cash performed a concert at the Washington Monument and rang a replica of the Liberty Bell. He also performed a benefit for the American Freedom Train that carted historical artifacts for public viewing across the nation that year.

In the summer of '76, *Johnny Cash and Friends* aired Sunday nights on CBS. Shot at the new Grand Ole Opry House in Nashville (not the Ryman Auditorium), the program showcased Cash as the Mount Rushmore-like figure he had become. The show also featured comedians Steve Martin and Jim Varney, June Carter Cash performing comedy routines as "Aunt Polly," and a generous heaping of gospel songs. Also in '76 came the first of *The Johnny Cash Christmas Specials* that would be annual televised holiday fare until 1985.

Any misgivings the onetime Great Rebel may have had about his new status as an American totem were swept aside by the matter that had been getting Cash's undivided attention when he and June signed up for a correspondence course on the Bible in 1975. For the next three years, at home and on tour, they assiduously worked on lesson plans from the Christian International School of Theology, then based in Phoenix, Arizona. Johnny had learned of the school through his sister Joanne and her husband, Harry Yates.

"John was an avid student of history," Yates said. "He loved history more than anything—except he loved the Bible more, and of course, Bible history would be his greatest thing to talk about. He loved the Old and New Testaments. He loved to go to Israel and see all the places where Jesus walked because it was historical. It was really his passion."

Few knew at the time that Cash was working towards an Associate of Theology degree—and that he was even considering giving up show business to become a full-time minister. He eventually abandoned the latter idea on the ground he would be labeled a "celebrity preacher" who attracted people who wanted their picture taken with him more than anything else. June reminded him that he could reach far more people through his music than the ministry.

Johnny's thirst for the scriptures was unquenchable—especially the Apostle Paul, a special fixation because Cash so related to him as a man.

"The Apostle Paul inspires me," Cash said. "There's a man who set out to conquer the world in the name of Jesus Christ and did it . . . I can relate to him."

It should not come as a surprise that Johnny was drawn to Paul.

The great apostle was once a very wicked man. The mere mention of his name sent shivers down the backbone of many a first-century

Christian, as Saul made it his mission in life to hunt them down and kill them.

The Bible described him as a behaving like a "wild beast," breathing out threats (Acts 9:1).

But the Lord got hold of the notorious Saul and transformed him into the great Apostle Paul.

Saul knew he was the worst of sinners who was a recipient of God's grace.

Johnny knew the same was true of him as well.

Cash often retreated to Bon Aqua, a 107-acre farm about an hour's drive from Hendersonville, to do his coursework. He came to own the place in 1972 after he discovered an accountant had embezzled money from him. Rather than prosecute, Cash had the thief give him title to all the properties he'd purchased with the stolen funds. Bon Aqua was one of them. The two-story farmhouse there was built in 1847 by a retired veteran of the Mexican War. It became Cash's special sanctuary where he read and studied, wrote songs, and took long walks to reflect in peace. He once called it the "center of my universe."

"John was pulled in a lot of different directions and had so many demands on his time that it killed his creativity for a while," said niece Kelly Hancock. "It was go, go, go for so many years, and Bon Aqua was a light in the dark for him. He could go there and decompress, sit on the front porch and listen to the birds and the cows. It brought him back to who he was, which was a country boy from Arkansas."

Mornings at Bon Aqua started with coffee and reading the Bible, which Cash said "sets me up for a good day." During his sixty credit hours of study to obtain his degree, Johnny consulted many, including Pop Carter, Rev. Jimmie Snow, and Pastor Harry Yates.

That Cash had a brilliant mind is attested to by Dr. Wilford S. Hamon, president of the Christian International School of Theology.

"I graded some of his course work and found his answers to the questions and theological essays were as good as any preachers' courses I had graded," said Dr. Hamon, noting that only 30 percent of people who started the course actually finished it. "John took courses in the Old and New Testaments but concentrated on courses on the books of the Bible that Apostle Paul wrote. He also took a special course on the life and ministry of Paul."

These, of course, prepared Cash to write his 1986 book covering that subject called *Man in White*.

Cash completed the coursework for his degree on March 6, 1977. The following May, Dr. Hamon flew to Nashville to personally present it to him in a small ceremony at the House of Cash. Pat Robertson's Christian Broadcast Network heard about it and arranged to record the event. Cash sported a black mortarboard and gown as he proudly posed for pictures.

In the early 1980s, Cash called Dr. Hamon as he was about to embark on a trip to Israel. His intention was to baptize some friends in the Jordan River, and Cash wanted to be sure his ministerial credentials qualified him to do so.

"He met the requirements, so Christian International Ministerial Association ordained John as a minister of the Gospel of Jesus Christ," Dr. Hamon said. "John did not want his ordination to be made public, and we honored his request. Very few people ever knew that John had been ordained. It is probably one of the secrets that the world did not know about Johnny Cash."

The Man in Black was also a man of the cloth.

28

A CONTRAST IN KINGS

"I confess right up front that I'm the biggest sinner
of them all. But my faith in God has always been
a solid rock that I've stood on, no matter where I
was or what I was doing. I was a bad boy at times,
but God was always there for me, and I knew that.
I guess maybe I took advantage of that."

—JOHNNY CASH

John R. Cash was a seeker, and when seekers look for something
and find it, they become very committed to it. Every undertaking
was epic. Every task was done at full steam or with no enthusiasm
whatsoever. There was little middle ground.

Cash's fame had become a high-speed treadmill, and he had
become a slave to the grind. He had family obligations, charity

projects, award dinners and benefits, Billy Graham Crusades and endless touring. He had little down time because of his massive obligations to others and his own lifestyle.

His career ultimately suffered because of his long list of obligations. Cash wanted to take young John Carter with him everywhere, which meant bringing a nanny and a bodyguard on tour. The regular traveling troupe, including the Carter Family, was expensive, too. He also took a contingent of thirty people to Israel during this time, a considerable expense that included first-class airplane accommodations, five-star hotels, and guided tours.

It took a financial toll. There was little time to write or reflect. Cash seemed distracted.

What preparation did Johnny Cash have for such an enterprise? He had gone literally from picking cotton in Arkansas to worldwide fame.

He had an unusual and very special God-given talent for touching people through music. Not only that, people just connected to Johnny as a person.

But he had not been properly prepared to effectively be a CEO of a massive organization.

Johnny liked solitude and observing people.

This became fertile soil for his songs.

He needed to "un-plug" in order to "plug-in'" and connect to people.

But, disconnected from that, going from project to project to keep feeding the "machine" that his band, family, and large organization had become was a daunting task to say the least. It was not playing to his strengths but to his weaknesses.

I know a bit about this myself.

When I started out as a young pastor at the age of twenty, my primary focus was on teaching the Bible and helping a small group of believers to grow spiritually.

Fast-forward many decades, and we have far more people on our staff then we had in our church in the early days and thousands that attend one of our multiple campuses.

That, of course, requires attention to detail, and I often find myself spending more time on administration than I do on what I think I am really called to do.

Johnny was experiencing that on a far larger scale, and when Johnny was under pressure, he would often turn to familiar crutches and vices.

Since 1968, Cash's career had careened from legitimate to ludicrous, and by the late '70s, he had in some ways become a caricature of himself. Contemporaries Kenny Rogers, Dolly Parton, Merle Haggard, and Glen Campbell were far outselling him. By then, the Outlaw movement had kicked in, led by Waylon Jennings, Willie Nelson, Jessi Colter, and Tompall Glaser. Their renegade sound was orchestrated by Hollywood producer Ken Mansfield, who brought Los Angeles-style production techniques to Nashville. Cash was friendly with the aforementioned artists, and in November 2018, I asked Mansfield why his outlaw buddies didn't invite Cash to join them.

"I've asked myself that same question over the years, and the only thing I can come up with is that Cash wasn't an Outlaw at that point in his career but more of an icon," Mansfield said. "It felt like he was unapproachable in a way—like James Dean or Steve McQueen—and wasn't the kind of person you could really pin down and put a defining tag on."

Mansfield first met Cash and June though Waylon Jennings in the 1970s. To Mansfield, Jennings was a one-of-a-kind figure, an outlaw on the outside and the inside who wasn't afraid of anyone or anything, except maybe himself.

"Waylon was the most charismatic man I had ever known," said Mansfield, "and I had worked with the Beatles, Buck Owens, Roy Orbison, and Glen Campbell. But Johnny Cash's charisma towered over Waylon's. Waylon was almost deferential to Cash in a way. It was interesting to watch and experience."

Cash's enduring charisma notwithstanding, the public's tastes had changed. A new traditionalist movement had taken root. Record buyers were now putting their dollars behind country artists such as Waylon Jennings, Willie Nelson, George Jones, Charley Pride, Dolly Parton, Loretta Lynn, Conway Twitty, Crystal Gayle, Ronnie Milsap, and Kenny Rogers.

Cash's late 1970s output—*The Last Gunfighter Ballad, Look at Them Beans, Strawberry Cake,* and *The Rambler*—was stale and out of touch. He swung and missed at a song called "The Gambler," written by Don Schlitz two years before and brought to Cash at a recording session in July 1978 by Larry Butler, who played piano on the road for Cash and moonlighted as a producer. The problem was that Johnny had gone back to his old ways and was using amphetamines again. According to Marshall Grant, during the session, Cash repeatedly ducked into the bathroom, emerging higher every time, with the result that the day-long session spun out of control. Nevertheless, they ended up with what Grant considered a great recording of "The Gambler," only to have Cash select three other songs from his *Gone Girl* album to showcase the LP. None of them made a dent on the country charts and all were quickly forgotten.

Larry Butler also produced Kenny Rogers, and he took "The Gambler" to him. Rogers' version became an instant smash, hitting No. 1 on the country singles charts and No. 16 on the pop charts, and most importantly, reviving his flagging career and pushing him into the superstar realm.

Marshall Grant said that Cash had climbed back aboard the amphetamine rollercoaster on January 29, 1977, in New Haven, Connecticut. Before the band's 5 p.m. sound check, Grant was told by a security guard that Cash was already there. That was odd because Cash never showed up for a sound check when he was straight. When Grant saw Johnny's eyes as he walked off the stage, he made a beeline for his dressing room and accosted him.

"Why, John? Just please, tell me why?" Grant asked. "You've had all these good years. You've got the world by the tail. You're *the* man in country music. You have a great family, a great wife. You've got everything a man could dream of. Why have you turned your back on them?"

Cash's response was that he was going through "the change of life" and would be fine. That night, Cash did a decent show. No one in the cast or crew noticed anything unusual. But when Grant saw June backstage, her own eyes said it all. She knew.

Months later, on August 16, 1977, Elvis Presley died. He and Cash hadn't seen each other in some time, but The King's death hit Cash hard. They had come up through the ranks together to become the biggest entertainers in the world—Elvis in rock and roll, Cash in country music.

"I didn't try to invade his privacy," Cash said. "I'm so glad I didn't, either, because so many of his old friends were embarrassed when they were turned away at Graceland. He and I liked each other, but we weren't that tight."

The two were just about the mirror image of each other in their respective musical genres. Both had reached the top in a very short amount of time, and their stardom crossed over into other mediums— film, television, touring, and even domination of Las Vegas.

Elvis had his flirtation with amphetamines in the Army and movie years. He first took them to keep up during field maneuvers on training exercises. He also liked how they kept his weight down.

In the concert years of the '70s, Elvis switched from uppers to downers to bring himself down from the high of performing. The pills started Presley on a toboggan slide whose end was a crash landing no one could have predicted or imagined.

The last three and a half years of his life were a mental and physical meltdown. Many have pointed to Elvis's divorce from his wife Priscilla as the catalyst for his unraveling, but there were many other factors as well. The common denominator linking all those things was his escalating abuse of prescription medication. His medicine cabinet was filled with industrial-sized bottles of Nembutal, Seconal, Benzadrine, Dexadrine, and Tuinal. He was also taking Demerol and Dilaudid— stuff they gave to last-stage cancer patients.

Elvis experienced periods of wild mood swings, erratic behavior, compulsiveness, and weight gain. He became totally unreachable, even by the people who loved him. After tours, he wouldn't come out of his room for weeks.

The only time Elvis appeared to sober up was when his daughter Lisa Marie came to visit, which wasn't for long stretches due to his problem. Her visits were just a brief interruption in a long, downhill slide.

Addiction killed Elvis Presley, and did it in the most humiliating and gut-wrenching way. Prescription drugs robbed Elvis of everything— music, family, friends, finances, and his future—and there wasn't a thing anyone could do about it.

Cash was perilously close to walking over the edge of the same cliff, but he didn't take that final step like Presley.

"[Cash] survived what Elvis didn't survive," noted Rodney Crowell, Johnny's former son-in-law.

Years later, Cash was much more sentimental about Elvis when he spoke of his death. He told CBN's Scott Ross: "Elvis may have had a stronger relationship with God than I did. God gives us life and takes us away as He sees fit. I don't say Elvis died because of drugs. I say God decided it was time for him to die. I don't believe any of the trash I've read about him. God's the final judge for Elvis Presley and Johnny Cash too. That's solely in the hands of God."

When asked to explain his own fall from grace in the 1970s after declaring to the world that he'd cleaned up, Cash said, "I never lost my faith during that time, but I lost my contact with God because anyone on drugs or alcohol chronically becomes very selfish. You don't think about anyone else. You think about where your next stash is coming from or your next drink. I wasted a lot of time and energy. I mean, we're not talking just days, but months and years."

Drugs were Johnny's Achilles heel, and they hounded him over the years.

"Everybody was well aware that John struggled and was on the fence," said former House of Cash employee Rick Scott. "In that era, people were experimenting with a lot of things, drugs, alcohol, even religion. He was struggling, and it was pretty evident why: his childhood was tough to overcome. One day, it was totally God, and the next day it would be a demon."

Despite bad decisions Cash made, God still was at work in and through him.

When our lives go off the rails, God is more than willing to forgive and restore us.

There is a fascinating passage where God promises to Israel to restore that which had been eaten by the locusts (Joel 2:25). In the same way, the Lord can restore back to the Christian that which was lost if we will own up to our sins and turn from them.

From time to time, Cash would try to slow down his drug use—especially when he was participating in a Billy Graham Crusade.

At a February 1978 Crusade in Las Vegas attended by more than fifty thousand people over five days, Cash met musician Reggie Vinson. Vinson had worked and recorded with such esteemed artists as Alice Cooper, Chuck Berry, and John Lennon. He lived in Vegas at the time and had recently received Christ as his Lord and Savior by watching one of Graham's Crusades on television. When he told Johnny and June about his hot-off-the-press born-again experience, June shouted, "Thank you, Lord! Another sinner has come to the Lord. Let's all pray."

They prayed and opened their hearts to one another. "Johnny reminded me of an old-time gospel preacher with sincere words of truth," Vinson said. "He would laugh and carry on, and he could get serious and talk about what the Lord had done in his life." Vinson could tell Cash was very sensitive about the fact that some Christians continued to pass judgment on him because he sang secular music and played in some less-than-temple-like venues.

"Reggie, they don't know how far I've come," Cash said.

It was true: Johnny had come so far. Of course, he, like all Christians, still had a long way to go. He struggled in life, as all believers do in some way, shape, or form. Even the great Apostle Paul, whom Johnny admired and followed, admitted to his struggles and need to continue to grow spiritually.

"I'm not saying that I have this all together, that I have it made. But I am well on my way, reaching out for Christ, who has so wondrously reached out for me. Friends, don't get me wrong: By no means do I count myself an expert in all of this, but I've got my eye on the goal, where God is beckoning us onward—to Jesus. I'm off and running, and I'm not turning back" (Philippians 3:13 MSG).

Marshall Grant said at the time only he and June knew about Cash's relapse. "I'm certain nobody connected with the Crusades knew because he was straight enough to be the old, affable J.R.," Grant said.

He couldn't keep up the facade. Within a few years, the Billy Graham and Rex Humbard organizations would temporarily remove Johnny Cash from their Crusade rosters.

29

SWIMMING IN DIFFERENT DIRECTIONS

"I learn from my mistakes. It's a very painful way
to learn, but without pain, the old saying is,
there's no gain."

—JOHNNY CASH

The Christian life is not a playground; it's more like a battleground. Some days we advance, and other days we may have to retreat.

All of us constantly misstep and make mistakes. Some people who come to Christ never go back to their former lives, but others do not fall so nicely into that category. That was Johnny Cash's trap. He even rationalized his backsliding by saying, "You aren't a good Christian unless you've suffered."

There is some truth to that as the Bible tells us that trials, adversity, and hardship can strengthen us spiritually (James 1:3).

It's been said, "Christians are a lot like teabags: you don't know what they are made of until you put them in hot water."

However, sometimes we create our own problems by bad decisions.

We all go through spiritual "storms" in life—storm being a metaphor for hardship, conflict, or difficulty.

There are both perfecting and correcting storms.

First, there are those perfecting storms, meaning things we have no control of that happen in our lives. This was the kind of storm Job went through when all kinds of calamity befell him, including the loss of his fortune, health, and—worst of all—the deaths of his children.

The death of Johnny's brother Jack would fit into this category. For better or worse, it contributed to the man Johnny became later in life. It brought maturity and spiritual growth, but also a lot of pain into the singer's life.

But then there are those calamities and repercussions that we bring upon ourselves.

These would be correcting storms.

That was the case with the original "Chicken of the Sea," Jonah, who was called by God to preach to the people of Nineveh. Jonah caught a ship going in the opposite direction. Then the Lord sent a mighty storm to get the reluctant prophet's attention, and it worked.

A lot of Johnny's storms were ones he brought unnecessarily upon himself.

Cash's life was filled with contradictions, so it stands to reason that his devotion to God was likewise. That doesn't excuse his behavior, but it does help to explain him. He acted humble, but like most celebrities and famous people, he had an ego and insecurities that required constant stoking and stroking. There were struggles and inconsistencies and addiction, different shades of darkness, varying depths of sadness that came with his chronic abuse of drugs. He seemed to be swimming in different directions at all times, and too often was barely treading water.

His bad behavior wasn't confined to taking drugs. Out of the blue one day while on tour, Cash instructed Marshall Grant, who made the hotel arrangements for the band, to put him and June in separate bedrooms. When *The National Enquirer* caught wind of the new arrangement and the rumors of adultery swirling around it, the supermarket tabloid offered to handsomely reward anyone in Cash's camp who would provide proof of anything illicit and salacious going on.

Johnny Western said he was offered $2,500 to give up the name, but his cowboy code would not allow him to betray his friend and boss. The tabloid snoops then tried enlisting Cash's sister Reba, offering her $5,000. No deal.

While Cash was off the hook, June checked into The Mayo Clinic in Rochester, Minnesota, for treatment of her skyrocketing anxiety. When the tour ended, she flew to London alone and then asked an attorney to draw up divorce papers. Cash's behavior and lifestyle was grating on June, and their relationship was coming apart. Johnny flew to England to talk her out of leaving him.

Cash always went back to what was true and had a knack for turning his suffering around. It usually started with repenting and returning to the spiritual well. Sometime in the mid-1970s, the Cashes left Evangel Temple to become members of the Hendersonville Church of God. In March 1979, when John Carter turned nine, Johnny presided over his baptism in the Jordan River by Church of God pastor John Colbaugh and was baptized again himself for the third time in his life. It was a proud day.

"I have no greater joy than to see my children walking in truth," Cash said more than once about his offspring.

With his family fractured due to bad decisions in the past, it was a wonderful thing for Johnny to see his son being raised in a cohesive, God-fearing home. Like Cash stated, it is always a great source of joy for Christian parents to see their children internalize their faith and make it their own.

In March and June of 1979, Johnny and June appeared at Billy Graham Crusades in Tampa and Nashville. That year, he also released the gospel double-album *A Believer Sings the Truth*, calling it the album he'd always wanted to do. It was not a commercial success (it sold thirty thousand copies) but Cash's devotion to gospel music was still a vital part of who he was.

"Gospel music was the thing that inspired me as a child growing up on a cotton farm, where work was drudgery and it was so hard that when I was in the field I sang all the time," Cash said. "Gospel songs lifted me up above that black dirt."

Cash also jumped head-first into his book on the Apostle Paul. He spent hours roaming through bookstores and scouring libraries for other books and articles. Cash considered Paul a hero and was endlessly intrigued by his education and his transformation from fierce persecutor of Christians to the most famous of Jesus's followers. Johnny first wanted to write a formal biography of Paul, but, worried that he wasn't a good enough biblical scholar, he decided to write Paul's story as a novel. It would take another seven years for it to be published.

Cash had a minor and short-lived resurgence in 1979 when he recorded the album *Silver*, the title a reference to his quarter-century in the music business. While the single "Ghost Riders in the Sky" reached No. 2 on the country singles charts and was a solid radio hit, it wasn't enough to buoy the album, and it sank quickly.

Sadly, Johnny descended into pills once again. By the early months of 1980, he and Marshall Grant were barely speaking to each other. Cash was running out of money, having spent lavishly on drugs, Lear jets, properties, shopping sprees, payroll, and the constant touring necessities. He had a meeting with his bookkeeper in Nashville at which Cash pointedly asked how much Grant was getting paid. Grant heard about it, and after a show in Houston, as Cash's limo pulled away, he was further unnerved by a "God-awful, smirky smile" Cash fixed on him until the car was out of sight.

A few days later, a registered letter informed Grant that after twenty-five years, his musical services were no longer required. The language in the letter was so nasty Grant thought Cash must've written it while on a drug binge. Turned out, he was right.

Cash told people he fired Grant because he had stolen a million dollars from him and took kickbacks from airlines and hotels when arranging tours. Few believed it. Grant's devotion to Cash from their start together back in Memphis was well known. It was also a fact that Grant had no access to Johnny's money and, therefore, no opportunity to siphon off any of it. Kickbacks? Grant said he worked hard to drive the best bargain, including having baggage fees for their instruments waived, getting comped suites and food for Cash, and hiring additional security for John Carter on the road. Grant said his many years of experience and the connections he'd built up earned him all those extras and only benefitted the Johnny Cash organization.

Cash maintained that when he asked Grant several times to assemble the band to rehearse a specific song for an upcoming rodeo, Grant blew him off. On Cash's bus during a California tour in February, Cash was looking over a map in an effort to help the bus driver find the venue. Grant knew virtually every back road in America thanks to his years on the road, and seeing Cash puzzling over the map, he made it a point to embarrass him in front of everyone by brusquely ordering him to give him the map as if Cash were a clueless child.

Cash historian Mark Stielper found Grant's account of the situation plausible enough. He doesn't give Cash a pass while saying the fault for the breakdown of the relationship was not entirely Johnny's— nor was it sudden.

"Marshall Grant was growing more and more insufferable and forgot who was the boss, as he frequently did over the years," Stielper said. "Cash was not in the mood to be scolded anymore, even if he deserved it at times. One minus one left zero."

In December 1980, Grant filed suit against Cash for $2.6 million in lost wages and damages resulting from allegedly slanderous statements.

In depositions, Cash was his own worst enemy—when he bothered to show up for them at all. He was usually high and rambled through one disjointed and incoherent story after another. Under cross-examination, he contradicted himself, and when pressed, he refused to answer any more questions or tried to change the subject.

Grant's lawsuit was settled without a trial, but it took nine years to reach a conclusion. Neither party was allowed to disclose the terms of the settlement, but within hours, the word around Nashville was that Cash agreed to pay Grant close to $1 million. It would be more than a decade before the old friends spoke again. Meanwhile, prompted by Grant's suit, the children of Luther Perkins also sued Cash for monies supposedly owed to their late father. Their case was reportedly settled for a smaller sum than Grant's.

"Will the Circle Be Unbroken?" was a Christian hymn long identified with Johnny Cash and June Carter. Now it was also a question asked by Cash's family and friends as his behavior continued its spiraling descent. They could only pray, "By and by, Lord, by and by."

30

——

WHERE'S WALDO?

"I have people who say to me, 'I want you
to sound like you did in 1955 on Sun.'
I can't sing that way anymore, and people don't
record that way anymore . . . But honesty in
performance and freedom of delivery,
that's where it's at."

—JOHNNY CASH

The 1980s weren't kind to Johnny Cash.

The decade was filled with setbacks, mishaps, and misadventures that surely would have killed a lesser man. Cash experienced a precipitous drop in popularity, a fight to stay relevant, lukewarm record sales, a worsening drug addiction, marital woes, a robbery at gunpoint, financial problems, and health scares that nearly took him out.

One of the last was courtesy of an ostrich named Waldo.

Waldo lived in the exotic animal compound behind the House of Cash offices, and in September '81, he was the sole survivor of a cold spell that croaked the rest of the ostrich population there, including Waldo's mate. In his grief and isolation, Waldo went rogue. As Cash walked through the compound, the eight-foot bird materialized and crouched in front of him with wings out, hissing menacingly. Cash froze, and for several moments, they stood there like a couple of gunfighters. Waldo backed off, but a few minutes later, he returned, fully locked and loaded. By then, Cash had wisely armed himself with a six-foot-long stick, and the battle was joined.

Johnny's home run swing missed because the 250-pound Waldo leaped straight up into the air. He came down with his razor-like claws extended, breaking two of Cash's ribs and ripping open his stomach. Only the big metal belt buckle he wore prevented Johnny from being disemboweled. Before Cash managed to get a lick in with the stick and drive Waldo off, the ostrich broke three more of his ribs.

(Waldo won the battle but lost the war. According to those in the know, the battling ostrich's final resting place—semi-final, actually—was Cash's freezer.)

Cash was stitched and bound up at the hospital and sent back home with a bottle of painkillers. Under the circumstances, he needed them. But as his ribs and wounds healed, he kept taking them because he "liked the way they made me feel." Soon he was going around to different doctors to keep himself well stocked. When the painkillers upset his stomach, he started drinking wine to settle it down. It also took the sharp edges off the amphetamines he'd begun adding to the mix.

Three months later, Cash and his family faced a danger that made Waldo seem as threatening as Big Bird. It happened at their Cinnamon Hill retreat in Montego Bay, Jamaica. Cash started visiting the country in the early 1970s and fell in love with the land, the great weather, and its people. Almost immediately, he and June became a part of the community by performing a number of benefit concerts there. They were also on hand to inaugurate the S.O.S. Children's Village in nearby Barrett Town when it first opened in 1972. Afterward, they demonstrated their Christian faith by making time to visit and care for orphans at the site whenever they visited, and they also financially supported them over the years.

Cash lived like a baron inside his Caribbean retreat, which was built in 1747 and was once a sugar plantation. His every need was seen to by a full-time staff of housekeepers and cooks. The opulence and relaxed atmosphere was in marked contrast to the poverty and violence rampant just beyond Cash's front gate. Cash confidant and friend Mark Stielper visited the compound four times, remembering, "The drive from the airport to the house was terrifying. It was littered with artifacts from many killings—memorials, bullet holes, police presence. John told me, 'Do not stop for anyone or anything until you get to my gate.'"

On an evening in late December 1981, the Cashes had just sat down to dinner with Johnny's sister Reba and her husband Chuck Hussey, cook and housekeeper Edith Montague, archeologist Ray Fremmer, and John Carter and his friend Doug Caldwell, when three men wearing nylon stockings over their heads burst into the room.

"Somebody's going to die here tonight!" yelled one of them.

The intruders were armed with a machete, a knife, and a pistol. They told Cash that if he didn't fork over $1 million, they would kill a member of his family. Cash stayed calm, said he didn't have that kind of money around, and invited the bandits to help themselves to several thousand in cash in a briefcase underneath a bed and to June's jewelry, worth a considerable amount.

For two terrifying hours, the thieves held them hostage. They were forced to lie on the floor, and at one point, a pistol was put to John Carter's head and a swatch of June's hair was cut off. Finally, the thieves locked everyone in the basement and escaped in June's Land Rover with an estimated $50,000 in loot.

The hostages freed themselves by battering down a two-inch thick mahogany door with a coat tree and summoned the police. Two of the intruders were apprehended as they tried to board a plane for Miami at Donald Sangster International Airport. They were later killed attempting to escape from prison. The third intruder was killed a few weeks later resisting arrest.

It's long been rumored that the robbery was an inside job, masterminded by a relative of one of Cash's staff at Cinnamon Hill. In any case, it didn't keep Johnny and his family from coming back to Jamaica, though after that, he hired an armed security detail for the estate and carried a gun there himself.

Back home, Johnny returned to business as usual on the tour-record-promote grind. Not that there was much to promote or brag about. *Rockabilly Blues* (1980) and *The Baron* (1981) were mostly forgettable efforts save for the Top 10 single "The Baron," which got a boost from the success of the movie *Urban Cowboy*. The John Travolta-Debra Winger popcorn flick became a cultural phenomenon and boosted the popularity of country music across the board.

Cash received more attention from a made-for-television drama called *The Pride of Jesse Hallam* that aired on CBS in March 1981. He played an illiterate coal miner from Kentucky who learns how to read and write and gets his high school diploma. Cash received stellar reviews, with the *New York Times* saying, "His acting techniques may be leaden, but he projects a natural and disarming sense of solidity. The deep, resonant voice booms out with authority while hinting at a basic gentleness. On screen, Mr. Cash dominates with enviable ease. He's just there."

The departure of Marshall Grant resulted in a radical reconfiguration of Cash's backup band. He recruited Joe Allen, one of Nashville's most respected bass players, to replace Grant, and he also brought aboard W. S. Holland, Bob Wootton, Earl Ball, Jerry Hensley, Jack Hale, Jr., Bob Lewin, and Marty Stuart (who would become the boss's son-in-law when he married Cindy Cash). The new band was called the Great Eighties Eight, but they were only pretty good. The new band members did not help revive Cash's sagging career.

Johnny's turning fifty years old resulted in bizarre outbursts and behavior. The milestone coincided with his daughter Rosanne's success as a recording artist; she scored five No. 1 country hits in the 1980s. While Cash was proud of her, he couldn't help but feel somewhat territorial.

"When I was having my hit records, my dad and I felt competitive with each other," Rosanne Cash told *Rolling Stone's* Anthony DeCurtis. "He admitted it later. I mean, he would ask me about my contract and how many points I was getting. We went through that phase. But when he felt that I was pulling away from him, he gave me a lot of space. I think it probably hurt him some."

Cash was hurting, so he hit back. One incident manifested when he threw a hatchet over the head of producer Brian Ahern during the studio sessions for *Johnny 99*, his 1983 album; it stuck in the wall behind Ahern. Once, Johnny abandoned a recording session when struck by a sudden hankering for milk and cheese, and on his way to buy some, he drove his silver Mercedes into a ditch, and the car caught fire. It made the evening news.

When *Johnny 99*—which contained the Bruce Springsteen songs "Highway Patrolman" and "Johnny 99"—tanked, Cash was at the end of his rope, professionally and personally. He and June had terrible screaming matches and knock-down, drag-out fights. During a tour stop in Montreux, Switzerland, June told him she was leaving him after the final show. But she didn't follow through.

In November 1983, Cash trashed a hotel room in Nottingham, England, during a drug-induced hallucination that so convinced him there was a Murphy bed behind one of the room's walls that he ripped away the wood veneer with his bare hands. A large sliver imbedded itself in his right hand. The resulting wound became badly infected, and Cash's hand swelled to almost twice its normal size. He told the press he had been bitten by a poisonous spider.

Back in Nashville, Cash went to Baptist Hospital to have his infected hand treated. Doctors ran him through a battery of tests, and discovered Cash also had a bleeding ulcer. They ended up taking out his spleen and several feet of intestine. Manager Lou Robin was so concerned he called June, who was still seething from his bizarre behavior and had stayed behind in London, and implored her to come home immediately because Johnny might be dying.

 He wasn't, but not for lack of trying. Johnny called daughter Kathy from his bed in the intensive care unit and asked her to bring him a six-pack of beer and some pills. She refused, so he hung up on her. Cash eventually succeeded in having Percodan, amphetamines, and even Valium smuggled in to him. He hid the Valium under the dressings on his large abdominal incision.

When he started fading in and out of consciousness two days later, his doctors were mystified until they found half the Valium under his dressing. The other half had seeped through his incision into his blood stream. Between that and the morphine Cash was already getting, he was perilously close to an overdose.

All visitors were barred except June, though an exception was made for Johnny's mother. Cash later recalled feeling Carrie's hand on his forehead and hearing her pray, "Lord, You took one of my boys, and if You're going to take this one, he's Yours to take. But I ask You, let him live and teach him to serve You better. Surely, You have work for him to do."

What an amazing prayer for his mother to pray. Having already lost Jack, she did not want to lose Johnny as well. The evangelist Billy Sunday once said, "There is more power in a mother's hand than in a king's scepter." Carrie Cash's prayers were heard and answered.

Johnny's physical condition slowly improved, but doctors said he was doomed without psychological therapy to break his addictions. Through the hospital, the family contacted the Betty Ford Center in Rancho Mirage, California, co-founded a year earlier by the former First Lady, who herself suffered for years from alcohol addiction.

To convince Cash to check into the drug and alcohol treatment facility, June and Cash's children staged an intervention led by a specialist from the hospital. They each read letters to Johnny that expressed their worries and detailed how his addiction had impacted their lives. John Carter, now a teenager, reminded his father of several embarrassing episodes played out in front of his friends, and when he finished, a chastened Cash hugged him tightly and declared, "I want to go. I want to get some help."

Johnny always wanted to be a good father, and he took special pride in John Carter's baptism, but now the legendary singer was behaving more like a child.

It was time for a change.

The Bible promises that God "causes all things to work together for good for those who love Him" (Romans 8:28 NKJV).

These episodes and this intervention would get Cash back on track . . . again.

31

ROCK BOTTOM
AND TOP OF THE POPS

"Many times, I was aware enough to pray,
and many times, in my pain and mental terror,
I felt that warm presence of the Great Healer,
and I always knew that I would live and that I
wasn't finished for Him yet."

—JOHNNY CASH

We are all mere flesh-and-blood humans.

No matter our skin color or how beautiful or handsome we may be on the outside, we are basically the same. Regardless of our talents or abilities, we are not really all that different from one another.

Deep down inside, we all long for the same thing.

We are essentially born with a hole in our heart.

It's a hole that nothing, no person or experience, can fill. The finest education, the greatest morality, even being deeply religious cannot fill it.

It's a hole only God can fill.

It's a longing for a relationship with God, and it's a longing for Heaven itself.

C. S. Lewis called it the "inconsolable longing." He wrote, "If I find in myself a desire which no experience in this world can satisfy, the most probable explanation is that I was made for another world. If none of my earthly pleasures satisfy it, that does not prove that the universe is a fraud. Probably earthly pleasures were never meant to satisfy it, but only to arouse it, to suggest the real thing."

Johnny Cash wanted that relationship with God, but he would get pulled back time and time again to his old ways.

Most of us have no idea of the caliber of temptation that comes to those who possess great wealth and power. Johnny was no exception to that rule.

However, he was a Christian, now and he had God's promise that, with every temptation, there was always a way out (1 Corinthians 10:13).

The problem for Johnny was he did not always want to look for that escape route. It reminds me of the words of the famous raconteur and Victorian bon vivant, Oscar Wilde: "The only way to get rid of a temptation is to yield to it."

Johnny had done that one time too many.

But unlike Wilde, Cash knew where to go when he fell.

He would return to the Lord.

That is really the mark of the true Christian—where they end up.

Johnny always knew where home was spiritually for him. It was in the church and staying close to God.

So thank God that He's the God of second and third chances, ad infinitum.

Johnny Cash was given more chances than most, and therefore tested the infinity of God's patience more than most.

But to his credit, whenever he was knocked down, Cash got up, dusted himself off, and humbled himself before God. Whatever his faults—and there were many—he was smart enough to know that all beginnings and endings were in the hands of the Creator.

At the Betty Ford Center, where Cash spent Christmas 1983, addiction therapy and recovery is based on a twelve-step set of principles. Doctors devised an individualized treatment plan for him so that he could learn to live his life without the crutch of drugs or alcohol. Cash lived in a dormitory and, as did the other patients, had to clean toilets, vacuum floors, make beds, and perform other daily chores.

"They make a big deal out of that, but it's just like cleaning up your room if you're camping out somewhere or in a dormitory," Cash told British morning TV hosts Mike Morris and Lorraine Kelly. "I did it as a matter of course, and that's what anybody else would do in those places."

Other things that took place in rehab, like board and guessing games, stripped away all the artifices of superstardom, Cash said.

"We'd sit around on the floor playing guessing games and kids' games and find ourselves really laughing at it," Cash said. "Just bring you back to the basics. It made me realize that I was human and just like everyone else."

He also met with a counselor and attended group lectures on addiction; a daily talk was delivered by Betty Ford herself, who had been addicted to alcohol and the medication taken for arthritis. Her April 1978 public admission about abusing alcohol and drugs ended several years of speculation by friends and the press fueled by her frequently slurred speech.

Other celebrity patients at the Ford Center during Cash's stay there included rocker Ozzy Osbourne and movie star Elizabeth Taylor. Cash and Taylor discovered they were born one day apart in 1932. It was the start of an unlikely friendship, and they would exchange birthday cards for years.

It took about three weeks of treatment for Cash to achieve what he called his "awakening." During that time, his counselor was tough on him, accepting no excuses and demanding "rigid honesty" from Cash.

"I've had people say that they felt so bad that they thought they were going to die," Cash later reflected. "I remember a time during my hospitalization I felt so bad I was afraid I was going to *live*. I didn't want to feel that way anymore."

Cash also came to the realization that drugs kept him separated from his Creator and his spiritual life.

"The problem with Christians, and me as a Christian, was that the alteration of the mood vexes the spirit of communication and worship and commitment to God," Cash said. "And it's like anything else that can come between you and God as an idol to take the place of God . . . it's a road to ruin."

When not doing chores or having a session, Cash resumed work on his novel about Saint Paul and wrote letters of apology to his children and others. He was visited by Gene Autry, Kris Kristofferson, Lou Robin, and, during "Family Week," June and John Carter Cash. June's thoughts about divorcing Johnny evaporated as soon as she saw him and held his face in her hands.

His forty-three-day stint at Betty Ford was a journey of self-discovery for Cash that resulted in a renewed vigor and focus when he returned to Hendersonville. His new clarity enabled him to recognize struggles his own children were having. Daughter Cindy had her own drug problem, and Johnny sent her to Loma Linda Hospital in California, where she spent three months in recovery.

But, in time, Cash returned to his old, kind self, said House of Cash employee Rick Scott.

"The most special quality John possessed was his approachability," Scott said. "I've been around a lot of superstars, none of them bigger than John, and most are standoffish. But that was not John. It was always about you and what was going on in your life. 'How are you,

Rick? How ya doing?' He was the kind of man that would stop and have a cup of coffee with you, literally. This was a busy man, especially back then."

By March 1984, Cash was back touring, and a month after that, he was in the studio again. The question many Cash fans have asked ever since is, "Whatever possessed him?"—because the result was a song called "Chicken in Black" (originally titled "Brain Transplant"). Written by Gary Gentry, it was a novelty song about a bank robber called the "Manhattan Flash," who has a startling personality change after a brain transplant. The single debuted in the summer of 1984, accompanied by a cartoonish, embarrassing music video in which Cash wore a superhero costume.

Columbia executives actually thought it might be a winner for Cash in the vein of "A Boy Named Sue." It sort of sounded like it musically. Later, Cash would claim it was his idea to do the song as a means of sticking it to Columbia as his contract approached its end in '86. Not so, said Cash historian Mark Stielper.

"It was not a mistake when it was done," Stielper said. "Yes, it turned out campy and terribly embarrassing, but it was one of those 'A Boy Named Sue' and 'One Piece at a Time' moments in Johnny Cash's career where it called for a little lightening up. All these comedy songs are running through his career. They are all strategic. They were there to balance out a very serious man . . . but in this case, it didn't work."

The song and video were universally panned, with even Cash's family and friends piling on. Daughter Rosanne sensed an air of desperation about the song and said the video was too painful to watch. Waylon Jennings told Cash he looked like a "buffoon" in the costume. Stung by the reaction, Cash demanded that Columbia reclaim not only the video from TV stations but also all unsold copies of the record from the stores (of which there were plenty). The incident poured lighter fluid on Cash's already highly flammable relationship with Columbia Records.

Cash quickly moved on, getting to work on a new album with Chips Moman, the Grammy Award-winning producer, engineer, and songwriter whose American Sound Studio in Memphis helped define some of the greatest records of the 1960s.

Following a European tour, Cash headed to Montreux, Switzerland, to tape *Johnny Cash: Christmas on the Road* for CBS, for which Moman was sound producer. Cash's guests on the show included Waylon Jennings, Kris Kristofferson, and Willie Nelson. Cash, Jennings, and Kristofferson were good pals, but he barely knew Nelson. That changed as the four of them got together to jam after taping each day's segment of the holiday special. They were pleasantly surprised at how well their voices blended, and once back in the States, they cut an album over the course of just a couple days.

Released in late May 1985, *Highwayman* and its first single (Jimmy Webb's "Highwayman") both reached the top of the country charts and remained in the Top 10 for several months. Cash was back after a decade in the doldrums, albeit as one-fourth of a superstar quartet. The partnership spawned numerous tours, three studio albums, a live album/DVD, and a 1986 TV movie, a reworking of the 1939 classic *Stagecoach*.

"Those four were like grownup kids, having fun together, teasing each other, and having a ball. When they went out on stage, people went nuts because they were four big giants," said sister Joanne Cash Yates. "They were friends, and they protected each other from anything that could be harmful. It came at a very needed time in all of their lives."

In October '85, Cash released his seventieth album, *Rainbow*, the one he'd started before he got involved with and sidetracked by the *Highwaymen* project. *Rainbow* took so long to complete that Columbia lost interest in it and ended up pressing a minimal number of copies and doing even less to promote the album. Not surprisingly, it went nowhere commercially. Critics booed its downbeat vibe and lack of cohesiveness and wondered what was responsible now for putting Cash in such a funk.

The answer was his father. At age eighty-eight, Ray Cash's health was in steady decline. He was partially blind and often was confined to bed. As his condition steadily deteriorated, his children and grand-children sat as his bedside and sang gospel songs and hymns.

Cash's feelings about his father were wildly ambivalent. He loved Ray, but after all those years, he still harbored resentment about the way his father had treated him as a child in Dyess. Ray, in turn, was proud of what his son had achieved but made no secret of his belief that success in show business was not all it was cracked up to be.

Ray Cash died on December 23, 1985, from complications of Parkinson's disease.

In his second autobiography, written twelve years later, Cash said that his father never once told him he loved him. "It would have meant an awful lot for me to have heard it, just once, before he died," said Cash.

Undoubtedly, that explains why, though Johnny passed close by his dad's grave in Hendersonville almost every day, he hardly ever stopped to pay his respects.

I understand that personally.

Never really knowing my father because my mother conceived me out of wedlock, I longed for that kind of connection through life. Like Johnny's father Ray, my mother Charlene never told me that she loved me.

It's funny that even as an adult you still long for that. Johnny longed for it, and so did I.

Despite Ray's ambivalence toward Johnny and statements like "God took the wrong son" that haunted Cash throughout his life, he was deeply loved by his Heavenly Father.

That would be demonstrated time and time again.

32

KICKED TO THE CURB

"Nashville got to watering down and slickin' up
the country music . . . A lot of producers
and record companies made the fatal mistake
of continuing to try and record that
syrupy country music."

—JOHNNY CASH

Every music genre is a harsh mistress, and entertainment careers tend to run hot and cold, especially when you hit forty. Johnny Cash— legend that he was—was nearing his mid-fifties when his contract with Columbia Records came up for renewal in 1986.

Music is and always will be a young person's game. They have their ear to the street, set the trends, and buy the music. And they sure weren't buying Johnny Cash music in the 1980s.

By then, the good old boy network on Music Row had dramatically changed. The colorful mavericks and iconoclasts who took chances and reaped big rewards died off or retired, and their record companies were taken over by big media conglomerates. Once run by people who loved the music business, the labels were now in the clutches of buttoned-up bean counters who were "risk averse"; they disdained originality and avoided sticking their necks out. They mostly relied on ledgers, analysts, and demographics. They sucked the soul right out of the industry, and artists who didn't fit their mold and who failed to get with the program were dropped from rosters and quickly shown the door.

A whole new crop of new country artists started to emerge. Dwight Yoakam, The Judds, George Strait, Randy Travis, Alan Jackson, Travis Tritt, and many other fresh faces began dominating the airwaves. They would be followed by a seismic change in country music led by Garth Brooks, Brooks & Dunn, Clint Black, Vince Gill, Tim McGraw, Faith Hill, and the huge crossover artist Shania Twain. Country was becoming more mainstream, and the artists more youthful, buffed out, and video-friendly. The aging Cash did not fit that bill.

After the cringe-worthy single "Chicken in Black" and the album *Rainbow* belly-flopped, Columbia—the record label Cash helped build—kicked him to the curb in July 1986, after three decades. Cash was a loner, and while that was very attractive and exciting, sometimes loners find themselves . . . alone.

It was especially humiliating for Cash, who was touring in Canada at the time, to learn he had been dropped through an article in *The Nashville Tennessean* and not from Columbia/Epic/CBS Nashville head Rick Blackburn, with whom Cash thought he was on friendly terms. The stinging newspaper headline read: " 'Man in Black' without a Label."

Years later, Blackburn said he'd made what he thought was an off-the-record comment to a reporter about Cash's contract not getting renewed and that he'd hoped to go to Cash's home on the lake and have a frank conversation with Johnny about how to make the numbers work so they could keep him on the Columbia roster. But then the newspaper article appeared, and that was that.

Cash's sacking impacted him greatly, said niece Kelly Hancock, who, along with her mother Reba, visited Johnny and June the next morning to console him.

"Mom and I went over to their house and were sitting down with [him] and June when Johnny made the comment, 'You know, it's really sad to read that you've lost your record contract in the newspaper,'" Hancock recalled. "I remember him being in shock because of the lack of respect afforded to him. I think the lack of respect threw him for a loop."

Nashville artists Dwight Yoakam, Ricky Skaggs, and Marty Stuart publicly denounced Cash's sacking, stating that he was an icon who deserved better treatment. Producer/music executive Ken Mansfield, who was once deeply involved with the roster of artists at Capitol Records, said Columbia's was a short-sighted decision even if the numbers didn't make sense.

"When you have a leader in [the] field like Johnny Cash on your roster, then the door is open to other artists being attracted to your label," Mansfield said. "It also influences artists on your label because they will see a legendary artist like Johnny Cash and his great success and they will do one of two things: they will either mold themselves after him, or they will try and not compete and be their own individual. And the ironic part is, Cash did it just by being Cash. He didn't try being the best guitar player, the best singer, or the best performer—he was just himself."

Cash's take was that his relationship with Columbia had eroded over the years. He said it was hard to get excited about an album when label executives came to regard him as a long shot and weren't willing to put serious money or muscle into pushing his records. Columbia and all the other record companies in Nashville were now putting their chips on the younger generation. "Youth appeal" was their mantra.

"I got so tired of hearing about demographics, the 'new country fan,' the 'new market profile,' and all the other trends supposedly working against me that I just gave up and decided to have fun with it," Cash wrote in his second autobiography.

However, what was fun to him didn't result in a cacophony of ringing cash registers. Three Johnny Cash albums were released in 1986—*Class of '55, Heroes,* and *Believe in Him.* The first release was essentially a nod to the past that fell way short of the mark. *Class of '55* teamed Cash with his one-time Sun labelmates Carl Perkins, Jerry Lee Lewis, and Roy Orbison, and was producer Chips Moman's tribute to Memphis, where all four got their start. Cash sang lead on just one track, the maudlin Elvis tribute "We Remember the King." Released by the newly formed and short-lived America label, *Class of '55* got to No. 15 on the country album charts and No. 87 on the Pop charts.

Heroes, a duets album with Waylon Jennings also produced by Chips Moman and released by Columbia, peaked at No. 13 on the country album charts.

Believe in Him was an album of classic gospel songs actually recorded in 1982 for Priority Records, a subsidiary of Columbia. Originally titled *Johnny Cash—Gospel Singer,* the ten-track album remained in the vaults until Word Records bought the rights and released it in '86. Commercially, it didn't have a prayer.

But Cash was never a one-trick pony. When his music wasn't clicking, he could turn to other artistic endeavors, such as acting. *Stagecoach,* a remake of the 1939 classic Western, featured Cash as Marshal Curley Wilcox. This made-for-TV version aired in May 1986 and also featured Cash's fellow Highwaymen—Kris Kristofferson, Willie Nelson, and Waylon Jennings—and actor John Schneider.

The Dukes of Hazzard star developed a close relationship with Johnny and June during filming and was especially impressed and inspired by their strong Christian faith.

"I lived with Johnny Cash for a year, and if somebody as rough-around-the-edges as Johnny could say that Jesus was his Savior, there had to be something to it," Schneider told writer Tammy Leigh Maxey of *Pivot Point Magazine* in 2011. "If Johnny Cash felt the need to keep a Bible in the trunk of his Mercedes next to his fishing pole, there had to be something to it."

Neither Johnny nor June ever preached to Schneider, but the way they conducted themselves, interacted with each other, and made God a daily part of and partner in their lives led him to follow suit.

"It was Johnny who led me to Christ," Schneider said. "He was so different from many of the other Christians I'd seen, and he didn't fit the stereotypes I had of guys in argyle sweaters happily dancing through the flowers with big smiles on their faces because life was so perfect. I just watched as Johnny's and June's lives were held together by the love of Christ.

"Johnny and I would be fishing, and suddenly he'd look at his watch and start heading back to the house, saying something about needing to spend some time with the Lord. It intrigued me that this rough man's man would have these priorities, and pretty soon, I was asking questions, wanting what he had. Johnny and June kept circling and trying to talk sense into me without being sappy. And it worked. They understood that I had to be ready; so they waited patiently. That was very different from anything I'd seen before."

Johnny understood the importance of being a good example.

He was not doing these things to impress people; he did them simply because this was who he was. Despite his struggles and setbacks, Johnny always knew where "home" was.

He knew how his life was stabilized and grounded when he took time for prayer and study of Scripture. He also knew what happened when he neglected that and how agitated and stressed he could become.

One definition of being a consistent Christian is "long obedience in the same direction." It's not about emotional highs and lows. It's about discipline and focus.

Johnny had it perhaps better at this stage of life, despite his artistic setbacks, than any other.

In October 1986, *Man in White*, Cash's paean to the life of St. Paul, was published by Harper Collins. Cash did his best to promote the novel, even appearing at booksellers' conventions, but reviews were sometimes harsh—Kirkus Reviews said *Man in White* was "strictly for those with the patience of Job, and then some"— and sales were dismal. Still, Cash had demonstrated that he had the discipline and imagination to research and author—without a ghostwriter—a serious literary work, adding another layer to his voluminous canon.

It was several months before another label picked up Cash, and he had to go through the humiliating process of auditioning for music executives, many of them half his age. Cash wrote about his experience with Jimmy Bowen, at the time the president of MCA Nashville. Cash decided to approach Bowen, a rockabilly singer turned producer, the way he did Sam Phillips in the 1950s—just go in with a guitar, sing some songs, and sell himself. It was more or less a hat-in-hand situation.

Cash gave Bowen a private half-hour concert in his MCA office. At the end of it, he asked, "Well, what do you think?"

"Let me think about it," Bowen said as if he were giving the brush-off to a pesky salesman.

Cash packed his guitar in his case, snapped the clasps, left the building, and never heard a peep back from the music executive— no note, no phone call, not a word. It was a depressing pattern.

Bowen recalled the incident differently in his 1997 autobiography *Rough Mix*. He wrote that his relationship with Cash dated back to the late 1950s, when he was a singer and Cash a hot touring act despite a reputation for showing up only when he felt like it. A music associate had talked Bowen into putting up a $20,000 deposit for a half dozen shows. Cash was a no-show for all six gigs, and Bowen was out all his hard-earned money. Thirty years later, Bowen was a white-hot record executive, and when Cash came to his office to play for him, it was uncomfortable for both of them.

"He'd play me eight, ten, twelve bars and just quit," Bowen wrote. "After the third or fourth song, the poor man said, 'Y'know, I haven't been this nervous in my whole life.' And I said, 'Me, neither.' My God, to have Johnny Cash *audition* for me."

It must have been unsettling for a man who sang from his heart to have his guts turned inside out by people who had never achieved anywhere near the heights of success he had experienced.

"Cash was going in and auditioning for twenty-five-year-olds when he had already been in the Country Music Hall of Fame for six years," said Cash historian Mark Stielper. "He would sit in their offices, and one in particular made him sit there and wait for over an hour past his appointment time, then called him in and said, 'You really don't have anything that we're going to be able to sell.' It was not the best time in Johnny Cash's career."

Cash was a respected artist but an irrelevant figure. That's a no-man's land that's confusion, and it's where no artist likes to be.

Finally, Steve Popovich of Mercury Records, an artist-friendly executive, came to Cash's rescue with a modest offer that would have been unthinkable in Cash's glory days. Popovich was an ally of Cash's from his Columbia Records days and met with the singer at the House of Cash. Cash was despondent and down on himself, and Popovich did his best to prop up the legend, assuring Johnny that he was beloved by millions and that all it would take for him to be back on top again was the right song and the right producer.

Mercury announced its signing of Cash in an August 1986 press release that proclaimed "the world is waiting for more great Cash music."

Cash chose "Cowboy" Jack Clement, an acquaintance from the Sun Record days, to produce his first record for the new label—*Johnny Cash is Coming to Town*. In hindsight, it wasn't such a wise choice. What Cash needed to do was offer up something different right out of the box to make people sit up with a real jolt; but the new record leaned too much on nostalgia. The first single from the album was a remake of a Porter Wagoner song, "The Night Hank Williams Came to Town."

"Hank Williams died in 1953, so the first opportunity for Johnny Cash to come out with a new creative direction that is going to redefine him after the loss of a record contract is a song about somebody who'd been dead for thirty-four years," lamented Mark Stielper. "And so, this album was an exercise in futility. He missed the opening, which colored the relationship with Mercury."

Released in April 1987 and touted as the big comeback album, *Johnny Cash is Coming to Town* made Columbia Records head Rick Blackburn look like the savant of Music Row as it stalled at No. 36 on the album country charts. The single fared no better than No. 43. According to Cowboy Jack Clement, Cash was unfocused and unsure of himself during the recording sessions, and rather than stick to one approach to the music, he tried several, resulting in a very uneven, clunky product.

Cash had failed to seize the day musically, and the dry spell continued.

It turned out to be the least of his worries. Six months after his release from Betty Ford, Cash was back on pills, though nowhere near his former abuse level. And as he started the second song at a May 1987 concert in Council Bluffs, Iowa, Cash began slurring his words and started to shake. June rushed out from the wings, guided Johnny backstage, and called for an ambulance.

At Mercy Hospital, he was treated for stress, exhaustion, and an irregular heartbeat. It was Johnny's thirty-seventh show that year, and he had seventy-seven more to go, including a European tour. Somehow, Cash also found time to cut two more records for Mercury. The first was an album of duets called *Water from the Wells of Home* that paired Cash with Paul McCartney; Waylon Jennings; Hank Williams, Jr.; Glen Campbell; the Everly Brothers; Emmylou Harris; Roy Acuff; and his daughter Rosanne Cash, who by then had several No. 1 country hits under her own belt.

McCartney fondly recalled in an interview their first and only collaboration.

"We were on holiday in Jamaica. He [Cash] lives there, has a house there. And we go to dinner with him. He was there with Tom T. Hall, the country writer, and he said, 'Let's write a song, Paul.' There was a peak off to the distance, so I said, 'Yeah.' Who was I to refuse? So we wrote one," McCartney said.

The second album, *Classic Cash: Hall of Fame Series*, essentially offered new versions of hits from the Sun and Columbia records days. The duets album only reached No. 48 on the country charts. The other didn't chart at all.

Cash was fifty-five now, with the worn-out, frazzled body of a man twenty years older. Professionally, he was in even worse shape. Yet something inside kept pushing him onward. To stop was unthinkable. Rest? He'd get plenty of that when he was dead.

33

―

INTO THE FIRE

"I'm not obsessed with death, I'm obsessed with
living. The battle against the dark one and the
clinging to the right one is what
my life is about."

—JOHNNY CASH

In the late 1980s and for the next dozen years, Johnny Cash learned
how true it was that when you don't have your health, you don't have
your wealth. Years of abuse and neglect had worn his body and
immune system down to the danger point. His "live-now-pay-later"
attitude had caught up with him, and the "Payment Due" invoice
was staggering.

The first part of Cash's life, he battled grinding poverty. The
second part he devoted to cigarettes, booze, and drugs. The final
battle would be to regain a semblance of health.

Cash was hardly unique in this respect. Many of his hard-drinking,
pill-popping contemporaries were either in the same woeful boat or

six feet under. Carl Perkins and his brother Jay were seriously hurt in a car accident driving to New York City to appear on the *Perry Como Show*. Jay never fully recovered and died in 1958, and Carl dove into a bottle for consolation and stayed there for years. Elvis Presley abused drugs for years and died in August 1977 at age forty-two. In 1984, doctors cut away a third of Jerry Lee Lewis's stomach because of perforated ulcers. In December 1988, Roy Orbison died of a heart attack at age fifty-two, and that same month, Waylon Jennings, fifty-one, had a triple coronary bypass operation.

Like them and many others who paid the piper for their unchecked indulgences, Johnny Cash's name now showed up more on medical charts than musical ones.

The Bible talks about reaping what you sow (Galatians 6:7), and Johnny was seeing that in real time. Thankfully, when we sin and are sorry for it and repent of it, God lovingly forgives us and gives us another chance.

But that does not mean we will still not have to face the consequences of those actions in other ways. As an example, if you were to rob a bank and then get arrested, if you asked God to forgive you for your sin (and crime), He certainly would. However, that does not mean that you would not go to jail.

Johnny Cash never robbed a bank (well, except for the time he robbed one as "The Manhattan Flash," the "best bank-robber in New York," in his video "Chicken in Black"). He was now seeing those "chickens come home to roost" in his health, and it was a sad thing indeed. He already looked much older than his years, and his body felt the same way.

The same thing was happening to his sister, Reba, according to her daughter, Kelly Hancock. She said her mother and uncle were workaholics, but Reba took on more responsibilities over the years, and the stress began to show.

"My mother had to field a lot of things for Uncle John, and as you can imagine, he got requests for a million different things from a million different people," Hancock said. "She took on the burden of standing between him and the world, and she became his protector. It was a big role because there was a lot to protect him from."

Hancock said Reba began suffering chronic migraines and was diagnosed with emphysema as a result of forty years of heavy smoking. In 1989, the untimely death of her son Rick ultimately pushed her over the edge.

"The stress, the lifestyle, the emphysema, and then after my brother Rick's passing, health-wise, it was all downhill from there," Hancock said. "She'd had enough of the work environment. Her body was no longer capable of handling the daily stresses, and she didn't want to be there anymore. She was tired and run down."

Cash started off 1988 run down as well, and he checked into the Eisenhower Medical Center in Palm Springs, California, in March. He was treated for laryngitis and bronchitis. Johnny had his annual physical check-up nine months later at Nashville's Baptist Hospital, and while there, visited his friend Waylon Jennings, who was there for a heart bypass surgery. Cash wasn't looking so hot himself, and the doctor ordered an angiogram.

"Don't you find anything because I'm going to Jamaica on vacation," Cash warned. A while later, the doctor came in and asked who he had to talk to about canceling the trip.

"That bad?" Cash asked.

"That bad," confirmed his doctor, who found 90 percent blockage in two coronary arteries and scheduled him for double bypass surgery on December 19.

A half-hour before he was wheeled into the operating room, Cash astonished his surgeons by smoking a cigarette. "Most patients are not brave enough to smoke thirty minutes before surgery," said one of them almost admiringly.

In the three-hour operation performed by Dr. Robert Hardin, chief of surgery, and his associate, Dr. Kenneth Laws, blood vessels were harvested from Cash's leg to bypass the coronary blockages.

The surgery itself was uneventful, but in the intensive care unit, Cash developed double pneumonia (perhaps that last cigarette wasn't such a good idea), and his condition was listed as critical.

Cash later recalled that at one point, as he fought for every breath, he heard a voice cry out in alarm, "He's slipping . . . he's slipping!" And then:

"Their voices receded and everything got quiet and dark and calm and peaceful. Then a light grew around me, and soon it enveloped me, and it was more than light: it was the *essence* of light."

Cash described it as a safe and warm place that grew brighter and more beautiful with every moment. He began to drift to its very center, feeling a sense of joy unlike any he'd ever experienced before.

Then his eyes flew open as he was abruptly snatched back by the doctors frantically working to revive him. At first, Cash felt overwhelming sorrow and started to cry. Then he became angry and tried to communicate that he wanted to go back to that realm of light and joy, but the tube in his throat prevented him from getting the words out. After a few moments, he calmed down and realized he was where he was supposed to be.

Having a near-death experience was not unusual to Johnny Cash. Many have reported something very similar to what he experienced. For Johnny, it was a reminder that life would not go on forever, especially the way he was living. But it was also a reminder that on the other side, in eternity where his beloved brother Jack was, there was a place of light and peace.

Rumors abounded that the Man in Black was on his death bed, and Music City journalists got busy preparing obituaries in case Cash crossed over the rainbow. But he summoned the will and fortitude to survive yet another brush with death. Waylon Jennings had his triple bypass done at the same hospital just a week earlier, and he and Cash cheered each other up by trading insults about whose heart was smaller and blacker and who was the most famous big shot in the cardiac unit.

Cash was discharged on January 3, 1989, with a stern lecture about changing his diet, getting more exercise, and, most of all, giving up the cancer sticks. Calling his month-long hospitalization "a great soul-searching experience," the fifty-six-year-old entertainer vowed to give up smoking, though he wouldn't be successful for several years. Nicotine, Cash said, was even tougher to quit than amphetamines.

In March, Cash began recording a second album with the Highwaymen called *Highwayman 2*. Later, he recorded *Boom Chicka Boom*, a solo album for Mercury. Then he toured for the rest of the year starting in April and continued paying on the installment plan for his workaholic ways. In May, he went to the hospital in Paris after suffering severe chest pains (not, as he told the press, a "torn ligament"). Doctors suggested he cancel his next show, so, of course, he didn't and even gave a longer performance than usual. That resulted in a three-day hospital stay.

You could not argue with Cash's work ethic. He wanted to deliver for his audiences, and they loved him for it. But it took its toll. In August, recurring bronchitis and laryngitis forced the cancellation of three shows. Acting on fears of a potential relapse into pill abuse, just before Thanksgiving Cash entered Nashville's Cumberland Heights Alcohol and Drug Treatment Center for two weeks of "relapse prevention therapy." Any rest he got seemed only to happen in hospitals and healthcare facilities.

Johnny's suffering increased tenfold in January 1990 after a dentist removed an abscessed tooth and a large cyst was scraped away. In the process, his jawbone was undermined, which Cash found out a few months later when the mandible fractured as he was chewing on a piece of steak. It left the lower part of his face grotesquely swollen, and also permanently damaged nerve endings, resulting in chronic pain Cash likened to being burned by a blowtorch. Still, he soldiered on.

Contemporary Christian artist and musician Dennis Agajanian, a good friend of mine who had played with Cash at Billy Graham

Crusades since the 1970s, recalled his friend's show-must-go-on attitude.

"His jaw was way out there and swollen, and I felt so bad for him," Agajanian said. "But I never heard him complain about it or bring attention to it. Cash was a tough man—and a real man."

Agajanian said Cash was a one-of-a-kind presence, the likes of which he has not seen before or since.

"There aren't that many people who can walk into a room—and I don't care how big of a star they are, even a president—who command all the attention," Agajanian said. "To my mind, there were only two people who had that kind of charisma and could pull it off—Johnny Cash and Billy Graham."

Repeated operations on the jaw (Cash later confirmed he'd had thirty-four surgical procedures) did nothing to alleviate the pain and altered Cash's appearance. The lower left side of his face was constantly swollen, and Cash developed a habit of pulling up his shirt collar on that side when being photographed. He instructed a camera crew filming a documentary of the Highwaymen to shoot him only from his good side. Cash was well aware of his tendency toward abuse and did his best to gird himself from addiction.

"I didn't ever kick the drug habit, and I don't think I ever will," Cash confessed to Ralph Emery, a Nashville radio and television personality. "There'll always be that craving there for it. That comes by every day and then passes, thank God. We don't say, 'We're recovered.' We say, 'We're recovering.'" Cash said the sensations sometimes lasted a few seconds; sometimes it was hours.

"I make a daily commitment to God and ask him to take away the desire," Cash said. "And for many, many days, He done that."

As excruciating as it was, all his physical pain was nothing compared to the heartache Cash suffered as his eighty-six-year-old mother slowly died of cancer.

Carrie Cash was her son's heart and soul, his bedrock, his backbone, his encourager, and his inspiration. She had remained determinedly

cheerful and committed to God and her family through so many personal trials—Ray's long-term alcoholism, Jack's death, Johnny's battles
with drugs, and his divorce from Vivian. Carrie had told Johnny that
God had His hand on him, and she never let him forget it.

It had been Carrie's idea years earlier to open and go to work at
the House of Cash gift shop. She recognized that having a place to
sell Johnny Cash souvenirs and merchandise (as well as her own line
of cookbooks) would keep interest in her son's career percolating, and
she saw how much it would mean to fans to buy them from Johnny's
own mom. He was hesitant at first, but the gift shop became a rousing success thanks to the warm attention Carrie paid to thousands of
fans every year who got to tell the folks back home they'd met Johnny
Cash's mother. From time to time, Carrie even corralled Johnny into
dropping over for an impromptu meet-and-greet. Each time, he sub-
dued his congenital shyness to please his mother.

Visitors naturally cottoned to Carrie, said former House of Cash
employee and singer-songwriter Rick Scott.

"Carrie was absolutely the sweetest woman and as country as they
come," Scott said. "She was right there in that museum every single
morning, greeting people as they came in. She made people feel welcome and made them feel like they were family. She was wonderful
for that job. Very salt of the earth."

It was bladder pain that first sent Carrie to the doctor. She thought
it was an infection, and so did doctors; they prescribed antibiotics.
There was no improvement, so more tests followed, and Carrie's bladder cancer was finally detected around Thanksgiving. Surgery didn't
eradicate it, and by the time the cancer spread to her lungs, the only
resort left was to send her home under hospice care.

Johnny carried on as best as he could. Nashville producer and
musician Billy Smiley worked for Word Music at the time and was
producing a Christian punk band from Austin, Texas, called One
Bad Pig. The band wanted to record "Man in Black," and Mark
Maxwell, the A&R director at Word Music, made a few calls that

resulted in an invitation for One Bad Pig to attend a party at Cash's Hendersonville home. Cash immediately "fell in love with the band," according to Smiley, and agreed to drop by at its recording session the next day.

"He came to the studio," recalled Smiley, "and quietly said, 'Before we start, I'd love for you guys to pray with me.' He had just seen his mom, and he said, 'She's in a bad way, and I'd appreciate your prayers.' So all these rock guys got in a circle with him—and we all prayed. Then, when we said 'Amen,' Cash looked at everybody and said, 'Let's rock!'"

The Cash women—Reba, Louise and Joanne—took turns being with Carrie during the day, and a hospice nurse stayed overnight. She was given morphine, which caused her to occasionally hallucinate. As the end neared, the entire Cash family serenaded Carrie with gospel tunes.

Recalled sister Joanne Cash Yates: "The last song we sang to her, around seven o'clock in the evening, was 'O Come, Angel Band.' I was sitting by momma's bedside when, all of a sudden, she opened her eyes real wide and took in this deep breath and said, 'Ahhhh . . .' It appeared to me as if she saw something glorious. Then she closed her eyes. I yelled to everyone, 'She's leaving us!'"

The lyrics to the song sum up exactly what was happening to this saintly woman.

She was being escorted by angels into the presence of God.

This what happened to the beggar Lazarus when he died.

The Bible says, "The time came when the beggar died and the angels carried him to Abraham's side" (Luke 16:22 NIV).

The Cash family sang for their beloved mother:

The latest sun is sinking fast, my race has nearly run
My strongest trials now are past, my triumph is begun
O come, angel band, come and around me stand
O bear me away on your snow-white wings to my
*   immortal home.*

Holding hands, the Cash children circled the bed, and then in unison, everyone spontaneously took a step back, making the circle larger. It was something Joanne didn't think about until her brother brought it up a few weeks later.

Johnny had been clutching Joanne's hand when their mother died. Now he said to her, "Baby, remember when we were all holding hands and took a step back at the same time?"

Joanne answered affirmatively, and Johnny continued, "Did you not see the angels?"

"When I told him I didn't," said Joanne, "Johnny said that he saw angels come down through the ceiling, go under Mama's bed and bring her upward. He said, 'I saw the angels take her home.'"

The death of Carrie Cash on March 11, 1991, provoked a flood of tributes from family and friends and a flood of tears from her famous and famously tough son. It was the first time anyone could ever recall seeing Johnny Cash cry in public.

After Carrie's funeral, Johnny could hardly bring himself to go inside the museum gift shop anymore.

34

THEN CAME BRANSON

"What's the difference between Jurassic Park
and Branson? Blue hair."

—JOHNNY CASH

Years of brutal touring had taken a toll on Cash's health, and he knew it was time to get off the road. Touring was an easy money grab for superstars like him and a surefire way out of a financial pinch. But with Cash's health and career on the downgrade, he couldn't rely on that anymore.

According to Cash historian Mark Stielper, Johnny couldn't outright retire because of obligations to his family and members of his touring band—at times as many as forty people relied on him for their income. Stielper said Cash often used advance money for future tours to pay the bills from the last tour.

Cash's attempts to set himself up financially for the future all sadly fell short for one reason or another. A few years before, he'd asked the Henderson Regional Planning Commission to rezone ninety-five acres he'd purchased near his house at Old Hickory Lake so that he could build and sell approximately two hundred houses, each priced between $75,000 and $175,000. But the Commission said no after some thirty homeowners from the area voiced objections to Cash's plan on the grounds that the cheaper homes would affect the value of their own properties.

Johnny once invested in a downtown Nashville office building with Waylon Jennings, but operational costs were so prohibitive they ended up selling out after a couple of years.

Then there were their personal spending habits. Johnny often joked that June had "a black belt in shopping," but he didn't do anything to rein her in. His own spending habits weren't anything to write home about, either.

With his recording career at its lowest ebb, Johnny had to let some employees go, reduce the size of his band, and impose salary cuts on the musicians who stayed. He also sold his publishing catalog for some quick cash—though he didn't get as much as he thought he would after it was discovered that ex-wife Vivian owned half of the lucrative early catalog. Johnny and June were even reduced to hocking jewelry to pay their large domestic staff.

Enter a developer who came to Cash with a proposition to build a $35 million entertainment complex in Branson, Missouri, called "Cash Country."

The Ozark Mountain town of Branson (pop. 3,700 at the time), four hundred miles from Nashville and two hundred miles south of Kansas City, started out as a rural tourist stop known mostly for the fishing in nearby Table Rock Lake. For years, the only musical game in town was the Baldknobbers Hillbilly Jamboree Show, featuring the area's finest fiddle players and a country comedy duo called Droopy and Stubb. Branson's transformation into a major tourist attraction began in 1983 when the Roy Clark Celebrity Theatre opened. The Highway 76 venue was so successful that travel-weary music stars such as Mel Tillis, Ray Stevens, Jim Stafford, Mickey Gilley, Moe Bandy, and Boxcar Willie soon opened their own theaters in Branson, luring millions of tourists there who spent to the tune of $1.5 billion annually. In December 1991, *60 Minutes* aired a feature calling Branson the "live music capital of the entire universe." Country star Conway Twitty called it "Hillbilly Heaven."

Not so many years before, the idea of Branson turned Cash's stomach.

"Many of my friends came here and built theaters, and they liked it," Cash told *Rolling Stone* writer Steve Pond. "I thought, 'I'll never do that. I'll just keep hittin' the road until I'm too old to bop, and then I'll drop.'"

But Cash's fortunes and circumstances dramatically changed in the early 1990s. His career was at an all-time low; he hadn't had a bona-fide country hit in a decade, and album sales were sluggish.

All of a sudden, Branson didn't seem so bad.

"It's a place where folks can come, and I can settle down and do what I like without having to hit the road," Cash said. "I feel good about it." To Steve Pond, he sounded like a man trying very hard to convince himself this was a good career move.

The developer, who'd made his fortune on outlet malls, envisioned Cash Country as a music theme park whose eighty acres would include three theaters (one of them devoted solely to gospel music), a horse arena, a go-cart track, an amusement park, a water park, an auction house, a Cash museum/souvenir shop, a thirty-five-unit hotel, three motels, and a 20,000-square-foot shopping mall.

The best part of the whole deal was that Cash wouldn't have to invest a dime in the project, only lend his good name to it and agree to do three months a year in one of the 2,500-seat theaters—in return for which he would get a royalty, $30,000 per day and a percentage of the box office after it reached a certain threshold. A similar deal for Dolly Parton in 1986 made her a bundle of cash and put Pigeon Forge, Tennessee, on the map as the home of "Dollywood."

What was not to love about it?

Plenty, according to those who urged Cash to run the other way. Daughter Rosanne shuddered picturing Cash Country amidst Branson's T-shirt shops, all-you-can-eat buffet restaurants, water slides, miniature golf courses, RV campsites, and the Wal-Mart that sat near the curve in the highway—and groaned when her father said he hoped she would perform there. Johnny's son-in-law Rodney Crowell considered the budget-class resort town the last stand for creaking stars of yesteryear, and the specter of Cash moldering away in such a musical wax museum depressed him beyond words.

Mark Stielper personally appealed to Johnny not to do it.

"At the time, the Branson concept was ideal: make the people come to you. Many artists were building their own theaters, beguiled by the idea of getting off the road," Stielper said. "June and John were over sixty, their biggest days apparently behind them. I argued against the move on the grounds that it was a surrender. I even prepared a paper making that case. I lost, then he lost."

Having signed on the dotted line, Cash threw himself wholeheartedly (at least outwardly) into his new role as a Branson booster. He shopped at Wal-Mart with the locals, signed autographs for two hours at a nearby fishermen's convention, and taped a segment of *Larry King Live* at the site of his theme park.

He also gamely sat still for interviews with local disc jockeys whose on-air hijinks and repartee must have made Cash wonder what he had gotten himself into. One deejay had Cash record a message for his personal answering machine; another endlessly and pointlessly blathered on about Elvis. Yet another deejay blindsided Johnny and June in the worst way, saying, "I bet you don't remember the first time I met you." When Johnny shook his head uncertainly, the jock gleefully proclaimed, "It was 1966, and you were in bad shape."

Striving to be gracious, June smiled wanly, nodded her head, and muttered, "He coulda been"—whereupon the guy whooped, "You, too!" and chortled, "In fact, Johnny, we were taking bets on how long you'd be alive—and the longest anyone would bet on was two years!"

While Cash intrepidly did his part, his lighting director and production manager, Jay Dauro, huddled with the architect designing the stage in the theater where Johnny would perform and sensed problems right off the bat.

"Branson at that time was in a big boom period, and they were using architects from the area," Dauro said. "Many of them had very little experience in theater design, and the folks working on Cash Country didn't, either."

Dauro moved to Branson to devote himself full-time to the project, and with his input, a design was created for a proscenium stage with a fairly aggressive thrust that would've given audiences a close-up experience with Cash and his band.

But Dauro and the rest were just building castles in the sky. The deal that sounded too good to be true ended up exactly that way.

"The developer lost sight of the ball," said Dauro. "The ball is being able to put people in the seats and put on a show. You don't get any money until you're doing that. The theater lobby was beautiful, but the stage never got done. The lobby is definitely a draw, but nobody's buying a ticket just to come and look at a lobby. The developer just lost sight of what had to get done first to get up and running."

The developer's pipe dream landed him in a federal bankruptcy court in Kansas City, with about five thousand creditors (including fans who purchased advance tickets to Cash's shows) on his heels. The uncompleted theater in Branson was sold for $4.1 million to satisfy their claims. Cash's lawyers won a $1.6 million settlement from him in 1993.

Johnny was crushed and humiliated by the Cash Country fiasco, but he needed the money too much to say anything but *danke schön* when Jim Thomas, one of the buyers of Green's theater, offered him the opportunity to perform at Branson's Wayne Newton Theatre in the spring of 1993.

Newton kept a large and luxurious apartment on site, but on his strict orders, it was off-limits to Johnny and June. They set up housekeeping backstage at the theater, a cramped cinder-block setting as drab as some of the shows they gave during their run in Branson. Johnny was listless and often rambled pointlessly to the blue-haired crowd about past glories such as *The Johnny Cash Show* and *The Gospel Road*. On a good night, half of the theater's three thousand seats were filled. Sometimes, fewer than three hundred people turned out for a show. Where were Droopy and Stubb when you needed them?

As it turned out, the collapse of Cash Country had fortuitously designed the final act of Cash's career. Had the Branson theme park gotten off the ground, Cash very well may not have launched the greatest and most magnificent comeback in popular music history.

It was clear that The Creator had something else in mind for Johnny Cash.

35

THE WANDERER COMES HOME

"I'm doing what I feel like I was put on this world to do. I just want to do more of the same, but I want to do it better. I want to make some records that people will pay attention to."

—JOHNNY CASH

A wonderful thing happened to Johnny Cash when his ego was stripped away over time—it was the necessary evil needed to bring him to the end of himself. His painful trials and tribulations led him through the valley of the shadow of death. His torrid past was not for naught, either, because he used it to keep others from making the same mistakes he had made. He dedicated the final decade of his life to sharing the knowledge that life apart from Christ was as useless as his vanity because it got him nowhere and led to an unfulfilled life.

For most of his adult life, Cash thought he was ten feet tall and bulletproof, but his health scares, the deaths of his parents, financial woes, and career nosedive showed him the things of this world were not that important compared to all eternity. In his more vulnerable state, he realized he was no longer indestructible and it was God who was in charge, not Johnny Cash. He began to seek God's will for his life more earnestly, and songs like "Turn Your Eyes Upon Jesus" became increasingly sweet and meaningful.

Cash's brother-in-law, Pastor Harry Yates, said, "As Johnny was going through his downward spiral, I believe it finally put him in a position to do what God wanted him to do. After his hospitalization, somewhere deep in John's subconscious, because he did not die, he must have come to the realization that God kept him here for a purpose and he had not accomplished all of the things he needed to do. He had an opportunity to reflect on himself, his family, his music, and his God. One day, he just woke up and said, 'Okay, God, I'm done doing what I want to do, and I'm finally ready to do Your will.'"

Even though Cash related early on to the Apostle Paul and his weaknesses in the New Testament, his latter-day tribulations aligned more with those of Job in the Old Testament. God said in Matthew 5:45 that it "rains on the just and the unjust" (KJV). Like Job, Johnny Cash experienced torrential downpours in his life and yet managed to weather those storms, often without recognizing that he survived because of God's amazing grace and not through his own design. Job and Johnny shared the same rags-to-riches story; both suffered the loss of their wealth and health. But Job said, "Though God slay me, yet will I trust in him" (Job 13:15b NKJV). Job remained faithful to God when everything was going well for him, and then also when he lost everything. Johnny was not as consistently faithful as Job, and even though his wealth was restored, his health was not.

We experience adversity in our lives because we live in a fallen world where we continually fight three things: the world, the flesh, and the devil. Johnny Cash had gone toe-to-toe with all three up to this point, but he was finally ready to give up the fight because the world and its enticements no longer held the sway it once had in his life. His physical self was failing him, his ego was practically gone, and the devil no longer had the stranglehold on him of days gone by.

Johnny was homesick.

In some ways, he was homesick for a home he'd never had but, in his heart of hearts, really wanted.

Despite the fact that Cash was a symbol of country roots of hearth and home to millions of Americans, he was in many ways a wanderer, singing for his supper and getting ready for the next gig, living out of a suitcase and from paycheck to paycheck. No wonder so many ordinary people related to Johnny. He really was one of them.

The home Cash really longed for was in a relationship with God.

And in the closing stretch of his life, it was a longing for Heaven.

C. S. Lewis summed it up this way: "All the things that ever deeply possessed your soul have been but hints of Heaven. Tantalizing glimpses, promises never quite fulfilled, echoes that died away just as they caught your ear . . . If I find in myself a desire which no experience in this world can satisfy, the most probable explanation is that I was made for another world . . . Probably earthly pleasures were never meant to satisfy, but to arouse it, to suggest the real thing."

God was not done with Johnny Cash.

As Cash came to the end of himself, he also came to the beginning of God.

In the secular realm, the Cash name was being writ large in important places. Johnny rang in 1992 as a new member of the Rock and Roll Hall of Fame. Other artists in that year's class included Booker T. & the M.G.s, the Jimi Hendrix Experience, Sam & Dave, Bobby "Blue" Bland, the Isley Brothers, and the Yardbirds, including guitarist Eric Clapton.

In his lifetime, Cash was also inducted into the Grand Ole Opry, the Country Music Hall of Fame, and the Nashville Songwriters Hall of Fame. In addition, he was a recipient of the National Medal of Arts in recognition of his numerous musical contributions.

Given his status as country music's most visible star, Cash wasn't sure he belonged in the Rock and Roll Hall of Fame. He never considered himself a true rock 'n' roller, and he worried that performers who were would resent his inclusion. Cash's doubts on that score were groundless. Music historians correctly maintain that he, Elvis Presley, Jerry Lee Lewis, and Carl Perkins were early pioneers of rock and roll and imbued the genre with the rebel spirit that enhanced its appeal.

Any notion he wasn't welcome in the Rock and Roll Hall of Fame was wiped away by the thundering standing ovation that greeted Cash when he stepped up to the podium after a heartfelt introduction by Lyle Lovett.

He said of the award: "I'm extremely proud of it, and whether I belong here or not, I'm going to show it off at home."

Johnny's mind was actually set at ease even before the program began when he was standing at a urinal in the restroom and heard someone singing "Loading Coal," an obscure number from his *Ride This Train* album. When Cash turned around, there stood a smiling Keith Richards. Right there in the bathroom, he later gleefully recalled, "We sang the chorus together. That's when I guess I knew everything was going to be okay."

Another surrealistic moment occurred during the jam session after the dinner when Cash sang "Big River," backed by Richards and John Fogerty on guitar, who played inspired solos. At the end of the night, Cash joined esteemed rockers Jimmy Page, Carlos Santana, Neil Young, Steve Cropper, and U2's The Edge in a version of Jimi Hendrix's "Purple Haze," along with Noel Redding and Mitch Mitchell, surviving members of Hendrix's band, The Experience.

The ceremony gave Johnny a chance to connect with U2 lead guitarist The Edge (David Howell Evans), who inducted The

Yardbirds that year. Cash had already met two other of his band-mates—lead singer Bono and bassist Adam Clayton.

It took place in November 1987 when U2 was in Memphis's Sun Studios to record "Jesus Christ" for the Woody Guthrie tribute album *A Shared Vision*. The studio hadn't been functional since 1969, but U2 hoped to capture the magic of that historic place and pay homage to the greats whose photos adorned the walls—Presley, Cash, Lewis, Orbison, and Perkins.

As a student of popular music, Bono was intrigued by the early history of Sun Records and the era of early rock and roll. He was especially interested in trying to understand the spiritual conflicts of these Southern artists and how they co-existed with their carnal music, hedonistic lifestyles, and their Christian values. Like Cash, Bono was a spiritual provocateur who often drew outside the conventional lines of Christianity while snubbing the usual behavior of a rock star.

"Johnny Cash was a saint who preferred the company of sinners," Bono noted.

Clayton reflected that he connected with Cash on a different level.

"My first forays into learning to play the guitar and singing a tune would have been based on Kris Kristofferson tunes and Johnny Cash tunes because they connected with rock 'n' roll, they weren't straight country," Clayton said. "At thirteen or fourteen, I was aware of Johnny and the prison gigs and that sort of thing, but when the Sex Pistols came along, you couldn't admit to that. It wasn't a reference point that was even helpful."

Producing the Sun music session for U2 was "Cowboy" Jack Clement, Cash's longtime friend. When he found out about Bono's hero worship of Johnny, he got on the horn. Soon afterward, Bono and Adam Clayton were headed to the house on Old Hickory Lake three hours away.

In a subsequent *Rolling Stone* interview, Bono shared details about his meeting with the man he regarded as one of the "father figures" in his life.

Bono and Clayton were instantly charmed by Cash's self-deprecating and zany sense of humor. Cash took them on a tour of his house, property, and ranch, and at the zoo, he gave them a blow-by-blow account of his life-and-death duel with the late, unlamented Waldo. Cash also gave Bono and Clayton black stage shirts so big the skinny Irishmen could have fit in one together. They treasured them and their host's kindness.

"I considered myself a friend, he considered me a fan—he indulged me," Bono said.

Dinner was a huge spread the guests assumed was in their honor but turned out to be a photo shoot for the cover of June's new cookbook. Before they ate, Cash asked everyone to hold hands and bow their heads and said a prayer of thanks.

"Then, when he was done," recalled Bono, "he turned to me and Adam Clayton and said, 'Sure miss the drugs, though.' It was just to say, 'I haven't become a Holy Joe.' He just couldn't be self-righteous . . . And that just made you like him even more."

At lunch, they discussed Irish poets, scriptures, and where the Cash name originated. The Nashville legend told Bono that he was from a baronial family in Scotland, but Bono explained that the Cashes were a horse-loving, travelling people from County Wexford in Ireland.

"He only half-guffawed when I broke the news," Bono recalled.

Afterwards, Cash and his guests jammed and started to write a song called "Ellis Island." They didn't finish it before Bono and Clayton had to go, but an even more momentous collaboration was ahead.

In February 1993, Cash was in Dublin to play a concert with Kris Kristofferson. Afterward, Bono invited him to Windmill Studios, where U2 was working on an experimental music project with producer Brian Eno. The day before, Bono had written a song titled "The Preacher" (later renamed "The Wanderer"), inspired by the Old Testament book of Ecclesiastes. Bono said the story is about the "intellectual wanderlust" of a man who is searching for God in a post-apocalyptic world and expresses concern about society's diminished view of Jesus Christ ("They say they want the Kingdom but they don't want God in it").

"He tries wealth. He tries experience. He tries everything," Bono said. "You hurry to the end of the book to found out what, and it says, 'It's good to work,' 'Remember your Creator.' In a way, it's such a letdown. Yet it isn't. There's something of Johnny Cash in that."

Many critics and fans alike believe it is the greatest song Bono has ever written. But he couldn't get it down right on tape; something was missing. When he heard his friend Johnny Cash was coming to Dublin, Bono realized Cash was exactly what the song needed and asked him to sing the lead on "The Wanderer."

Cash not only delivered the goods, but he gave Bono an "a-ha" moment.

"I remember trying to sort out some phrasing problems with the lyric and Johnny stopping me, saying, 'No, I like it when the rhythm's uneven. I get to do the unexpected," Bono recalled Cash saying. For the Irishman, it was "another lesson from a master."

Cash recorded the song with U2 and afterwards told an Irish reporter, "I don't know if it will ever be released or even what it's called!" To his surprise and delight, "The Wanderer" became the tenth and final track on the album *Zooropa*. "The Wanderer" introduced Cash to an outside audience unfamiliar with his work or past. U2 was as big as they got—arguably the most powerful and important rock band since the Beatles. That July, *Zooropa* became a number-one album in ten different countries and sold more than seven million copies worldwide. Every one of those young listeners had to take notice and ask, "Who is this Johnny Cash fellow?" And the reviews and reception of the haunting last song on the album were especially fulsome.

Thanks to "The Wanderer," Cash felt renewed artistically. One of the first things he did upon returning to the States was cancel his remaining shows in Branson.

"I have no plans to come back at all," he told a reporter. "I don't think I'm doing myself or my fans a favor being there."

God had other plans for His faithful servant. The craggy sexagenarian was about to undergo a career renaissance no musical artist his age had ever experienced.

36

—

RESURRECTION

"I'm on my way to doin' my best work right now.
I've got another chance, and I'm grabbing at
the brass ring again."

—JOHNNY CASH

Johnny Cash understood for the first time in his life that there were no coincidences because he had a renewed relationship with life's Grand Architect. He was growing in his faith by leaps and bounds by reading the Bible, praying, and relying on the Holy Spirit for guidance. He dedicated everything he did to the Lord and found a renewed purpose for himself. In the process, Cash rediscovered his muse.

Occurrences others would have chalked up to randomness, happenstance, or a cosmic roll of the dice Johnny now recognized as God's providential arrangement of circumstances. What he didn't know—none of us do—is how God would choose to present those circumstances to him. So he was wary when a balding, bushy-bearded man made an appointment to meet Cash backstage at a small dinner theater in Santa Ana, California, on the night of February 27, 1993, and said he wanted to produce Johnny's music.

To Cash's manager Lou Robin, the man looked like "a wino." He turned out to be Rick Rubin, at age thirty already a legend in rap and hip-hop music circles. He started the rap label Def Jam Records with Russell Phillips in his New York University dorm room. He helped popularize hip-hop music through his work with The Beastie Boys, LL Cool J, Public Enemy, and Run-DMC. A few years later, he set up shop in Los Angeles and produced heavy metal/rock acts like the Red Hot Chili Peppers, Slayer, the Black Crowes, and Tom Petty and the Heartbreakers. Rubin and Russell made music history by melding rap and metal when they paired Run-DMC and Aerosmith for the single "Walk This Way." MTV had called Rubin one of the most influential producers of the previous twenty years.

And now he wanted to record Johnny Cash—why? Rubin later explained, "I had worked pretty much exclusively with young artists, either making their first album or their second album. There might have been minor exceptions to that, but I felt like it would be an exciting challenge to work with an established artist or a legendary artist who might not be in the best place in his career at the moment."

Rubin also saw in Cash a mysterious and dangerous figure, which played well with Generation X.

"From the beginning of rock and roll, there's always been this dark figure who never really fit," Rubin said. "He's the quintessential out-sider. In the hip-hop world, you see all these bad-boy artists who are juggling being on MTV and running from the law. John was the originator of that."

Cash was dubious. "What're you gonna do with me that nobody else has done to sell records for me?" he asked Rubin.

"Well, I don't know that we *will* sell records," the rap mogul said. "I would like you to sit in my living room with a guitar and two microphones and just sing to your heart's content, everything you ever wanted to record."

As it happened, Rubin's notion happened to jibe perfectly with something Cash had been contemplating for some time—recording a batch of cowboy-country, folk, and love songs, just him and a guitar, and call it *Johnny Cash Late and Alone*.

No hard sell was required. "That sounds good to me," Cash told Rubin.

Thus began one of Johnny's most fruitful professional collaborations, his "third career," and the renewal of Cash's passion for recording. The stark acoustic records that comprise the American Recordings series would ultimately give the legend back his voice.

Cash still owed Mercury another album even though his last one, 1991's *The Mystery of Life*, was an unmitigated disaster. Cash claimed the label pressed only five hundred copies, but that may have been an exaggeration on his part born of his frustration with the label. Rubin got him out of doing the final album by promising Mercury a royalty on Johnny's future record sales for his American Recordings label (out of Johnny's proceeds, of course).

For months, Cash and Rubin sent cassette tapes and CDs back and forth between Nashville and Los Angeles and discussed the material they would record. For three days in mid-May, Cash sat in the living room of Rubin's Hollywood home just off the Sunset Strip with his guitar and recorded thirty-three songs. It reminded him of the early days at Sun Records when Sam Phillips put him in front of a microphone for the first time and told him to have at it. Even so, Cash still had butterflies.

"He was not an ego-driven person," Rubin said. "He did not come from a place of confidence. For all his success, he was somewhat insecure."

The songs Cash recorded were ones from his back catalogue he felt hadn't been properly done before, tunes written by Willie Nelson, Nick Lowe, Dolly Parton, Tom Waits, Kris Kristofferson,

Leonard Cohen, and heavy rock artist Glen Danzig (one of Rubin's selections).

A pall was cast on the undertaking when Johnny's seventy-one-year-old brother Roy died of cancer on July 8 in Memphis. "You might really say he died of a broken heart," said Pastor Harry Yates, "because after his wife died (in 1985), Roy stopped eating. He never got over Wandene's death."

Like their mother, Roy was always supportive of and encouraging to his younger brother in Johnny's quest to become a recording artist. Roy also contributed to that by introducing his brother to Marshall Grant and Luther Perkins, the Tennessee Two, who created the signature back-up sound for Cash. History has often neglected the role Roy played in his brother's life, but Cash always knew and acknowledged it.

Roy was buried in the Mississippi County, Arkansas, cemetery alongside his wife and their son, who died of leukemia at age three, and near the grave of Jack Cash.

The final album sessions took place between October and December 1993 and were split between Rubin's living room and Johnny's studio, The Cash Cabin, on his property in Hendersonville. By then, he and Rubin were fast friends who eagerly exchanged ideas and philosophies. Before each recording session, they prayed together. Near the end of Cash's life, they did daily communion together over the phone.

Rubin said Cash was the most spiritually committed person he'd ever met. One night, he recalled to a reporter, "We had a dinner party at my house with Johnny and June and some musicians and film directors, and before dinner, Johnny had everyone hold hands, and he said a prayer and read from a Bible.

"Some of the people at the table had never experienced that before, and some were even atheists. But his belief in what he believed was so strong that what you believed didn't matter so much because you were in the presence of someone who really believed, and that felt good, and that made you believe really in him more than anything else. It was really beautiful."

Before the album called *American Recordings* was released, Rubin wanted to preview the songs in front of a live audience at a small venue. He chose The Viper Room, a hipster club in West Hollywood on the Sunset Strip whose coterie of owners included actor Johnny Depp. The much-hyped gig received a lot of attention with Cash hanging out at the club to do promotion and interviews with local and national media.

Playing at The Viper Room the night before Cash's performance were The Wallflowers, the popular rock band formed by Bob Dylan's son, Jakob. At around nine o'clock, keyboardist Rami Jaffee arrived at the club to sound check his organ. Afterwards, he headed for the owner's office with an unlit cigarette in his mouth—and froze in the doorway when he saw who was sitting there.

"It was the Man in Black, larger than life, alone and oddly doing nothing," Jaffee recalled. "I was frozen with shock, lighter on, cig dangling, mouth kinda open, and Johnny says, 'Well, son, you gonna have a seat and light that thing or just stand there?'

"I can't remember what we talked about other than chuckling chit-chat and naming a few famous friends we had in common, and me trying not to geek too hard with 'I'm such a big fan' patter," added Jaffee, who a few years later played piano on "Father and Son," one of the most haunting and beautiful tunes Cash would record at the end of his life.

Johnny Depp himself introduced Cash on the night of December 3, 1993, with the simple declaration, "Ladies and gentlemen, I can't believe I get to say this: Johnny Cash!"

At that moment, a seismic shift took place in the life and career of John R. Cash. Suddenly, Johnny was cool again.

What is cool?

One could give a thousand explanations.

Why are some actors and artists cool in their later years as well as at their beginning? It's not easy to say.

Elvis Presley was the very personification of cool for a time.

Then he went into the Army, made corny movies, ended up wearing knit jumpsuits in Vegas, and was never the same again.

James Dean died too young to ever see if he could continue to maintain his coolness.

Steve McQueen had it, never lost it, and was dubbed "The King of Cool."

To me, being cool is to be real and authentic.

It's not the person who morphs with the latest trends.

It's the person who stays true to who he is.

It's authenticity, being real, and original.

Johnny was that in spades.

Fact is, Cash was always cool.

The 150-member audience was a veritable Who's Who of the music and entertainment industry, and included Tom Petty, Graham Nash, Pierce Brosnan, Roseanna Arquette, Juliette Lewis, Shannen Doherty, Randy Quaid, Henry Rollins, Dwight Yoakam, and Flea of the Red Hot Chili Peppers. They went collectively nuts during Cash's forty-five-minute set, and after he finished, he asked June, standing in the front row, "What do I do now?" "Sing your hits," she suggested. He did, which, of course, brought more rapturous applause.

Cash savored the memory of that night.

"It was kinda like playing a bloody honky-tonk in the Fifties," he said. "That kind of attitude like, 'Let's have fun!' And it's a very fun place, smaller, actually, than the early years. If I feel like I can just go onstage with my guitar and sing my songs, I can't do wrong no matter where I am."

Just four weeks earlier, twenty-three-year-old actor River Phoenix had fatally overdosed on the sidewalk underneath The Viper Club's purple awning. Later, Johnny Depp recalled Cash's appearance there as a "great cleansing" and an "exorcism" of a dark cloud that had been enveloping the club since Phoenix's death.

At the 1994 South by Southwest alternative music fest in Austin, Texas, Cash delivered a keynote address, and Rubin premiered the noirish black-and-white video to the old folk song "Delia's Gone," in which Johnny tossed dirt on the face of the murdered Delia (model

Kate Moss) in her open grave. MTV objected to some of the grim imagery in the video, which delighted Rubin, who wanted to present Cash as a dangerous agent provocateur. Cash also did an unannounced gig that same night on March 17 at Emo's, a metal-tattoo-hipster joint in Austin, that went over like gangbusters.

"By playing this club, Johnny Cash was being introduced to an audience who had never even considered him—Generation X," said Raoul Hernandez, then Assistant Music Editor for the *Austin Chronicle*. "Emo's was an in-your-face dive bar and emerged in the post-punk and grunge era. It was the beginning of Alternative Nation, and this was one of their clubs. Inside it had Frank Kozik's artwork and murals—it was a very extreme place."

The stage there was four feet high, and Hernandez said when the six-foot-two Cash, garbed in black tuxedo shirt, waistcoat, and black boots, materialized on it, you could almost hear the collective dropping of jaws.

"Johnny Cash was the Grand Canyon. I remember looking up, staring at his boots, his knees," Hernandez said. "Solo acoustic, he drew from his as-yet-unreleased *American Recordings* debut, then got rhythm when his Tennessee Three joined him. They were the Horsemen of the Apocalypse, and when they tore twang on 'I Walk the Line,' my head spun harder than at any music moment because that song was a part of my DNA growing up."

According to Hernandez, Austin was a savvy but somewhat jaded music market, and at the time, a lot of national music acts gave it a wide berth. Cash changed that.

"People here know what's real and what's not, and if they don't like someone, they'll stand with their arms crossed and say, 'Come on, dude, show us what you've got,'" Hernandez said. "But when Cash played Emo's, that room was giddy. People knew how lucky they were to be there. Everybody was grinning from ear to ear, patting each other on the back and saying, 'Can you believe we made it in?' The room was electric, and everyone just melted into a puddle.

"It was a very important gig for the city because, after Johnny Cash played Emo's, suddenly Austin started getting those big acts and one-of-a-kind superstars that we hadn't gotten before. It was clear to me that this gig opened doors, and then there was nobody we couldn't get."

Loud, sustained hosannas greeted *American Recordings* upon its release on April 26, 1994. *Rolling Stone* magazine awarded it five stars and said it was "unquestionably one of [Cash's] best albums." The new, stripped-down sound was viscerally intimate, both intense and ambitious, its subjects touching on God, murder, salvation, forgiveness, and, of course, trains. It was a major artistic breakthrough, a vivid acoustic collection that stunned the music world and reintroduced a mythic American artist to rock audiences.

"The first time I heard it, I said, 'All right!' because I knew that John was back in the ballgame at a level that was comparable to the times when he was the most popular," said friend and recording artist Kris Kristofferson.

Cash was pleased with every aspect of the album and its reception.

"The reaction was like the '50s all over again. It was like that kind of excitement," he said. "I had the freedom of choice in the studio. I did an album I wanted to . . . exactly the way I wanted to. It felt so good to me. It felt good to my producer, and the reaction from the fans and critics was beautiful."

American Recordings earned Cash a Grammy for Best Contemporary Folk Album. *Rolling Stone* later placed it at No. 336 on its honor roll of the "500 Greatest Albums of All Time." It marked Cash's artistic rebirth as a postmodern punk and brought the Man in Black back into the spotlight as "The Godfather of Cool."

He didn't intend to blow it this time.

37

HIP ICON

"There's always been that side of me, and it has
been brought to the fore again. But there's a
rebel in all of us . . ."

—JOHNNY CASH

Sixty-three-year-old Johnny Cash was suddenly relevant again. College students and a new generation of metal heads, alt-rockers, punks, and goths now had an almost frenzied interest in the "hip icon," as one reporter called Cash.

They saw in Cash a resilient, larger-than-life figure who had been through the wars and come out alive; a flawed hero who never complained or explained; an old warrior who didn't look back in anger or regret but only ahead to what tomorrow might bring—a towering, spellbinding American original.

Cash's mid-1990s resurgence was as sweet as they came. It wasn't that long ago that Nashville hastily cast him aside and Branson treated him like a dinosaur. Though bemused and at times bewildered by the adulation of his new young fan base, Cash was grateful that people were paying attention again. He was in demand, his calendar was filled with tour dates, festivals, photo shoots, TV appearances, award shows, and galas. Hipsters, actors, and supermodels now showed up at his gigs to revel in his presence, hoping that some of that perceived mystical juju would rub off on them. The mystery of Johnny was very simple: his bedrock faith in Jesus Christ that had brought him back from the brink of death more than once. Now, he was simply, as Jesus said, "letting his light shine." The new generation, raised on grunge, post-punk, and alt-rock offerings basked in its warm glow. Now they wanted to see the legend in person and hear him sing his old Sun Studio songs mixed in with his new material from *American Recordings*.

Cool has a way of cutting through the generations.

"Growing up, we always knew The Man in Black was cool because that was his whole persona," said Will Turpin, bassist for Collective Soul, the band that had more radio hits in the 1990s than any other group that decade. "During his 1990s comeback, you started to learn things about his life and picked up on the fact that he had seen a thing or two. He was an absolute rock and roll rebel. Rock and roll can be defined by someone's lifestyle just as much as the sound of music . . . and everybody picked up on that real quick during his comeback."

Turpin believed Cash was at a good place in his life and career when he emerged as an icon to a younger generation.

"The middle part of an artist's career is always the toughest, but once you get through the other side there's a comfort and a confidence that comes with that," said Turpin, whose own career now spans a quarter-century. "Then maturity sets in and you're able to create from the right spot. I think when you're able to be yourself again and stand on that ground and be confident, that's when the best stuff comes out."

According to producer, songwriter, and musical artist Anthony J. Resta, popular music since its inception has always been tied to two things: rebellion and pain.

"Generation X not only connected to Cash's legendary rebelliousness, but the pain in his storytelling was something that twenty-somethings at that time could relate to," said Resta, whose own career lifted off around the same time as Cash's comeback. "Johnny Cash painted real pictures of angst."

Cash was grateful for the accolades, but he shrank from considering himself an American icon. When a foreign reporter called him that during an interview, Johnny ruefully said, "I see the pimples on my nose and I see a fat jaw where the pain has left me severely swollen, thinning hair, whatever. Icon? No. I don't see him. He's not in my mirror . . . no, thanks anyway."

Johnny was no longer the young buck trying to establish himself. He had done that decades ago. This was a mature, seasoned Cash who appreciated the flush of newfound success but refused to give up the hard-fought-for spiritual ground he had gained of late.

The Johnny Cash Renaissance took its gravelly-voiced avatar to the famous Glastonbury Music Festival on June 26, 1994. Also performing there were Elvis Costello, Peter Gabriel, Oasis, Rage Against the Machine, Radiohead, and the Beastie Boys—none of whom mesmerized the crowd of eighty thousand fans the way Cash did sitting on a stool on the iconic Pyramid Stage, playing a thirteen-song set with John Carter backing him on rhythm guitar. Afterward, June came out for an encore of "Jackson." Organizers called it one of the most memorable performances in Festival history, and Cash counted it as one of his all-time favorite gigs (chiefly because most of the crowd was the age of his grandchildren). His hip quotient increased tenfold.

"We saw younger audiences coming to the shows," said Jay Dauro, Cash's lighting designer and stage manager. "I can remember when we had a young girl come in with dyed fire-engine red hair, and John just loved it. He thought that was just great. He was enjoying it and had a blast."

In September came another magical night when Johnny returned to New York City's Carnegie Hall. It wasn't the music alone that made it special. In what Cash would recall as an exercise in healing for both of them, daughter Rosanne joined him for a duet of "I Still Miss Someone."

Cash's raging popularity with artists and audiences less than half his age didn't keep him from hanging and working with old friends. He showed up at a Billy Graham Crusade in Atlanta in October.

I remember it well because I was there.

The Graham team was not really aware of the resurgence of Cash's career among the youth culture. In a way, Johnny was living in two worlds, but this time, it was not from compromising his faith. In fact, he was as open about his belief and trust in Jesus Christ to his more secular audiences as he was on the stage of the Billy Graham Crusade.

He was in a great place spiritually and career-wise.

That same month, Cash met up with the Highwaymen in Los Angeles to start work on their third album, *The Road Goes on Forever* (released in April 1995).

But the good times didn't last as long as he hoped.

Cash's second collaboration with Rick Rubin, *American II: Unchained*, was beset by problems, mostly medical ones. Repeated surgeries on Johnny's troublesome jaw left him in constant pain, for which he took so many prescription drugs he was in danger of getting hooked again.

On top of that, June and their son John Carter, now in his early twenties, were struggling with their own addictions. June had concerned herself with her husband's and children's issues all those years to the neglect of her own. Now, thanks to mistreatment of various physical maladies with pharmaceuticals, she spent most days and nights in a virtual stupor. June entered a treatment center, and Cash relied on faith, prayer, and God's grace to keep his family intact. They had switched roles, and ironically, Johnny was now the rock in the relationship for both wife and son.

Drug abuse, Cash once said, "runs through this family like a turkey through the corn. Man, it's terrible."

The sessions for *Unchained* provided a timely distraction. The album was recorded in late 1995 and early '96. Rubin wanted to build on the momentum of *American Recordings* and also take things sonically in a different direction. This time, he had Cash record with a full band behind him, but not Cash's own troupe. Instead, Cash had Tom Petty & the Heartbreakers as session musicians.

"I never asked them to play with me on a record," Cash recalled. "Tom called Rick Rubin just before the sessions and asked if he could come over and play. And when I got there, they were all there, his whole band. So I felt really good about that. He [Petty] said, 'Forget who we are. Let's just make some music.'"

The result, Rick Rubin said, was a fun and easy creative vibe that felt like musician summer camp.

"The Heartbreakers are such a great band, especially with the added excitement of playing with Johnny and without the pressure of it being their own album. It was no risk and all fun," Rubin later recalled to *Rolling Stone*.

Mick Fleetwood, Lindsay Buckingham, Flea from the Red Hot Chili Peppers, and Marty Stuart also played on the album.

Petty had known Cash since the early 1980s and by his own admission was "in awe of him."

"He was one of those people you don't encounter much," Petty later recalled. "It's easy to say, I guess, when someone's a big, iconic celebrity and they're gone. But he really was a fascinating person who had really lived a rich life and who I felt lucky just to be around. And to be his friend was amazing."

Rocker Lenny Kravitz also befriended and was briefly room-mates with the Cashes at this time. He bunked at Rubin's Hollywood home during the recording of *Unchained*. Kravitz was working with Rick Rubin on another project while the latter produced his second effort with Cash. He recalled in 2018 that Cash and Carter were present when he received a phone call from Cedars-Sinai Medical Center with the news that his sixty-six-year-old mother, actress Roxie Roker, had just succumbed to breast cancer.

"I got the phone call when I was in the house, and I'm standing there with the portable phone in my hand, just taking this in, and Johnny and June are walking down the stairs," Kravitz said. "So, Johnny said to me: 'Hi, you're back. How are you?'"

Kravitz told them that his mother had just passed.

"I was a bit fazed and out of it," he recalled. "And the two of them just came up to me and surrounded me and held me."

Though they barely knew him, they "took the time to have a very human moment with someone who was going through something very heavy," Kravtiz said, "and it was beautiful."

That special moment was the basis of Kravitz's 2018 song "Johnny Cash."

Cash was more confident this time than he'd been making *American Recordings*, and was fairly brimming with ideas for the new album. He went so far as to tell Petty that he wanted to make "a record that will offend Johnny Cash fans."

Consisting mostly of cover tunes, *Unchained* had a hard country-rock sound and featured material by Soundgarden, Beck, Hank Snow, Tom Petty, The Carter Family, and Cash himself.

Petty recalled the sessions as charmed, loose, and spiritual—especially the day the tape machine broke in the midst of a particularly hot moment in the studio.

"June came out in the room, where everyone was looking pretty low," he said. "And she said, 'I think if we sing a hymn, maybe God'll fix the tape machine.' Not a procedure I had seen before! And John said, 'Yeah, let's sing a hymn.' And June said, 'Yeah, but we've gotta hold hands,' and so we did. And I swear, within minutes, the machine worked. I always thought that was pretty interesting. That *that* would be their instinct if something was broken: 'We'll sing a hymn.' "

Hymns didn't fix everything. Progress on the album was slowed by Cash's medical issues. In addition to his jaw problems, he suffered from a nervous condition that left him stumbling, shaking, and sometimes unable to sing. He frequently had to lie down.

It helped when *Unchained* was released to some of the most stellar reviews of his career. *Entertainment Weekly* stated the album was a "travelogue of Cash's sticky psyche—the repentant sinner wrestling with dark desires." *Rolling Stone* gave it another five-star review and named it one of the best ten albums of 1996. Years later, the magazine was still hailing it as a "masterpiece."

Cash later received a Grammy for Best Country Album, and his version of Soundgarden's "Rusty Cage" was nominated for Best Male Country Vocal performance.

Dogged as ever, Cash went back on the road in the USA and Europe and toured especially hard in 1997 to promote *Unchained*. The grind took a toll. He began forgetting the lyrics to some of his biggest songs; he shortened his sets and cut back on banter with the audience. Cash even had a crew member lay down colored tape to mark his route from his dressing room to the stage.

The handwriting was clearly on the wall, and after a private appearance at Ford's Theatre in Washington, D.C., Johnny and June informed the band and crew that they intended to retire by the year 2000 and would only do selected engagements after that.

But the Farewell Tour was drastically shortened by another ominous development.

On October 25, Cash was in Flint, Michigan, for a show. Things got harrowing before he even went to the Whiting Auditorium, when Johnny and June were trapped in a glass elevator in their sixteen-story hotel. By the time they were rescued, Cash had suffered a full-blown panic attack, and he was still unnerved when he took the stage just after 8 p.m.

A half-hour into the show, Johnny dropped his guitar pick and almost toppled head-first into the front row trying to retrieve it. There was a ripple of laughter in the sellout crowd of 2,100 as a band member rushed over to help Cash steady himself.

Cash was embarrassed and decided on the spot that it was time to go public with what was wrong with him so there would be no speculation and snickering about drugs and booze.

He was sorry for the way he was behaving, he told the Flint audience, but he had just found out he had Parkinson's disease.

Again there was some tittering from the crowd—he was joking, right?—which instantly ceased when Cash snapped, "It ain't funny."

Then this colossus in black drew himself up and took a deep breath. He looked out at the auditorium full of people and, as if everyone there was his personal friend, bared his soul with as stirring and powerful a declaration as you'll ever find by a general or a statesman in the history books.

"It's all right," he said. "I refuse to give it some ground in my life."

The audience was momentarily stunned. Then came an explosion of applause and cheering.

He finished the show and walked off stage under his own power to a thunderous standing ovation.

After forty-two years and countless miles on the road, Johnny Cash was going home for good.

Days later, he was in a coma.

38

(SPIRITUAL) HOUSE OF CASH

"The Master of Life's been good to me. He has
given me strength to face past illnesses,
and victory in the face of defeat. He has given me
life and joy where others saw oblivion. He has
given me a new purpose to live for, new services
to render, and old wounds to heal."

—JOHNNY CASH

Johnny Cash's spiritual house had been put in order a long time ago. He made peace several times with the Lord throughout his lifetime and was ready for whatever was on the other side of the door when God called him through. He'd had several near-death experiences and had no fear of what awaited him. Now, as his health deteriorated, Johnny was at peace because his faith was in Christ and not in himself.

"I never questioned God, I never doubted God, I never got angry with God," Cash said. "I can't understand people saying they got angry at God. I walked with God all the way through this. That's why I didn't fear. I never feared anything. Not at all. I can honestly say that."

Cash relied throughout his life on the grounding in the faith he got as a youth in Dyess. He always harkened back to his conversion at age twelve in Dyess. He was buoyed by the prayers of his mother and grandmother for his salvation and the knowledge that God heard and answered the prayers of the faithful.

And that is true faith.

I think all of us hope for clear sailing in the sea of life. But we will all have shipwrecks, things that happen that don't make sense. The Bible says, "When your faith is tested, your endurance has a chance to grow. So let it grow, for when your endurance is fully developed, you will be perfect and complete, needing nothing" (James 1:3–4 NLT).

If your faith can't stand a test, it isn't genuine faith. You need to get rid of it and replace it with real faith in a real God. When Christians go through a crisis, their faith should not be destroyed. They should not lose their faith. Their faith should grow stronger because they're clinging to the Lord in the midst of it. The faith that can't be tested is the faith that can't be trusted.

Johnny's faith was tested many times in his life, and it only grew stronger, not weaker.

And because of his faith, Cash had no fear of death. But that didn't mean he wouldn't fight to live.

Now he had to.

On October 29, 1997—four days after the concert in Flint, Michigan—Cash checked into Nashville's Baptist Hospital with severe shortness of breath. He was diagnosed with double pneumonia. His pulmonary function was so poor doctors put Cash in a medically induced coma and on a ventilator.

When they felt his lungs were strong enough to work on their own, the ventilator was removed. But then Cash could not be awakened.

After ten days, doctors told his family to hope for the best but expect the worst.

June reached out to fans worldwide through the internet, asking for a prayer vigil for Johnny the following Tuesday evening. On that night, while Cash fans prayed around the world, Johnny's family gathered around his bed in the intensive care unit, held hands, and prayed, too. A few hours later, June felt her husband squeeze her hand. The following morning, he was sitting up in his hospital bed, sipping coffee.

"It was incredible," Lou Robin, Cash's manager, told *Billboard* magazine. "He was in critical condition at that point and the next morning had turned the corner."

When Cash was well enough to have visitors, one of the first to come was former bandmate Marshall Grant. He had called June when he heard about Johnny's condition and said it was time to forgive and forget. When Grant arrived at Cash's hospital room, Johnny was wearing horn-rimmed glasses and reading a book. Grant was shocked by his pale, almost emaciated appearance. For half an hour, they talked and cried and forgave each other. The past was buried.

When you harbor grudges towards others, it just eats you up inside. American novelist Anne Lamott once said, "Not forgiving is like drinking rat poison and then waiting for the rat to die."

Johnny needed both to extend and receive forgiveness in his life, because when you forgive someone, you set a prisoner free . . . yourself!

Johnny was initially diagnosed with Shy-Drager Syndrome, a neurodegenerative disorder that destroys the central and sympathetic nervous system. Victims of Shy-Drager usually die within eighteen months.

Thanks to his faith, Cash was prepared for whatever would come. "I didn't really worry about it," he told journalist Patrick Carr. "I never thought, 'Oh, man, I gotta get things in order.' I just was there in agreement that I had Shy-Drager's Syndrome or something bad wrong and that I was going to die."

That prospect held no terror for him.

"I thought it was going to be pretty nice and peaceful on the other side, so I guess maybe that's why I didn't worry about it," he said. "I knew it was going to be all right when I got over there. I thought of it in Christian terms—that I would be there with God in eternal bliss. Ecstasy."

This is one of the amazing traits of a Christian when it comes to their view of death. It's not that the Christian wants to die. Fact is, no one loves life more than the follower of Christ. At the same time, that terrorizing threat that death holds over us is gone.

The Bible talks about how God wants to free people who are "held in slavery by their fear of death" (Hebrews 2:15 NIV).

Cash often sang about death. In his song "Ain't No Grave," Johnny sang:

There ain't no grave can hold my body down.
When I hear that trumpet sound,
I'm gonna rise right out of the ground.
Ain't no grave can hold my body down.[3]

And he meant it.

When Cash later learned he didn't have Shy-Drager's, he said, "I was kind of disappointed when I realized I wasn't going to die—you know, more of this pain!'"

The pain was only half of it. When Cash emerged from the coma, his legs would not support him. He was put on meds and essentially sent home to die.

Over the course of the next two years, Cash reported intermittent improvement in his overall health and suspected he had been misdiagnosed.

"An old man knows in his bones if he's got a debilitating disease," he said. "And I knew I didn't have that one."

Additional tests showed that to be the case. Instead of Shy-Drager's, he had diabetic autonomic neuropathy, which is not a specific disease but a collection of symptoms affecting his blood pressure, respiration, and vision, caused by nerve damage. It wasn't Shy-Drager's, but he was far from out of the woods.

It also didn't keep him out of the studio. *American III* (and *American IV*) were recorded mostly at The Cash Cabin in Johnny's compound in Hendersonville. When his strength permitted, Cash made brief trips to Los Angeles to finish the tracks.

Due to his faltering health, on both albums Cash's voice quavers and creaks. It frustrated and embarrassed him, but actually gave the songs an ethereal, almost haunted aspect that made them even more poignant.

It wasn't just age and poor health that put the quaver in Johnny's voice. His loved ones and close friends were starting to die off.

In January 1998, sixty-five-year-old Carl Perkins died. The year before, Perkins had surgery to repair blockage in the right fork of his carotid artery. He seemed to be recovering until he suffered three mild strokes in late November and early December. Cash, who often referred to Perkins as one of his oldest and closest friends, was too ill to attend his funeral.

Helen Carter died in June of that same year at the age of seventy after a long span of poor health. Thirteen months later, Anita Carter passed at the age of sixty-six. Her death hit particularly hard. She suffered from rheumatoid arthritis for many years, and the drugs used to treat it eventually wore out her pancreas, kidneys, and liver. Like movie star Steve McQueen, she even sought alternative treatment in Mexico. Like McQueen, the treatments were for naught. She died under hospice care at Johnny and June's home in Hendersonville. Johnny's illness didn't prevent him from giving the eulogy before Anita was laid to rest near her parents.

"Of the ones who are still left, I talk to Marshall Grant, who played bass for me for so long. He and I are still friends," Cash told *Rolling Stone's* Anthony DeCurtis. "Jack Clement and I are still really close. We don't really do a lot of good ol' days sessions, but if something comes up, we'll argue about who's right about it. But I don't see many of them, no. I don't see many people at all since I got sick."

Truth was, Cash missed being out on the road—the travel, the camaraderie, and especially the approval of the audience, which he once said "gives me a high like none you can get."

His daughter Rosanne confirmed he missed the sights, sounds, and excitement of life on the road.

"It depresses him. He's not used to sitting around," she said. "He's a very powerful person, and to not feel well, that's really hard for him. He spent over forty years on the road, and suddenly he's not out there. When that energy comes to a screeching halt, there's a lot to deal with just inside yourself."

He couldn't get used to just sitting around and not being the boss. The payroll that once supported up to forty people now had a mere handful on it. The museum in the House of Cash that had attracted so many enthusiastic fans was shuttered in 1995.

Any one of Johnny's ailments alone would have been bad enough; but now infirmity and illness came in droves. His asthma compounded the chronic obstructive pulmonary disorder in his lungs; his jaw, in which a platinum plate had been implanted, was a constant source of pain; and he had trouble keeping food down. He was partly deaf in his left ear, partly blind from glaucoma, and suffered from damaged nerve endings and abscessed feet—all that, plus diabetes.

As Cash's condition declined, public acclaim for him grew swiftly. In 1996, Vice President Al Gore—a fellow Tennesseean—nominated Cash for the Kennedy Center Lifetime Achievement Award. President Bill Clinton presented it to him.

At the end of 1998, the National Academy of Songwriters honored Johnny with its Lifetime Achievement Award, and in February 1999, Cash received the same honor from the Grammys.

In April 1999, the industry gathered at Hammerstein Ballroom in New York for Turner Network Television's *All-Star Tribute to Johnny Cash*. Many of Johnny's closest friends and greatest admirers—U2,

Bruce Springsteen, Bob Dylan, Willie Nelson, Kris Kristofferson, Sheryl Crow, Dave Matthews, Emmylou Harris, Norah Jones, and Mary Chapin Carpenter—sang their favorite Cash songs. Up to the last minute, it wasn't certain Johnny would be up to performing himself, but he thrilled everyone there and watching on TV by standing in front of an audience for the first time in eighteen months and singing "Folsom Prison Blues" and "I Walk the Line." Two years later, President George W. Bush presented Cash with the National Medal of Arts.

All that was fine, but Johnny wasn't ready to be considered a relic or has-been; he still had a passion for pushing boundaries by creating and recording new songs. He worked in the Cash Cabin amidst the goats, deer, peacocks, crows, emus, and two buffalos—Rufus and Clementine—who wandered the grounds. Sometimes, sessions were disrupted when the two thousand-pound bison started scraping their horns against the cabin's air-conditioning unit. When Rufus and Clementine went the way of Waldo the ninja ostrich after they gored Johnny's father's pet pig, the family had meat for a whole year.

Cash was unable to put in long days at work on *American III: Solitary Man*, and the good-natured Rubin didn't press him. "He's been fine; we just have to take breaks," the producer told *Rolling Stone*. "Whenever he feels comfortable, we record. It's been very pleasant."

Rubin selected a bumper crop of strong pop, rock, and folk songs for Johnny to sing, including Tom Petty's "I Won't Back Down," U2's "One," and Neil Diamond's "Solitary Man," which became the album's title track.

Cash was self-conscious about his increasingly brittle singing voice, but nobody else had a problem with it. Critics were positive and *Solitary Man* peaked at No. 11 on *Billboard's* Country Album charts in October 2000, even though Cash was unable to go on tour in support of the album. The cherry on top of the sundae was another Grammy for Best Male Country Vocal Performance.

"I wouldn't trade my future for anyone's I know," Cash wrote in the liner notes to *Solitary Man*. "I believe that everything I've done and lived through is what has brought me to this part of my life right now. I like to say I have no regrets. And I really don't."

Radiating the old signature fierce determination, Cash said he didn't even think about death.

"What's to think about?" he asked. "I enjoy my life now."

Johnny was simply reflecting the words of Apostle Paul, about whom he'd written a book: "To live is Christ and to die is gain" (Philippians 1:21 NIV).

39

THE MAN COMES AROUND

"I'm thrilled to death with life. Life—the way God
has given it to me—was just a platter. A golden
platter of life laid out there for me.
It's been beautiful."

—JOHNNY CASH

You've probably heard the hoary cliché that the moment a person is
born he begins to die. Like most clichés, it's based on the truth.
As we age, our bodies decline, an irreversible, immutable process no
pill, no surgery, and no exercise can prevent. Each one of us is allotted
so many days on this earth, and God knows and numbers all of them.
He knows us when we are in our mother's womb, the day we are born,
and the day we take our last breath. The Bible tells us to "number our
days, that we may apply our hearts to wisdom" (Psalm 90:12 KJV).

In other words, as we grow older, make every day count.

Johnny understood this.

Our Creator knows the seasons of our lives. The spring season is about love, hope, and birth. It was during this season Johnny was born and experienced his spiritual rebirth and put his faith in Jesus Christ. Summer represented his youth, enthusiasm, expression, and whole-hearted action for life. With autumn came adulthood and the many transitions in Johnny's life. It was filled with ups and downs, trials and tribulations. Winter, the last season, saw Cash grow old and infirmed.

Like Johnny's friend Billy Graham once said, "Growing old is not for sissies."

Billy wrote in his book, *Nearing Home: Life, Faith and Finishing Well*: "While the Bible doesn't gloss over the problems we face as we grow older, neither does it paint old age as a time to be despised or a burden to be endured with gritted teeth (if we still have any). Nor does it picture us in our latter years as useless and ineffective."

Ironically, it was at this point in Johnny's life he ministered most to others.

"John had a great faith in God, and it was the greatest faith that I had seen or ever will see," said niece Kelly Hancock. "He tried to share it with all of us, and he was very unimposing about it, too. But he was firm that God was the only way."

Jesus said there is good news for the person who knows Jesus Christ, and that good news is eternal life for the believer. His crucifixion and resurrection offers the ultimate, definitive proof of life after death; and because Christ was raised from the dead, we have faith that we will be, too. That's why the certainty of death has no sting or terror for the true believer.

Johnny Cash was not just a believer but also a very smart man with a keen intellect. He knew he was approaching his end of days. Each one was potentially his last.

A true Lion in Winter, Johnny Cash had no intention of quietly fading away. He would remain committed to living and creating and would dedicate the time left to him to his Creator, his family, and his muse.

"At my age, I believe I can feel just a little bit of what Johnny felt—being older and wanting to do just as much or more for the call of God on our life," said Johnny's sister, Joanne Cash Yates. "Johnny knew that he had a calling to do more even though his body challenged him. He pushed on and accomplished everything he could.

"Johnny's love for God was deep and real, as it is with me. I imagine he felt he had disappointed God because of his many mistakes in life and was trying to make up for lost time in the end."

In October 2001, another bout of pneumonia put Cash in a coma for eight days, and once again, his powerful will to live and God's grace pulled him through. When Johnny was able, he and June headed to Cinnamon Hill for sunshine and relaxation. Their sojourn was cut short when Johnny's condition nosedived to the point it was necessary to have him airlifted to Nashville and its top-flight medical facilities.

Through all the travails, Cash somehow doggedly continued to work. "I still just want to make records and sing on the radio," he said. "After I finally got on the radio, I just wanted to make better records, and that's still what I want to do."

And he did it.

For years, Cash yearned to write a modern gospel song in the same vein as "The Wanderer" that would speak to younger fans who had just discovered him. The result was "The Man Comes Around," a song about Christ's second coming and the final judgment. Cash spent more time working on it than any other tune in his catalogue.

Personally, I think this is the greatest song Johnny ever wrote. It is both biblical and personal, powerful and poetic.

From the first rapid strum of his guitar to the pounding piano chords, it is a picture of complexity and simplicity. The deft production skills of Rick Rubin, who understood that "less was more" in this case, added to the familiar voice of the American icon Johnny Cash, and the result was a match made in Heaven.

While Cash was crafting "The Man Comes Around," Rubin was busy selecting other songs for the new album—The Beatles' "In My

Life"; the Eagles' "Desperado"; Roberta Flack's "First Time Ever I Saw Your Face"; Simon & Garfunkel's "Bridge Over Troubled Water"; The Rolling Stones' "No Expectations"; Cat Steven's "Father and Son"; R.E.M.'s "Losing My Religion"; Depeche Mode's "Personal Jesus"; and Nine Inch Nails' "Hurt."

"When Cash sang "Personal Jesus," it took on an entirely different tone than Depeche Mode's version. They sang sarcastically; Johnny sang convincingly. And he sang it with a fellow Christian—the incomparable Alice Cooper.

"I did some of the high parts on that song but I never met him," Cooper said. "He had already done his vocal, so I recorded my part in a studio."

Cooper, who had met almost every music and acting superstar of the twentieth century, said Cash was the one superstar who eluded him.

"There was something about him in that he was like Steve McQueen. He was like James Dean. There was this coolness about him," Cooper said.

"He was more relatable than Dylan was. Dylan was very abstract and wrote a lot of things that sounded great, was deep, and some of it wasn't that deep. It was fun. Johnny Cash had this homespun kind of Americanism to him. There was an honesty about him. Nothing shady about him. Johnny Cash was that icon that every single person could go, 'Yeah, I listen to Johnny Cash.' He was an all-American character."

Rubin was especially enamored of "Hurt," an intense song that spoke of pain, addiction, suicide, and the relentless, graceless march of time as related by one who has hurt himself and the people who love him. (Cash called it "the best anti-drug song I ever heard.")

The producer had long been an admirer of rock singer-songwriter Trent Reznor. Rubin considered Reznor an exceptional talent and despite the glaring differences between an industrial rocker like Reznor and an iconic country artist like Cash, Rubin felt it could work.

Cash also screened potential album material. "I get my coffee early in the morning, and usually, every morning, I listen to some music, usually to songs that were submitted to me the day before," he said. "It's a painful process of weeding them out."

By then, Cash's eyesight was so faded that son John Carter printed out song lyrics in eighteen-point type so he could read them. Johnny also had difficulty playing guitar because poor circulation had robbed him of so much feeling in his fingers. Constantly swollen and sore feet required specially made shoes that limited his mobility.

June also had her issues and checked into Baptist Hospital with pneumonia, and doctors implanted a cardiac pacemaker to keep her heart beating normally. No sooner had she returned home when Cash went back to Baptist Hospital with liver and kidney problems. He was hooked up to a dialysis machine, and his weight dropped by some fifty pounds.

When it rained, it poured. Johnny's close friend and fellow Highwayman Waylon Jennings died on February 13, 2002, after a long struggle with diabetes-related issues. Cash's grief over his friend's passing was assuaged when Jennings' wife, Jessi Colter, told him that in the months before he died, Waylon had recommitted his life to Christ—and died with a smile on his face.

Waylon had lived a rough life, but he knew where to turn in the end. That was no doubt due in part to Johnny's friendship and example. Though not perfect, it was effective.

Somehow, through all the tumult, Cash continued work on what would be his swan song.

"Sometimes I came to the studio and I couldn't sing," he later recalled. "I came in with no voice when I could have stayed at home and pouted in my room and cried in my beer or milk, but I didn't let that happen."

Naturally, the songs in *American IV: The Man Comes Around* possessed a poignant frailty that reflected the human spirit and the fight for survival—classic Cash themes he knew from hard personal experience.

The result was an album of which he was especially proud.

"We put more blood, sweat and tears, and love into this one than anything we've done," Cash said.

The Lord did His part, too.

"He stood with me," Cash said. "I can never praise Him enough for all his blessings."

I think this was the greatest of the American Recordings series, and many others agree, including producer Rick Rubin.

"*Unchained* was hard to make because that was right when he got sick," Rubin said. "His body was still quite strong, but his psyche was confused because he didn't know what was hitting him. On *The Man Comes Around*, his body was weaker, but his psyche was stronger. He knew what was going on; he was more in control."

With its eclectic yet harmonious choices, everything seemed to work, from the beginning to the end of the album.

Released in November 2002, *The Man Comes Around* outperformed all of its predecessors. It reached No. 2 on *Billboard's* country album charts and on the pop charts logged in at No. 22. It won the Album of the Year Award at the 2003 Country Music Association Awards and was certified gold in March and platinum in November—Cash's first non-compilation to do so in thirty years.

It's doubtful any of that would have happened without the gut-and-heart-wrenching video of "Hurt," a song Cash was hesitant to record because he couldn't imagine reinterpreting the original in his own style. The "Hurt" video gave him even greater pause, with its stark, juxtaposed images of the powerfully built, dark-haired singer in his prime and Cash as he was now, frail and aged. Scenes of the now shuttered House of Cash Museum underlined the seeming desolation of a life and career at their end.

From the moment I first saw it and still today, I am moved by the video. It stands the test of time and shows a man confronting his own mortality. His brother Tommy Cash confirmed this in an interview with the BBC.

"I was there some of the days when they recorded that video," he said. "I could see that it was painful for him, yet it was a message he wanted to talk and sing about. He was really proud of that video, but it was sort of goodbye in a way."

When Johnny and June viewed the final cut of the video, they were conflicted about it. June thought it left the impression that Johnny was destitute. Rosanne Cash wept uncontrollably as she watched the video and vehemently urged her father to release it because it was part of his art—excruciatingly truthful. Her reaction persuaded Johnny to give his okay.

"Hurt" received instant accolades and got heavy rotation on MTV and other media outlets and platforms, which in turn spurred radio play and album sales. *The Man Comes Around* was the first album since *At San Quentin* to top the one-million mark in sales.

The video had far greater impact. To millions of people who weren't even born when he sang at Folsom Prison and hosted his TV show, it made Johnny Cash a beloved, awe-inspiring hero.

"Hurt" was nominated for six MTV Music Awards, and it won for Best Cinematography. It lost to Justin Timberlake's "Cry Me a River" for Video of the Year, but when Timberlake accepted the award, he said, "My grandfather raised me on Johnny Cash. I'm from Tennessee. And I think he deserves this more than any of us here tonight."

Days before his seventy-first birthday, Cash won another Grammy for "Give My Love to Rose," a song he originally recorded in the late 1950s, for Best Male Country Vocal Performance. ("Bridge Over Troubled Water," a duet with Fiona Apple, was also nominated for Best Country Collaboration with Vocals, as was *The Man Comes Around* for Best Contemporary Folk Album).

The comeback was now complete.

His legacy was now forever cemented.

The Man in Black was going out on top.

Unfortunately, his time was running out.

40

——

UNSHAKEABLE FAITH

"That great light is a light that now leads me on
and directs me and guides me. That great light
is the light of this world. That great light is the
light out of this world, and into that better world.
And I'm lookin' forward to walkin' into it
with that great light."

—JOHNNY CASH

On March 28, 2003, country music officially became the House of Cash when Country Music Television named Johnny the most important male artist in the history of the genre, above such luminaries as Gene Autry, Jimmie Rogers, Elvis Presley, Waylon Jennings, Willie Nelson, Merle Haggard, George Jones, and Hank Williams. CMT also established a new award in Johnny's name—the Johnny Cash Visionary Award.

The accolades and celebrations of his achievements gave Cash a boost as he faced mounting health crises. By the time he turned seventy, the ravages of time and disease had left their mark on the legendary singer-songwriter. Cash was frail, and his thinning white hair made him look twenty years older. Diabetes inexorably dimmed his eyesight. There wasn't a part of him that functioned properly and didn't hurt. He spent as much time in the hospital as not.

Cash checked into Baptist Hospital after Christmas '02 for an operation to remove an ulcer on his foot. He went home after New Year's, but a bad fall sent him right back. Then he went home, fell again, and spent the rest of the month in the hospital.

For two days in March, he was strong enough to resume work on a new album, then titled *American V: A Hundred Highways*. But then Cash was rushed back to the hospital with severe respiratory distress and had to be put on a ventilator again. He was too ill to attend the funeral of his sister Louise, who died of pancreatic cancer at 79 on April 4, 2003.

A month later came the cruelest blow of all.

While everyone focused on Johnny's issues and needs—especially June—her own health deteriorated. Doctors had warned her for months about a leaking heart valve that needed immediate attention, but with Johnny's problems and all, she kept putting it off. In early April, seventy-three-year-old June was whisked to Baptist Hospital and placed in the intensive care unit. She rallied and returned home, but on April 28, she was readmitted to the hospital. Nine days later, surgeons replaced the faulty heart valve, but too much damage had already been done. On May 9, June went into cardiac arrest. Her heart stopped for up to fifteen minutes, and she was put on life support. Doctors detected no brain activity and told Johnny his wife was clinically dead.

The decision to take June off life support was his, and he finally assented at the urging of his children. Her cardiac pacemaker kept June's heart beating until the end came on May 15. Johnny and the children were with her when she crossed over, singing hymns and praying.

"The strongest person of everyone in the Cash and Carter family was Johnny Cash," recalled Mark Stielper. "He was devastated. He was bereft. I held his hand in the hospital when June was dying, and he was the one giving others strength. When people would come in and try to comfort him, he was comforting them even more."

June's funeral at the First Baptist Church of Hendersonville three days later was open to the public at Johnny's insistence. More than 1,500 mourners and luminaries turned out, including Rev. Jimmie Snow.

"The first person I ran into at the funeral was John, who was in a wheelchair at the time. I went over and hugged his neck, and we talked a while," Snow said. "It was a good conversation, and I didn't want to take up a lot of his time, but I just wanted to let him know how sorry I was. I also said, 'You know, we'll all be there together one day.' He nodded his head."

Music was provided by a variety of country and rock artists, including Emmylou Harris, the Gatlin Brothers, Sheryl Crow, and some of the Carter clan. June's pallbearers were Mark Stielper, Thomas Gabriel Coggins, Kevin Carter Jones, Theodore Rollins, John Jackson Routh, and James Dustin Tittle.

At the end of the service, Johnny was helped to his feet and guided over to the casket to say farewell to his greatest ally, fiercest supporter, and the love of his life.

Back home, Cash and his children, grandchildren, and some close friends gathered at the bell garden where thirty brass bells were hung. After an opening prayer by Johnny, the bells were rung seventy-three times, for each of June's years on earth.

With her gone, no one expected Johnny to last much longer, and he himself must've sensed that his own time was nigh. He told John Carter he had to get into the studio as quickly as possible, and three days later he was.

"He suffered a lot of pain in his life, but this was by far the worst he'd ever had to deal with," said Rick Rubin. "But a strange thing happened. He became more driven about work. He booked a session for three days after June passed. He said, 'I don't want to do any of the things some people do when they lose their partner. I don't want to spend money and meet a lot of girls. I don't want to do anything of this world. I want to make music and do the best work I can. That's what she would want me to do, and that's what I want to do.'"

One of the songs Cash recorded after June's death was Cat Stevens' "Father and Son," which ended up being a duet with artist Fiona Apple. Rick Rubin enlisted keyboardist Rami Jaffee to lay down the piano track in California.

"I got a call from Rick Rubin's assistant that I come straight away to Rick's house off Sunset Plaza in the Hollywood Hills," Jaffee recalled in 2019. "When I asked who was the session for, she replied it was either for the Red Hot Chili Peppers or Johnny Cash but wasn't really sure. I hopped on my motorcycle in Malibu and immediately headed that way."

Jaffee first heard the song at summer camp when he was in his early teens. "The counselors there were really just older teens themselves and would sit around the campfire and play classic rock, country, and folk—the kind of songs that I've grown to feel in my blood," Jaffee said. "Not only was this Cat Stevens classic embedded in my soul in a good way, but when I heard Cash sing those words loud and clear in my earphones, it was just chilling."

Usually, Rubin let Jaffee do his own thing in the studio. This time, his instructions were succinct to the point of terseness:

"Play it super simple, don't second-guess anything, play from the heart—and walk away."

Jaffee did as ordered, and the results were nothing less than stunning. "Father and Son" was issued on *Unearthed*, released a few weeks after Cash's death.

"It was where country and pop culture felt dangerous like never before," Jaffee recalled of his collaboration with Cash. "And that last chapter with *American Recordings* . . . Johnny may have been in the bottom of the ninth inning, but he hit such a grand slam before he left."

Cash's work on the next Rubin-produced album was suspended long enough for a late June trip to the Carter Family Fold in Hiltons, Virginia, where he performed in front of an audience of about 1,600.

After being helped from his wheelchair to a chair on stage, he sang and strummed an acoustic guitar for a thirty-minute set backed by bassist Bobby Starnes and guitarist Jerry Hensley. Fragile as he was, Johnny exuded warmth and life force—for which he credited his wife, born seventy-four years ago that day. He returned to the same venue on July 5 for what would be his final public performance. At the end of his last song, "Understand Your Man," Cash received a standing ovation.

Johnny's longing for June weighed heavier on him every day. Not able to sleep alone in the bed they had shared, he had a twin bed put in his office amidst the things he loved most: his guitar, his Bible, a library of more than five hundred books, a TV (usually tuned to CNN), and a framed photograph of June he talked to constantly. He spent a lot of time on the phone with his friend Billy Graham, praying and receiving encouragement. He napped in the afternoon and at night slept as best he could, propped up by pillows to reduce acid reflux.

A team of caretakers watched over him day and night, among them health practitioner and nutritionist Phil Maffetone, whose job was to gradually wean Cash off the thirty medications he took daily.

Among family members who took turns being with Johnny were daughters Cindy, Tara, and Rosanne, who used the time to heal the breach between themselves and their father resulting from his divorce from Vivian and marriage to June, his drug addiction, and his constant touring.

Cindy traveled from Jackson, Mississippi, to stay with Cash for three months. One of their first excursions was to visit the Bon Aqua farm, during which the extent of her dad's physical problems became clear to Cindy.

"He kept thumbing through books that I kept noticing he wasn't reading, and that's when I realized he was blind," she said. "After he thumbed through about seven or eight books, he said, 'Let's walk through the house.' He had a collection of bottles that he had dug up on the property. I was told they were over a hundred years old. He said, 'I want you to take all of my bottles home.' I said, 'I don't want to take your bottles, Dad. They've been sitting here in the window sill for thirty years." He said, 'That's why I want you to take them. I don't want anything to happen to them.'

"That's when I realized he was saying goodbye to the farm. And about two months later, I said goodbye to him."

At the Henderson Lake house, Cindy frequently wheeled him outside to sit in the sun, and once took him to visit June's gravesite. Johnny cried for June constantly, and at her grave, he choked up and said, "I'm coming, baby. I'm coming." When Cindy said she didn't like to hear such talk, Cash apologized and said, "But I *am*—I'm coming to Heaven."

Tara came for three days in July. Knowing that it was likely their last time together, she taped her conversations with her dad. They also passed time playing a fun game Tara made up whereby she threw out a random topic and Johnny had to come up with a song about it. She never stumped him.

Vivian herself visited for a week in July. She had in mind to publish a book based on the thousands of letters she and Johnny had exchanged during his Air Force years, and she hoped he wouldn't object.

"If anyone on this planet should write a book about me, it should be you," Johnny told her. Her memoir, *I Walked the Line: My Life with Johnny*, was published in 2007. Unfortunately, Vivian never saw the finished product. She died on May 24, 2005.

Ann Sharpsteen, the book's co-author, said the last meeting between Vivian and Cash was cathartic for her friend.

"She was thrilled that [Johnny] was supportive about the book. He never told her the words outright—'I am so sorry.' But she came to the conclusion that sometimes people—particularly men—have a hard time saying they're sorry but show it in other ways," Sharpsteen said. "When Johnny gave his approval for the book, in her heart, that was his 'I'm sorry.' I remember talking to her immediately after that encounter, and she was teary and so happy. It makes me cry when I think about it. It was such a monumental, touching, and affirming final moment with him."

Rosanne Cash came in August, watching TV with her dad and reading to him from the Book of Job and the Psalms, and poetry by Will Carleton, one of Johnny's favorites. Her heart ached for him one afternoon as the sun started to go down and Johnny sighed, "The gloaming of the day is the hardest part."

Niece Kelly Hancock visited with Johnny as much as she could.

"This was a man who had such a great impact on my life and was like a second father to me," she said. "I had such a great love for and felt so connected to him. He watched the news non-stop, and I joked, 'You know you're an old man when you watch CNN all the time,' and he would laugh and say, 'You can go home now, okay?' I loved him very much."

On August 20, MTV's Kurt Loder filmed what would be Cash's final television interview, in which Johnny talked about his career, music, faith—and his imminent death.

"I expect my life to end pretty soon," Cash said. "I'm seventy-one years old, but I have unshakeable faith. I've never turned my back on God, so to speak. I've never thought God wasn't there. He is my counselor. He is my wisdom—all the good things in my life are from Him."

When Loder asked, "Where do you think we go?" Cash didn't hesitate. He smiled broadly and said, "When we die, you mean? Oh, well, we all hope to go to Heaven."

Sister Joanne and her husband Harry Yates lived ten minutes away and came over frequently. They read the Bible to Johnny and talked about spiritual matters. Recalled Joanne:

"I asked him one time, 'Are you afraid of death?' He said, 'No, Baby, I can't hardly wait to be with the Lord.' On a later visit, very close to the end of his life, he asked me, 'If you walked the shores of Galilee and you looked up and saw Jesus walking towards you and you knew He was going to say one thing, what would you hope He would say?' Well, chills went all over me, but I didn't know how to answer him other than I hoped He was pleased with me.

"Then I asked Johnny how he'd answer. Tears rolled down his face as he said, 'Come unto Me all ye that labor and are heavy laden, and I will give you rest. Take My yoke upon you and learn of Me, for I am meek and lowly in heart'" (Matthew 11:28 NKJV).

"What Johnny was saying to me that day," said Joanne, "was, 'I'm going home, and it's okay.'"

On August 21, Cash returned to the studio and recorded "Engine One-Forty-Three," an old Carter Family traditional based on the true story of an 1890 train wreck. It was the last full recording he would ever put to tape. (The song was released on 2004's *The Unbroken Circle: The Musical Heritage of the Carter Family*.)

Johnny hoped to attend the MTV Video Music Awards at Radio City Music Hall in New York City on August 28, and also talked about going to Los Angeles in September to meet with Rick Rubin. But those plans went a-glimmering on August 26 when Cash was rushed to Baptist Hospital with severe stomach pain. He was treated for pancreatitis.

Johnny returned home on Wednesday, September 10. The next morning, Phil Maffetone found him slumped in his wheelchair, his oxygen and blood sugar levels plummeting. Maffetone started to rub his extremities to get his circulation going, and Cash lifted his head, looked him in the eye, and said, "It's time."

As an ambulance sped Johnny to Baptist Hospital, family members were notified to get there as fast as possible.

Joanne recalled the last time she saw her brother, on September 11, 2003. She said:

"Most of his children were there, and so were Harry and me, and my sister Reba. I asked the kids if I could have a moment alone with him. Johnny was laying on his side, and I said, 'Just let go, Johnny . . . take the hand of Jesus.' He opened his eyes and looked at me, then closed them like, 'Okay.' He was all right. He was ready."

As his body began the process of shutting down, Cash squeezed the hands of Rosanne, Kathy and John Carter as they prayed. After several hours, the exhausted children went to nearby rooms to rest. In the middle of the night, a nurse summoned them back to Johnny's bedside.

They hugged and kissed their father and assured him it was okay for him to go, and at two o'clock in the morning on September 12, 2003, the man Kris Kristofferson called "Abraham Lincoln with a wild side" was gloriously reunited with his brother Jack, his parents Ray and Carrie, his brother Roy, his sister Louise, and his wife June at the throne of God. Johnny Cash was finally home.

And the ultimate gift: eternity in Heaven.

EPILOGUE

I wrote this book because of a lifelong fascination with and appreciation of the man Johnny Cash. I always knew of his deep Christian faith, but as I worked on this project with Marshall Terrill, I discovered many things I did not know.

I was not disappointed—just surprised.

I learned Johnny had more struggles and lapses than I was aware of, even into his later years. What did not surprise me was that he had a bedrock faith in Jesus Christ that sustained him to the end.

Johnny was a flawed individual . . . just like the rest of us. He sinned, and he was the first to admit it. But he knew where to turn when he was in need, which was often.

Johnny started and finished well, both musically and spiritually. He stands as a textbook example of a man who found that God gives second chances in life, and he took full advantage of that again and again.

I love what Johnny hoped to hear Jesus say to him when they met face to face: "Come unto Me all ye that labor and are heavy laden, and I will give you rest. Take My yoke upon you and learn of Me, for I am meek and lowly in heart."

These are the words of Jesus from Matthew's gospel.

If Johnny Cash were here with us today, he would want us to know that eternity is real, and God's promises are trustworthy.

And I am confident, based on his life and words and songs, that he would want you to find the same peace and satisfaction in a relationship with God through Jesus Christ that he had.

So what do you need to do?

No. 1—You need to admit your need for God.

That is hard for a lot of people. They think they make it on their own. One of Johnny Cash's great strengths was an awareness of his weakness.

He knew he was a sinner. The fact is, we all are.

The word "sin" means many things in the Bible. One definition of it is to "cross the line."

Johnny sang of how he "walked the line," but he also crossed it many times—as we all do.

This is when we break God's commandments, such as "You shall not steal," "You shall not commit adultery," "You shall not take the Lord's name in vain," "You shall not lie." And if you have broken just one of God's commandments, you have crossed the line.

The Bible says, "For the person who keeps all of the laws except one is as guilty as a person who has broken all of God's laws" (James 2:10 NLT).

Another definition of sin from the Bible is to miss the mark. God has set a mark for humanity, which is absolute perfection. We all miss that mark by a country mile. None of us is even close to perfect. And that is where Jesus comes in. Which brings us to . . .

No. 2—You must realize that Jesus Christ died on the cross for you. And why does Jesus dying on a cross matter to us some two thousand years later? Because we are all separated from God by our sin, Jesus died in our place. He paid the price for our sins.

He came to pay a debt He did not owe because we owed a debt we could not pay.

Jesus put it this way: "For God so loved the world that He gave His only begotten Son, that whoever believes in Him should not perish but have everlasting life" (John 3:16 KJV).

Johnny Cash believed that verse, and you need to as well if you want to have everlasting life and go to Heaven.

No. 3—You must turn from your sin and believe in Jesus. That is what Jesus said: "Whoever believes in Him should not perish." So what exactly does it mean to "believe"?

It is not mere intellectual assent to the fact that a man named Jesus lived and died two thousand years ago. It is putting your personal faith in Jesus, who not only died for you but then rose again from the dead three days later.

Now Jesus stands at the door of your life and He knocks. If you will hear his voice and open that door to your heart, so to speak, He will come in.

Have you done that yet?

Johnny Cash did it as a young man, had multiple lapses, and returned to the Lord as he grew older. His wife June Carter Cash did it as well. Johnny's friend and fellow country superstar Waylon Jennings did it at the end of his own life. At the peak of his fame, actor Steve McQueen prayed and asked Jesus to come into his life as well. They all had fame and fortune to an extent most people can only dream about. All of them saw their need for Jesus and turned to Him. And all these people are together right now in Heaven because of it.

What have you got to lose?

You could ask Jesus to come into your life right now in a simple prayer like this:

Lord Jesus, I know that I am a sinner.
But I also know that you are the Savior, who died on the
  cross for my sin.
I am sorry for my sin and repent of it right now.
Come into my life to be my Lord, my God, and my friend.
I receive you now by faith.
In Jesus's name I pray.
Amen.

Did you just pray that prayer?

If so, you can know with certainty that Christ is living inside of you right now.

You can also know that you will go to Heaven when you die.

I would love to help you in this commitment to Christ you have just made.

We have a special website (www.knowgod.org) set up that you can visit to find out more about what it means to be a follower of Jesus Christ.

ACKNOWLEDGEMENTS

In my research, I have consulted a veritable library of Cash books, articles, periodicals, YouTube videos, and literally thousands of pages on the internet. But my most valuable resource has been people who knew the man. You'll be reading quotes and contributions here from those who intimately knew Johnny Cash at the beginning, middle, and end of his life.

Three of them have been especially valuable: Johnny's sister, Joanne Cash Yates; her husband, Pastor Harry Yates; and Cash family historian Mark Stielper.

They say no one knows someone better than a sister, and that was certainly the case with Johnny and Joanne Cash. Their mother Carrie often commented that they were like "twins born six years apart." Joanne adored her big brother and is very protective of Johnny's legacy and understandably wary of inquiries about him. This gracious and devout lady agreed to help me solely in the hope that Johnny's redemption story might bring more people to Christ.

The incomparable Pastor Harry Yates, Joanne's husband, holds three doctorates, including a Ph.D. in Psychology and Counseling. This amazing Renaissance man has been a high school teacher, pilot, author, actor, lecturer, college instructor, Bible college president, record producer, and he founded the Nashville Cowboy Church in 1990. Harry intimately knew Johnny's heart, especially when it came to godly matters. Cash enjoyed hearing Harry's interpretation of the Word. "It made Johnny think," says Harry, who possesses the rare ability to guide you to a revelation or insight and make you believe you did it all by yourself. He's also as funny as a stand-up comedian, and that made the ride a lot easier.

Mark Stielper is a human encyclopedia on all things Cash. He was a successful Maryland businessman in hotel management when he met Johnny in 1983. They didn't talk about music or the entertainment business then so much as about the Apostle Paul. At the time, Cash was researching a book on the life of Paul he would call *Man in White*. Mark once considered entering the priesthood, and though he chose a different path, he maintained a keen spirituality and enjoyed talking over and debating theological matters with Cash. Sometimes, their discussions became intense debates, but never to the detriment of their friendship, for as it says in Proverbs 27:17, "As iron sharpens iron, so one person sharpens another" (NIV). Mark's generosity in his time and knowledge went way beyond the pale.

I'm endlessly grateful to have been blessed in this undertaking by their wonderful cooperation, guidance, and kindness.

Others who also helped enormously in this endeavor we'd like to thank in alphabetical order: Dennis Agajanian, Brenda Rose Bailey, Dick Boak, Joe Byrne, Alice Cooper, Jay Dauro, Karla Dial, Pete Ehrmann, Don Hancock, Dr. Bill Hamon, Sherilyn Miller-Hamon, Kelly Hancock, Ruth Hawkins, A J Henson, Raoul Hernandez, Cara Highsmith, Rami Jaffee, Keith Jones, Ken Mansfield, Anne Meyer, Deborah Millikan, Louise Nichols, Tom Phillips, Anthony J. Resta, Rick Scott, Ann Sharpsteen, Billy Smiley, Jimmie Snow, Will Turpin, Carolyn Terrill, Mike Terrill, Kat Vinson, Reggie Vinson, Erik Wolgemuth, and Robert Wolgemuth.

SELECTED BIBLIOGRAPHY

Bannister, C. Eric. *Johnny Cash FAQ: All That's Left to Know about the Man in Black*, Backbeat Books, 2014.

Bono, The Edge, Adam Clayton and Larry Mullen, Jr. *U2 by U2*, Harper Collins, 2005.

Bowen, Jimmy and Jim Jerome. *Rough Mix*, Simon & Schuster, 1997.

Cash, John Carter. *Anchored in Love: An Intimate Portrait of June Carter Cash*, Thomas Nelson, 2007.

Cash, John Carter. *House of Cash: The Legacies of My Father, Johnny Cash*, Insight Editions, 2011.

Cash, Johnny with Patrick Carr. *Cash: The Autobiography*, Harper Collins, 1997.

Cash, Johnny. *Man in Black*, Zondervan, 1975.

Cash, June Carter. *From the Heart*. Prentice Hall Press, 1987.

Cash, Rosanne. *Composed*, Viking, 2010.

Cash, Vivian with Ann Sharpsteen. *I Walked the Line: My Life with Johnny*, Scribner, 2007.

Chadwick, Julie. *The Man Who Carried Cash: Saul Holiff, Johnny Cash and the Making of an American Icon*, Dundurn, 2012.

Fine, Jason. *Cash*, Crown Publishers, 2004.

Grant, Marshall. *I Was There When It Happened: My Life with Johnny Cash*, Cumberland House, 2006.

Hawkins, Van. *A New Deal in Dyess: The Depression Era Agricultural Resettlement Colony in Arkansas*, 2015.

Hilburn, Robert. *Johnny Cash: The Life*, Little Brown and Company, 2013.

Light, Alan. *Johnny Cash: The Life and Legacy of the Man in Black*, Smithsonian Books, 2018.

Miller, Stephen. *Johnny Cash: The Life of an American Icon*, Omnibus Press, 2003.

Schwoebel, Tara Cash. *Recollections by J.R. Cash: Childhood Memories of Johnny Cash*, 2014.

Streissguth, Michael. *Johnny Cash: The Biography*, Da Capo Press, 2006.

Streissguth, Michael. *Ring of Fire: The Johnny Cash Reader*, Da Capo Press, 2002.

Thomson, Graeme. *The Resurrection of Johnny Cash: Hurt, Redemption and American Recordings*, Jawbone, 2011.

Turner, Steve. *The Man Called Cash: The Life, Love, and Faith of an American Legend*, W Publishing Group, 2004.

Waddell, Hugh. *I Still Miss Someone*, Cumberland House, 2004.

Willet, Edward. *Johnny Cash: The Man in Black*, Enslow Publishers, Inc., 2011.

Wren, Christopher S. *Winners Got Scars Too: The Life and Legends of Johnny Cash*, The Dial Press, 1971.

Urbanski, Dave. *The Man Comes Around: The Spiritual Journey of Johnny Cash*, Relevant Books, 2003.

Yates, Harry. *Help! I'm in the Ministry!*, 2000.

Yates, Joanne Cash. *My Fears Are Gone*, Bible Voice Books, 1978.

SOURCES

Chapter One

"I don't believe a man ever lived," Johnny Cash. *Man in Black*, Zondervan, 1975, pg. 7.

"His early years were misspent," Mark Stielper, personal interview, October 18, 2018.

"It wasn't a place that," Mark Stielper, personal interview, October 18, 2018.

"Well, that was worth something, wasn't it?" Mark Stielper, personal interview, October 18, 2018.

"What this meant was," Mark Stielper, personal interview, October 18, 2018.

"When word got out about," Mark Stielper, personal interview, October 18, 2018.

"There was no running water," Johnny Cash with Patrick Carr. *Cash: The Autobiography*, Harper Collins, 1997, pg. 15.

Chapter Two

"I think for the first time I knew what I was going to do," Johnny Cash. "Johnny Cash—The Lowdown—Interviews—Part 1," YouTube.com, April 5, 2013.

"According to my dad, the waters," Joanne Cash Yates, personal interview, June 1, 2018.

"He used to call me 'Baby,' because I'm the baby sister," Joanne Cash Yates, personal interview, June 1, 2018.

"J.R. was an extremely hard worker," A J Henson, personal interview, October 18, 2018.

"It wasn't an easy existence," Kelly Hancock, personal interview, February 16, 2019.

"J.R. would lead sometimes," Joanne Cash Yates, personal interview, June 1, 2018.

"The simple doctrine of the church," A J Henson, personal interview, October 18, 2018.

"My daddy would put us in the wagon," Joanne Cash Yates, personal interview, June 1, 2018.

"That really scared me," Joanne Cash Yates, personal interview, June 1, 2018.

"Whenever you have something shoved," Kelly Hancock, personal interview, February 16, 2019.

"He was a young man in an old, brown tweed suit," Johnny Cash. *Man in Black*, Zondervan, 1975, pg. 8.

"The 'Grand Ole Opry' on Saturday," Joanne Cash Yates, personal interview, June 1, 2018.

"He drew Mighty Mouse with the stroke of his pen," Joanne Cash Yates, personal interview, June 1, 2018.

"I knew there was two distinct ways to go in life," Johnny Cash. *Man in Black*, Zondervan, 1975, pg. 18.

"I left feeling awfully good that night," Johnny Cash. *Man in Black*, Zondervan, 1975, pg. 19.

Chapter Three

"Jack was the essence of a Christian," Joanne Cash Yates, personal interview, June 1, 2018.

"I didn't know you cussed," Johnny Cash. *Man in Black*, Zondervan, pg. 16.

"I think it bothered Jack," Johnny Cash. *Man in Black*, Zondervan, pg. 16.

"Jack you know if you don't belong to my church," Joanne Cash Yates, personal interview, June 1, 2018.

"I don't think he ever tried to talk religion," Johnny Cash. *Man in Black*, Zondervan, pg. 17.

"Throw away your fishin' pole and get in," Johnny Cash. *Man in Black*, Zondervan, pg. 22.

"Tell me something happy," Christopher S. Wren. *Winners Got Scars Too: The Life and Legends of Johnny Cash*, The Dial Press, 1971, pg. 59.

"We're going to lose him, J.R.," Johnny Cash. *Man in Black*, Zondervan, 1975, pg. 23.

"No. It's not your time," John Carter Cash. *House of Cash*, Insight Editions, 2015, pg. 31.

"He was saying strange things that I didn't understand," Joanne Cash Yates, personal interview, June 1, 2018.

"Will you meet me in Heaven?" Joanne Cash Yates, personal interview, June 1, 2018.

"Why is everybody crying over me?" Johnny Cash. *Man in Black*, Zondervan, 1975, pg. 25.

"It really scared her and she said John comforted her," Kelly Hancock, personal interview, February 16, 2019.

"I'll get up when *God* pushes me up," Johnny Cash with Patrick Carr. *Cash: The Autobiography*, Harper Collins, 1997, pg. 27.

Chapter Four

"Why, Lord? Why? Why? Why?" Johnny Cash. *Man in Black*, Zondervan, 1975, pg. 28.

"Daddy was in deep grief," Joanne Cash Yates, personal interview, June 1, 2018.

"Sometimes when you lose a gift," Johnny Cash with Patrick Carr. *Cash: The Autobiography*, Harper Collins, 1997, pg. 50.

"You're wasting your time," Johnny Cash with Patrick Carr. *Cash: The Autobiography*, Harper Collins, 1997, pg. 51.

"You'll never do any good as long," Johnny Cash with Patrick Carr. *Cash: The Autobiography*, Harper Collins, 1997, pg. 51.

"Ms. Fielder said, 'Well, J.R.,'" Joanne Cash Yates, personal interview, June 1, 2018.

"My dad used to drink all the time," Vivian Cash with Ann Sharpsteen. *I Walked the Line: My Life with Johnny*, Scribner, 2007, pg. 49.

"Mama did all of her biscuit making," Joanne Cash Yates, personal interview, June 1, 2018.

"You sound exactly like," Joanne Cash Yates, personal interview, June 1, 2018.

"God has His hand on you," Johnny Cash. *Man in Black*, Zondervan, 1975, pg. 38.

Chapter Five

"J.R. liked to be out front," A J Henson, personal interview, October 18, 2018.

"We were all from farming families," Louise Nichols, personal interview, October 2, 2018.

"Back then there were no alcohol," Louise Nichols, personal interview, October 2, 2018.

"J.R. loved Westerns," Louise Nichols, personal interview, October 2, 2018.

"They showed a serial and a cartoon," Louise Nichols, personal interview, October 2, 2018.

"I might go with you sometime," Johnny Cash. *Man in Black*, Zondervan, 1975, pg. 36.

"So long, Virginia North," Johnny Cash. *Man in Black*, Zondervan, 1975, pg. 36.

"Many people from Dyess," A J Henson, personal interview, October 18, 2018.

"How long you gonna work here?" Robert Hilburn. *Johnny Cash: The Life*, Little, Brown & Co., pg. 26.

Chapter Six

"Why he's almost human," Vivian Cash with Ann Sharpsteen. *I Walked the Line: My Life with Johnny*, Scribner, 2007, pg. 25.

"Boys grow up fast over here honey," Vivian Cash with Ann Sharpsteen. *I Walked the Line: My Life with Johnny*, Scribner, 2007, pg. 71.

"He said his military service was very hard," Kelly Hancock, personal interview, February 16, 2019.

"Spent twenty years in the Air Force," C. Eric Banister. *Johnny Cash FAQ: All That's Left to Know About the Man in Black,* Backbeat Books, 2014, pg. 7.

Chapter Seven

"You're the one who's been calling," Johnny Cash, 1993 interview, YouTube.com.

"There's something really squirrely," Robert Hilburn. *Johnny Cash: The Life*, Little, Brown & Co., 2013, pg. 67.

"We've got good songs, love songs," Steve Turner. *The Man Called Cash*, Word Publishing Group, 2004, pg. 52.

Chapter Eight

"John, the way I do it is by being what I am," Johnny Cash. *Man in Black*, Zondervan, 1975, pg. 50.

"Elvis was the most handsome man," Joanne Cash Yates, personal interview, June 1, 2018.

"Oh yeah, always talked about gospel music," Johnny Cash, "Johnny Cash on the Gospel," YouTube.com, October 14, 2014.

"That's why I feel so low this morning," Johnny Cash. *Man in Black*, Zondervan, 1975, pg. 56.

"Baby, are you ever tempted," Vivian Cash with Ann Sharpsteen. *I Walked the Line: My Life with Johnny*, Scribner, 2007, pg. 279.

"You don't ever need to worry, baby," Vivian Cash with Ann Sharpsteen. *I Walked the Line: My Life with Johnny*, Scribner, 2007, pg. 279.

Chapter Nine

"'I Walk the Line' would be a better title," Johnny Cash. *Man in Black*, Zondervan, 1975, pg. 57.

"Wait guys, wait!" Marshall Grant. *I Was There When It Happened: My Life with Johnny Cash*, Cumberland House, 2006, pg. 56.

"It was in my head too long," Johnny Cash. *Larry King Live*, 2002.

"The road is crushing," Mark Stielper, personal interview, October 18, 2018.

"I got something that will fix you right up," Johnny Western, personal interview, December 15, 2018.

"I loved everybody!" Johnny Cash. *Man in Black*, Zondervan, 1975, pg. 61

"I've always wanted to meet you," Andrew Leahey. "Flashback: Johnny Cash Makes Opry Debut, Meets June Carter," *Rolling Stone*, July 7, 2014.

"I can't remember anything else," Johnny Cash. *Love, God, Murder* liner notes, Legacy/Columbia, 2000.

"Someday I'm going to marry you," Johnny Cash. *Love, God, Murder* liner notes, Legacy/Columbia, 2000.

Chapter Ten

"Now we have a connecting door," Marshall Grant. *I Was There When It Happened: My Life with Johnny Cash*, Cumberland House, 2006, pg. 66.

"He gave Carl Perkins one when," Johnny Cash with Patrick Carr. *Cash: The Autobiography*, Harper Collins, 1997, pg. 78.

Chapter Eleven

"Hey, man, did you hear Johnny Horton died," Vivian Cash with Ann Sharpsteen. *I Walked the Line: My Life with Johnny*, Scribner, 2007, pg. 287.

Chapter Twelve

"I spent a good deal of time at John and Vivian's house," Kelly Hancock, personal interview, February 16, 2019.

"I found you can cultivate a taste," Johnny Cash. *Man in Black*, Zondervan, pg. 62.

"Look, with every husband, my diamond," Vivian Cash with Ann Sharpsteen. *I Walked the Line: My Life with Johnny*, Scribner, 2007, pg. 290.

"Almost overnight they took control," Vivian Cash with Ann Sharpsteen. *I Walked the Line: My Life with Johnny*, Scribner, 2007, pg. 291.

Chapter Thirteen

"She was great. She was gorgeous," Michael Streissguth. *Johnny Cash: The Biography*, Da Capo Press, pg. 75.

"Vivian, what is that on your coat," Vivian Cash with Ann Sharpsteen. *I Walked the Line: My Life with Johnny*, Scribner, 2007, pg. 294.

"As soon as Vivian saw him," Johnny Western, personal interview, December 15, 2018.

"I know that the hand of God was never off me," Johnny Cash. *Man in Black*, Zondervan, 1975, pg. 76.

"I am your God," Johnny Cash. *Man in Black*, Zondervan, 1975, pg. 78.

"John's behavior was really puzzling," Marshall Grant. *I Was There When It Happened: My Life with Johnny Cash*, Cumberland House, 2006, pg. 81.

"Artists prefer not to be starving," Mark Stielper, personal interview, October 18, 2018.

Chapter Fourteen

"Vivian, he *will* be mine," Vivian Cash with Ann Sharpsteen. *I Walked the Line: My Life with Johnny*, Scribner, 2007, pg. 298.

"I fully expected to see you blow up," Johnny Cash. *Man in Black*, Zondervan, 1975, pg. 75.

"We saw the smoke and heard the news," Don Hancock, personal interview, February 27, 2019.

"No. My truck did, and it's dead," Johnny Cash with Patrick Carr. *Cash: The Autobiography*, Harper Collins, 1997, pg. 152.

Chapter Fifteen

"I don't ever want out of this cell again," Johnny Cash. *Man in Black*, Zondervan, 1975, pg. 97.

"It was my first conviction of any kind," Julie Chadwick. *The Man Who Carried Cash: Saul Holiff, Johnny Cash and the Making of an American Icon*, Dundurn, 2017, pg. 192.

"There's something wrong with Johnny," Julie Chadwick. *The Man Who Carried Cash: Saul Holiff, Johnny Cash and the Making of an American Icon*, Dundurn, 2017, pg. 193.

"I think that came out of amphetamines," Steve Pond. "The Rolling Stone Interview," *Rolling Stone*, December 10, 1992.

"How are you doing?" Julie Chadwick. *The Man Who Carried Cash: Saul Holiff, Johnny Cash and the Making of an American Icon*, Dundurn, 2017, pg. 195.

"Why are you asking how I'm doing?" Julie Chadwick. *The Man Who Carried Cash: Saul Holiff, Johnny Cash and the Making of an American Icon*, Dundurn, 2017, pg.195.

"You need to do *something*," Vivian Cash with Ann Sharpsteen. *I Walked the Line: My Life with Johnny*, Scribner, 2007, pg. 305.

"No. It's too late," Vivian Cash with Ann Sharpsteen. *I Walked the Line: My Life with Johnny*, Scribner, 2007, pg. 308.

Chapter Sixteen
"When we shared the apartment together," Johnny Cash. *Larry King Live*, 2002.

"Is your show about over with for today?" Christopher S. Wren. *Winners Got Scars Too: The Life and Legends of Johnny Cash*, The Dial Press, 1971, pg. 184.

"You want to fight in front of your mother?" Christopher S. Wren. *Winners Got Scars Too: The Life and Legends of Johnny Cash*, The Dial Press, 1971, pg. 184.

"It was the worst thing I could ever do," Christopher S. Wren. *Winners Got Scars Too: The Life and Legends of Johnny Cash*, The Dial Press, 1971, pg. 184.

"Johnny's as complex as anything God or man," Christopher S. Wren. *Winners Got Scars Too: The Life and Legends of Johnny Cash*, The Dial Press, 1971, pg. 149.

Chapter Seventeen
"I had turned my back on my own mother," Johnny Cash. *It's Great to Be Alive*, YouTube.com, January 14, 2019.

"I lay down to die in the total darkness," Johnny Cash with Patrick Carr. *Cash: The Autobiography*, Harper Collins, 1997, pg. 170.

"I'm going to give your money," Johnny Cash. *Man in Black*, Zondervan, 1975, pg. 98.

"Whichever one you want," Johnny Cash. *Man in Black*, Zondervan, 1975, pg. 98.

Chapter Eighteen

"I've never known of anyone as far gone," Johnny Cash. *Man in Black*, Zondervan, 1975, pg. 100.

"Get set for the fight of your life," Johnny Cash. *Man in Black*, 1975, pg. 100.

"I felt Him with me," Johnny Cash. *Man in Black*, Zondervan, 1975, pg. 105.

Chapter Nineteen

"We all got soaking wet, but we all had a great time," Johnny Cash, *Larry King Live*, 2002.

"There was everything from jazz bands," Michael Streissguth. "Merle Haggard's Lost Interview: Country Icon on Johnny Cash, Prison Life," *Rolling Stone*, January 4, 2017.

"He had an affinity for these men," Kelly Hancock, personal interview, February 16, 2019.

"We're here for several reasons," Johnny Cash. *Man in Black*, Zondervan, 1975, pg. 110.

"I saw three-time murderers," Johnny Western, personal interview, December 15, 2018.

Chapter Twenty

"Don't give up on me, Lord," Johnny Cash. *Man in Black*, Zondervan, 1975, pg. 116.

"The times I was so down and out," Michael Streissguth. *Ring of Fire: The Johnny Cash Reader*, DaCapo Press, 2002, pg. 151.

"A part of me died with Luther," Michael Streissguth. *Johnny Cash: The Biography*, Da Capo Press, 2006, pg. 156.

Chapter Twenty-One

"I feel that this year, 1968," John Carter Cash. *House of Cash*, Insight Editions, pg. 116.

"I was just walking down the sidewalk," Christopher S. Wren. *Winners Got Scars Too: The Life and Legends of Johnny Cash*, The Dial Press, 1971, pg. 161.

"John sensed the TV show was going to take his career," Kelly Hancock, personal interview, February 16, 2019.

"They (ABC) got to where they wanted to book anybody," Johnny Cash, "Johnny Cash Talks Part #2," YouTube.com, February 1, 2017.

Chapter Twenty-Two

"Everybody in the entertainment industry," Joe Byrne, personal interview, January 17, 2019.

"He's a good man. He is what he appears to be," Johnny Cash, "Johnny Cash Talks Part #1," YouTube.com, February 1, 2017.

"If there's ever anything I can do," Juli Thanki. "For Johnny Cash, Billy Graham was a friend and a confidant," *USA Today*, February 21, 2018.

"I'd like to tell 'em some things," Juli Thanki. "For Johnny Cash, Billy Graham was a friend and a confidant," *USA Today*, February 21, 2018.

"I've always been able to share my secrets," Johnny Cash with Patrick Carr. *Cash: The Autobiography*, Harper Collins, 1997, pg. 209.

"They were Southern boys, and their culture was all about relationships," Tom Phillips, personal interview, March 3, 2019.

"Let's name him John Carter Cash," Johnny Cash. *Man in Black*, Zondervan, pg. 138.

"I'm not an expert on his music," Matthew Costello. "A Country Evening in the East Room," WhiteHouseHistory.org, May 12, 2017.

"We pray Mr. President, that you can end this war," Matthew Costello. "A Country Evening in the East Room," WhiteHouseHistory.org, May 12, 2017.

"This was a love fest," Mark Stielper, personal interview, October 18, 2018.

Chapter Twenty-Three
"God has given you your own pulpit," Robert Hilburn. *Johnny Cash: The Life*, Little, Brown & Co., 2013, pg. 396.
"He fell off the stage," Joe Byrne, personal interview, January 17, 2019.
"It was all right for the first year," Michael Streissguth. *Ring of Fire: The Johnny Cash Reader*, Da Capo Press, 2002, pg. 157.
"It was an all-star revue," Mark Stielper, personal interview, October 18, 2018.

Chapter Twenty-Four
"The preacher recognized me," John Carter Cash. *House of Cash*, Insight Editions, 2015, pg. 54.
"I think about the time that June and I went to Vietnam," Johnny Cash, "Johnny Cash on Burning the Flag," YouTube.com, October 11, 2018.
"John and I were both basically shy," Jimmie Snow, personal interview, June 2, 2018.
"I need to talk to you," Jimmie Snow, personal interview, June 2, 2018.
"I'd spent several years at that point," Jimmie Snow, personal interview, June 2, 2018.
"Why don't you come visit us," Johnny Cash. *Man in Black*, Zondervan, 1975, pg. 149.
"I thought you'd never ask," Johnny Cash. *Man in Black*, Zondervan, 1975, pg. 149.
"Twenty minutes in a hailstorm," Joanne Cash Yates, personal interview, June 1, 2018.
"After I asked Jesus to come into my heart," Joanne Cash Yates, personal interview, June 1, 2018.
"You really got it, Baby," Joanne Cash Yates, personal interview, June 1, 2018.
"Their faces were like beacons" Johnny Cash. *Man in Black*, Zondervan, 1975, pg. 152.

"I'm reaffirming my faith," Johnny Cash. *Man in Black*, Zondervan, 1975, pg. 154.

"When I pray with someone," Jimmie Snow, personal interview, June 2, 2018.

Chapter Twenty-Five

"Naturally felt good at a service," Johnny Cash. *Man in Black*, Zondervan, 1975, pg. 155.

"Love and fame cannot exist in the same body," Kelly Hancock, personal interview, February 16, 2019.

"This I believe; that Jesus Christ is the Son of God," John Carter Cash. *House of Cash*, Insight Editions, 2011, pg. 53.

"The most misquoted, misread and misunderstood man," Steve Turner. *The Man Called Cash*, Word Publishing Group, 2004, pg. 146.

"Lots of people go all their lives thinking Jesus," Stephen Miller. *Johnny Cash: The Life of an American Icon*, Omnibus Press, 2003, pg. 227.

"I want you to make me a film," Julie Chadwick. *The Man Who Carried Cash: Saul Holiff, Johnny Cash and the Making of an American Icon*, Dundurn, 2017, pg. 296.

"There's the mountain I dreamed," Johnny Cash. *Man in Black*, Zondervan, 1975, pg. 157.

"John walked up to me," Jimmie Snow, personal interview, June 2, 2018.

"The most devoted bunch of people," Michael Streissguth. *Ring of Fire: The Johnny Cash Reader*, DaCapo Press, 2002, pg. 131.

"This is my life's proudest work," Michael Streissguth. *Ring of Fire: The Johnny Cash Reader*, DaCapo Press, 2002, pg. 131.

Chapter Twenty-Six

"I don't have a career anymore," C. Eric Banister. *Johnny Cash FAQ: All That's Left to Know About The Man in Black*, Backbeat Books, 2014, pg. 342.

"He advised me to keep singing," Dave Urbanski. *The Man Comes Around: The Spiritual Journey of Johnny Cash*, Relevant Books, 2003, pg. XIX.

"Johnny Cash made it cool to be a rogue," Rick Scott, personal interview, February 25, 2019.

"I have tried drugs and a little of everything else," Steve Turner. *The Man Called Cash*, Word Publishing Group, 2004, pg. 151.

"Flesh to the devil and left only," Steve Turner. *The Man Called Cash*, Word Publishing Group, 2004, pg. 151.

"The establishment in America at that time," Tom Phillips, personal interview, March 3, 2019.

"Our property had been incorrectly surveyed," Jimmie Snow, personal interview, June 2, 2018.

"He'd give people cars, he'd pay off mortgages," Jimmie Snow, personal interview, June 2, 2018.

"On a Sunday morning a man in a red coat," Jimmie Snow, personal interview, June 2, 2018.

"All the money—and I mean," Marshall Grant. *I Was There When It Happened: My Life with Johnny Cash*, Cumberland House, 2006, pg.197.

"A first offender needs to know," Bill Demain. "The Time Johnny Cash Met Richard Nixon," *Mental Floss*, July 14, 2014.

Chapter Twenty-Seven

"Do you have something against Jesus?" Julie Chadwick. *The Man Who Carried Cash: Saul Holiff, Johnny Cash and the Making of an American Icon*, Dundurn, 2017, pg. 325.

"Great family man, and one of the wisest men I know," Julie Chadwick. *The Man Who Carried Cash: Saul Holiff, Johnny Cash and the Making of an American Icon*, Dundurn, 2017, pg. 329.

"It was so nice to hear from you," Julie Chadwick. *The Man Who Carried Cash: Saul Holiff, Johnny Cash and the Making of an American Icon*, Dundurn, 2017, pg. 353.

"John was an avid student of history," Pastor Harry Yates, personal interview, June 3, 2018.

"The Apostle Paul inspires me," Johnny Cash, "Johnny Cash Talks Part #2," YouTube.com, February 1, 2017.

"Sets me up for a good day," Johnny Cash with Patrick Carr. *Cash: The Autobiography*, Harper Collins, 1997, pg. 227.

"John was pulled in a lot of different directions," Kelly Hancock, personal interview, February 16, 2019.

"I graded some of his course work," Dr. Bill Hamon, personal interview, November 27, 2018.

"He met the requirements," Dr. Bill Hamon, personal interview, November 27, 2018.

Chapter Twenty-Eight

"I've asked myself that same question," Ken Mansfield, personal interview, November 27, 2018.

"Waylon was the most charismatic man," Ken Mansfield, personal interview, November 27, 2018.

"Why, John? Just please, tell me why?" Marshall Grant. *I Was There When It Happened: My Life with Johnny Cash,* Cumberland House, 2006, pg. 235.

"I didn't try to invade his privacy," Johnny Cash with Patrick Carr. *Cash: The Autobiography*, Harper Collins, 1997, pg. 93.

"(Cash) survived what Elvis didn't survive," Alastair McKay. "I Went Down, Down, Down and the Flames Went Higher," *Uncut*, February, 2009.

"Everybody was well aware that John struggled," Rick Scott, personal interview, February 25, 2019.

"Elvis may have had a stronger relationship," Scott Ross. "Recounting Johnny Cash," CBN, 1984.

"I never lost my faith during that time," Lee Habeeb. "The Johnny Cash You Never Knew," LifeZette, February 24, 2017.

"Thank you, Lord! Another sinner," Reggie Vinson, personal interview, March 24, 2018.

"When Johnny spoke he reminded me," Reggie Vinson, personal interview March 24, 2018.

"Reggie, they don't know how far I've come," Reggie Vinson, personal interview March 24, 2018.

"It was one of the most touching," Reggie Vinson, personal interview March 24, 2018.

"I'm certain nobody connected," Marshall Grant. *I Was There When It Happened: My Life with Johnny Cash*, Cumberland House, 2006, pg. 243.

Chapter Twenty-Nine

"I have no greater joy than to see my children," John Carter Cash. *House of Cash*, Insight Editions, 2015, pg. 48.

"Gospel music was the thing that inspired me," Barney Hoskins. "Johnny Cash on Work Ethic, Preachers, and Singing Gospel Music with Elvis," *The Bully Pulpit*, October 14, 1996.

"Marshall Grant was growing more and more insufferable," Mark Stielper, personal interview, October 18, 2018.

Chapter Thirty

"The drive from the airport to the house," Mark Stielper, personal interview, October 18, 2018.

"Somebody's going to die here tonight!" Johnny Cash with Patrick Carr. *Cash: The Autobiography*, Harper Collins, 1997, pg. 37.

"When I was having my hit records," Anthony DeCurtis. "Johnny Cash Won't Back Down," *Rolling Stone*, October 26, 2000.

"His acting techniques may be leaden," John J. O'Connor. "The Pride of Jesse Hallam Stars Johnny Cash," *New York Times*, March 3, 1981.

"Lord, you took one of my boys," Robert Hilburn. *Johnny Cash: The Life*, Little, Brown & Co., 2013, pg. 494.

"I want to go. I want some help," Johnny Cash with Patrick Carr. *Cash: The Autobiography*, Harper Collins, 1997, pg. 180.

Chapter Thirty-One

"They make a big deal out of that," Mike Morris and Lorraine Kelly. TV-am, 1991.

"We'd sit around on the floor playing guessing games," Johnny Cash, "Johnny Cash Part #1," YouTube.com, February 1, 2017.

"I've had people say that they felt so bad," Johnny Cash, "Johnny Cash speaks on the subject of drug abuse," YouTube.com, February 2, 2014.

"The problem with Christians, and me as a Christian," Johnny Cash, "Johnny Cash speaks on the subject of drug abuse," YouTube.com, February 2, 2014.

"The most special quality John possessed," Rick Scott, personal interview, February 25, 2019.

"It was not a mistake," Mark Stielper, personal interview, October 18, 2018.

"Those four were like grownup kids," Joanne Cash Yates, personal interview, June 1, 2018.

"It would have meant an awful lot for me," Johnny Cash with Patrick Carr. *Cash: The Autobiography*, Harper Collins, 1997, pg. 236.

Chapter Thirty-Two

"Mom and I went over to their house," Kelly Hancock, personal interview, February 16, 2019.

"When you have a leader in your field," Ken Mansfield, personal interview, November 27, 2018.

"I got so tired of hearing about demographics," Johnny Cash with Patrick Carr. *Cash: The Autobiography*, Harper Collins, 1997, pg. 251.

"I lived with Johnny Cash for a year," Tammy Leigh Maxey. "Flag of My Father," *Pivot Point Magazine*, March/April 2011.

"It was Johnny who led me to Christ," Tammy Leigh Maxey. "Flag of My Father," *Pivot Point Magazine*, March/April 2011.

"Johnny and I would be fishing," Tammy Leigh Maxey. "Flag of My Father," *Pivot Point Magazine*, March/April 2011.

"Well, what do you think?" Johnny Cash with Patrick Carr. *Cash: The Autobiography*, Harper Collins, 1997, pg. 252.

"Let me think about it," Johnny Cash with Patrick Carr. *Cash: The Autobiography*, Harper Collins, 1997, pg. 252.

"He'd play me eight, ten, twelve bars," Jimmy Bowen and Jim Jerome. *Rough Mix*, Simon & Schuster, 1997, pg. 71.

"Cash was going in and auditioning," Mark Stielper, personal interview, October 18, 2018.

"Hank Williams died in 1953," Mark Stielper, personal interview, October 18, 2018.

"We were on holiday in Jamaica," Paul McCartney, "Paul McCartney on Working with Johnny Cash," YouTube.com, March 15, 2014.

Chapter Thirty-Three

"My mother had to field a lot of things," Kelly Hancock, personal interview, February 16, 2019.

"Don't you find anything because I'm going to Jamaica," Johnny Cash, "Johnny Cash Talks Part #1," YouTube.com, February 1, 2017.

"Most patients are not brave enough," Jeff Woods. "Country music star Johnny Cash, who once locked himself . . ." UPI, December 19, 1988.

"Their voices receded and everything," Johnny Cash with Patrick Carr. *Cash: The Autobiography*, Harper Collins, 1997, pg. 259.

"His jaw was way out there and swollen," Dennis Agajanian, personal interview, October 24, 2018.

"I didn't ever kick the drug habit," Johnny Cash, "Johnny Talks Part 1," YouTube.com, February 1, 2017.

"He came to the studio," Billy Smiley, personal interview, June 4, 2018.

"Carrie was absolutely the sweetest woman," Rick Scott, personal interview, February 25, 2019.

"The last song we sang to her," Joanne Cash Yates, personal interview, June 1, 2018.

"Baby, remember when we were all holding hands," Joanne Cash Yates, personal interview, June 1, 2018.

"When I told him I didn't," Joanne Cash Yates, personal interview, June 1, 2018.

Chapter Thirty-Four

"Many of my friends came here and built theaters," Steve Pond. *Cash by the editors of Rolling Stone,* Crown, 2004, pg. 133-134.

"It's a place where folks can come," Steve Pond. *Cash by the editors of Rolling Stone,* Crown, 2004, pg. 133-134.

"At the time, the Branson concept," Mark Stielper, personal interview, October 18, 2018.

"Hillbilly Heaven," Dan Chu. *People*, October 21, 1991.

"I bet you don't remember the first time," Steve Pond. *Cash by the editors of Rolling Stone,* Crown, 2004, pg. 133-134.

"Branson at that time was in a big boom," Jay Dauro, personal interview, February 22, 2019.

"Branson Cash Country Theatre Cashes Out," Phil Mulkins. *Tulsa World*, September 15, 1992.

Chapter Thirty-Five

"As Johnny was going through his downward spiral," Pastor Harry Yates, personal interview, June 3, 2018.

"I'm extremely proud of it," Joseph Hudak. "Flashback: Watch Johnny Cash Perform 'Big River' at His Rock and Roll Fame Induction," *Rolling Stone*, January 15, 2015.

"We sang the chorus together," Robert Hilburn. "Johnny Cash Looks Back with a Smile," *Los Angeles Times*, February 2, 1992.

"Johnny Cash was a saint who preferred," Steve Turner. *The Man Called Cash*, Word Publishing Group, 2004, pg. 190.

"My first forays into learning to play," Graeme Thomson. *The Resurrection of Johnny Cash*, Jawbone Books, 2011.

"I considered myself a friend," BBC News. "'Great Man' Cash Remembered," September 12, 2003.

"Then, when he was done he turned to me," Matt Diehl. "Remembering Johnny," *Rolling Stone*, October 16, 2003.

"He tries wealth. He tries experience," Bono, The Edge, Adam Clayton, and Larry Mullen Jr. *U2 by U2*, Harper Collins, 2009, pg. 249.

"He only half-guffawed when I broke the news," Bono, The Edge, Adam Clayton, and Larry Mullen Jr. *U2 by U2*, Harper Collins, 2009, pg. 204.

"I remember trying to sort out some phrasing problems," Bono, The Edge, Adam Clayton, and Larry Mullen Jr. *U2 by U2*, Harper Collins, 2009, pg. 249.

"I don't know if it will ever be released," Joe Jackson. "Bono and My Part in His Success," *Sunday Independent*, September 12, 2010.

"I have no plans to come back at all," C. Eric Banister. *Johnny Cash FAQ: All That's Left to Know About the Man in Black*, Backbeat Books, 2014, pg. 278.

Chapter Thirty-Six

"I had worked pretty much exclusively with young artists," Johnny Black. "Johnny Cash: The Unplugged Album That Saved a Legend's Life," *Classic Rock*, June 10, 2016.

"From the beginning of rock and roll," Anthony DeCurtis. "Johnny Cash Won't Back Down," *Rolling Stone*, October 26, 2000.

"What're you gonna do with me," David Kamp. "American Communion," *Vanity Fair*, February 23, 2010.

"Well, I don't know that we will sell records," David Kamp. "American Communion," *Vanity Fair*, February 23, 2010.

"He was not an ego-driven person," David Fricke. *Cash by the editors of Rolling Stone*, Crown, 2004, pg. 149.

"You might really say he died of a broken heart," Pastor Harry Yates, personal interview, June 3, 2018.

"We had a dinner party," Terry Gross. "American Remembered: Rick Rubin on Johnny Cash," NPR, February 26, 2010.

"It was the Man in Black, larger than life," Rami Jaffee, personal interview, March 2, 2019.

"It was kinda like playing a bloody," Jancee Dunn. *Cash by the editors of Rolling Stone*, Crown, 2004, pg. 153.

"By playing this club, Johnny Cash," Raoul Hernandez, personal interview, January 10, 2019.

"Johnny Cash was the Grand Canyon," Raoul Hernandez, personal interview, January 10, 2019.

"People here know what's real," Raoul Hernandez, personal interview, January 10, 2019.

"The first time I heard it I said, 'Alright!'" Kris Kristofferson, "Cash vs. Music Row," YouTube.com, February 12, 2010.

"The reaction was like the '50s all over again," Johnny Cash, "Reelin' In The Years," YouTube.com, December 11, 2018.

Chapter Thirty-Seven

"Growing up, we always knew the Man in Black," Will Turpin, personal interview, February 16, 2019.

"The middle part of any artist's career," Will Turpin, personal interview, February 16, 2019.

"Generation X not only connected to Cash's," Anthony J. Resta, personal interview, February 11, 2019.

"I see the pimples on my nose," Johnny Cash, "Johnny Cash on the Gospel," YouTube.com, April 8, 2014.

"We saw younger audiences come to the shows," Jay Dauro, personal interview, February 22, 2019.

"Runs through this family like a turkey," Jason Fine. "A Day in the Life," *Cash by the editors of Rolling Stone*, Crown, 2004, pg. 168.

"I never asked them to play with me on a record," Johnny Cash, "Reelin' In the Years," YouTube.com, December 11, 2018.

"The Heartbreakers are such a great band," Will Hodge. "Johnny Cash's 'Unchained' at 20: Inside the Making of a Masterpiece," *Rolling Stone*, November 4, 2016.

"He was one of those people you don't encounter much," Nick Hasted. "Tom Petty: From the Unchained Sessions to 'I Won't Back Down,'" *Uncut*, February 16, 2009.

"I got the phone call when I was in the house," Mark Savage. "Lenny Kravitz: 'Johnny Cash held me when my mother died," BBC News, September 5, 2018.

"June came out in the room," Nick Hasted. "Tom Petty: From the Unchained Sessions to 'I Won't Back Down,'" *Uncut*, February 16, 2009.

"It ain't funny," Doug Pullen. "Remembering Johnny Cash's Last Visit to Flint," *The Flint Journal*, October 26, 2007.

"It's all right. I refuse to give it some ground," Doug Pullen. "Remembering Johnny Cash's Last Visit to Flint," *The Flint Journal*, October 26, 2007.

Chapter Thirty-Eight

"I never questioned God, I never doubted God," Patrick Carr. "Johnny Cash: The Spirit is Willing," CMT.com, July 9, 2002.

"It was incredible," Wes Orshski. "Johnny Cash: An American Original," *Billboard*, March 30, 2002.

"I didn't really worry about it," Patrick Carr. "Johnny Cash: The Spirit is Willing," CMT.com, July 9, 2002.

"I was kind of disappointed when I realized I wasn't going to die," Patrick Carr. "Johnny Cash: The Spirit is Willing," CMT.com, July 9, 2002.

"An old man knows in his bones," Jason Fine. "A Day in the Life of Johnny Cash," *Rolling Stone*, December 12, 2002.

"Of the ones who are still left," Anthony DeCurtis. "Johnny Cash Won't Back Down," *Rolling Stone*," October 26, 2000.

"It depresses him. He's not used to sitting around," Anthony DeCurtis. "Johnny Cash Won't Back Down," *Rolling Stone*, October 26, 2000.

"He's been fine; we just have to take breaks," Anthony DeCurtis. "Johnny Cash Won't Back Down," *Rolling Stone*, October 26, 2000.

"I wouldn't trade my future," Johnny Cash. *American III: Solitary Man* liner notes, American Recordings, 2000.

Chapter Thirty-Nine

"John had a great faith in God," Kelly Hancock, personal interview, February 16, 2019.

"At my age, I believe I can," Joanne Cash Yates, personal interview, June 1, 2018.

"I get my coffee early in the morning," Rick Rubin, Concert Live Wire.com, April 1, 2003.

"Sometimes I came to the studio and I couldn't sing," Johnny Cash, Live Wire.com, April 1, 2003.

"We put more blood, sweat and tears," Johnny Cash, Live Wire.com, April 1, 2003.

"*Unchained* was hard to make," David Fricke. *Cash by the editors of Rolling Stone*, Crown, 2004, pg. 151.

"I was there some of the days," Tommy Cash. *The Story of Johnny Cash*, BBC Four, 2010.

Chapter Forty

"The strongest person," Mark Stielper, personal interview, October 18, 2018.

"The first person I ran into," Jimmie Snow, personal interview, June 2, 2018.

"He suffered a lot of pain in his life," David Fricke. *Cash by the editors of Rolling Stone*, Crown, 2004, pg. 151.

"I got a call from Rick Rubin's assistant," Rami Jaffee, personal interview, March 2, 2019.

"He kept thumbing through books," Cindy Cash, "Memories from the Farm," YouTube video, December 13, 2016.

"If anyone on this planet should write a book," Vivian Cash with Ann Sharpsteen. *I Walked the Line: My Life with Johnny*, Scribner, 2007, pg. 7.

"She was thrilled that Johnny was supportive," Ann Sharpsteen, personal interview, January 16, 2019.

"This was a man who had such a great impact," Kelly Hancock, personal interview, February 16, 2019.

"The gloaming of the day," Rosanne Cash. *Composed: A Memoir*, Viking Books, 2010, pg. 181.

"I expect my life to end soon," Kurt Loder. MTV, August 20, 2003.

"I asked him one time," Joanne Cash Yates, personal interview, June 1, 2018.

"Most of his children were there," Joanne Cash Yates, personal interview, June 1, 2018.

ENDNOTES

Chapter 7   A Cherry Pink and Apple Blossom White Dream

[1] "Sunday Morning Coming Down," © Kris Kristofferson, 1969.

[2] "I Was There When It Happened," © Fern Jones and Jimmie Davis, 1955.

Chapter 38   (Spiritual) House of Cash

[3] "Ain't No Grave," © BMG Rights Management, Carlin America Inc., 1922.